Praise for Where's My Happy Ending

'As entertaining as it is instructive . . . funny and touching.'

Evening Standard

'As a divorced single mother, thank God there is none of that smug, married-couple twattery in this book. I loved it.'

Jane Garvey, BBC presenter

'Fantastically unsmug.' Woman's Hour

'The honesty, wit and wisdom in this book makes it a joy to read. There's a genuine drive to get to the bottom of our often questionable romantic philosophy. It's painful and funny – and painfully funny.'

Emma Freud

'The book is a hoot – hilarious and heartfelt; Anna and Matt have done it again. I didn't know how much I needed to read this, a book that goes deep into the nitty gritty, beyond the Disney lies and "They Lived Happily Ever Afters". As someone about to get married, I absolutely loved this, and will keep it firmly on my bookshelf to remind me that life and love can be messy and hard, but it doesn't mean we're doing it wrong.'

Emma Gannon

'They both write and engage with the reader so playfully and willingly. There's such intimacy and lightness at the same time that there's intensity and great substance. This is a delightful book that takes us into the depths of the modern human condition. An essential psychological exploration.'

Charlotte Fox Weber, Head of Psychotherapy
at The School of Life

'This book made us laugh, cry and remember where it all started for us. In a garage. With the smell of petrol in the air. Memories!'

Chris and Rosie Ramsey,
Founders of *Shagged, Married, Annoyed.*

'This book left me laughing so very hard and equally blubbing with tears, often within a few pages. I've never read anything that so perfectly captures the questions we all have about family and life and happiness, and that leaves you with such an uplifting finish that you want to go and hug all your loved ones harder than ever.'

Jools Oliver

'A glorious mix of writing that's both painfully honest and painfully funny.'

Ellie Taylor

Where's My Happy Ending?

Happily ever after and how the heck to get there

MATT FARQUHARSON
(Papa Pukka)

ANNA WHITEHOUSE
(Mother Pukka)

bluebird
books for life

First published in the United Kingdom 2020 by Bluebird,
an imprint of Pan Macmillan
The Smithson, 6 Briset Street, London ECIM 5NR
Associated companies throughout the world
www.panmacmillan.com

ISBN 978-1-529-01369-6

5 7 9 8 6 4

A CIP catalogue record for this book is available from the British Library.

Typeset by Palimpsest Book Production Ltd, Falkirk, Stirlingshire
Printed and bound by CPI Group (UK) Ltd, Croydon, CRO 4YY

Visit **www.panmacmillan.com** to read more about all our books
and to buy them. You will also find features, author interviews and
news of any author events, and you can sign up for e-newsletters
so that you're always first to hear about our new releases.

This book is for all the people wondering what's next

CONTENTS

An Important Note

We wrote this book together but separately. We agreed nine topics and the people we might speak to, and then we sat side by side, interviewing, researching, tapping away but agreeing not to show each other our words. We agreed to include our truest thoughts, but to share them with the page rather than each other. We did this to force ourselves to be honest: everyone has thoughts that they keep from their loved ones, and we felt that if we collaborated too closely, we might sanitize those thoughts too much. (No partner has ever answered the question 'Darling, how do I look?' with complete honesty, after all.)

Our chapters went over to Carole, our editor, who sent back notes and then, before we started chapter 10, we read what each other had written . . .

Some names and minor details have been changed at the request of interviewees.

INTRODUCTION

Matt

I met a girl and fell in love. She was twenty-four and I was twenty-nine, and within hours of meeting her I wanted to grow old with her. I was like a cat watching the red dot of a laser pen, or a toddler when someone's slicing cake. I found her funny and smart and I wanted to live with her in a small flat with big bookshelves where we could drink wine and make nice dinners.

We had a few years of living abroad and being together. We made our nests and did our jobs and had friends and meals and miscarriages.

And after a few years, we had our first daughter.

Those first days of parenthood were a combination of delirious happiness – the sensation that my heart had expanded to make room for someone new – and absolute boredom: the slow realization that this someone was not that different to an elderly and incontinent dachshund. She was a loaf-sized bundle that I would feed, cuddle, change and move from room to room over the course of a day, but was so blind and bewildered that she seemed to have no more connection to me than she would an Ikea hat stand.

In the giddy comedown after her arrival, something struck me, and it wasn't just her wildly twitching feet. I realized that we might have another one of these but, after that, the next 'big life moment' might well be cancer or divorce or retirement.

I had finished the grown-ups list and made all the big decisions. The next forty years would be left living with those decisions until I stopped living entirely. I put these thoughts down to a lack of sleep and added extra sugar to my vending-machine hot chocolate.

Then we had a second daughter, and all of a sudden it's twelve years after our first date and I have developed passive-aggressive snark about footwear storage, kicking shoes about the bedroom floor because I'm always tripping over them. At weekends, I hide from my wife and offspring in the toilet, reading the sports pages on my phone.

For this is how it tends to go: you're born, you grow up, and you get educated. You start work, probably get married and maybe breed. But then what?

All of a sudden, an aching chasm opens up – decades of 'how did I get here?' and 'is this the right place to be?'

In the old cliché, this would be the time for a mid-life crisis: perhaps a fling with an intern who has 'married man' on her bucket list, or developing an interest in motorbikes or cross-dressing. But I barely have time to flirt with my wife let alone a young substitute, I still don't have a driving licence, and I haven't got the hips for a cocktail frock.

So what, I wondered, do people do now? But then I realized I'd been wondering that since I earned my first pay packet at thirteen, delivering papers for News and Chews on the High Road. It's a question I asked myself on the day I left home, and when I got my first job and all through half a decade of drunken flat-shares. I'd been wondering it most of my life.

So I decided to ask someone. I went to Mount Athos to see if monks were happier without women in their lives. I went to a free-love eco-village to see if humping like rabbits makes you happy or just very tired (this was a theoretical test rather than a practical). I spoke to people who never wanted kids and to people who had loads of them. I spoke to porn-makers and feminist academics, neurologists and romance novelists. I even asked my mum.

And the question was always the same: where is the happy ending, and what do you do once you get there?

This is what I found.

Anna

It was the moment I saw a rogue toenail clipping in my make-up bag that things shifted. The toenail clipping was not mine. It was too gnarled and jagged from a haphazard go with the toenail clippers. Had it been mine, I would have disposed of it in the dedicated bin where all bodily trimmings and other dark bathroom secrets lurk. As it stood, The Person Responsible decided to just pop the clippers back in that paisley bag, their offcut now hanging brazenly alongside things with the words 'shimmer', 'blush' and 'peony mist' on them.

That was when I first sensed a wobble in the marital pillars. The Person Responsible is my other half, my life lobster, my *raison d'être*, the Ren to my Stimpy. He's the person I went on a grotty mini-break to Milan with after only five dates. We walked around that amour-inducing city with his digits in constant contact with my buns, buzzing with oxytocin; I was knickerless for the duration and felt positively breezy – both in terms of undercarriage and general mindset.

He's the one who I accidentally emailed the following to:

> **SUBJECT:** *Lunch*
> Yes, lunch next door sounds great.
> It's been four hours thirteen minutes since I last heard from him. I'm doing everything I can to stop myself emailing again. Speaking to my plant, doodling on Post-It notes. Googling names of children that go well with his surname. I want to be on him. Now. I will wait. I must wait. I don't want to scare him off. I love his eyebrows. I love him. I must wait.

This note was meant for my colleague Lisa, but instead it erroneously made its way to Matt. We'd been on two dates.

He's my everything.

Apart from when he's not and I'm foaming at the mouth like a rabid gerbil, wondering if my happiness is also lurking in the bottom of that bathroom bin.

Or when I'm immersed in the administrative quagmire of 'ring doctor about possible bunion', 'buy new dustpan', 'fill in school-trip form' (The Forms – a whole chapter could be dedicated to The Forms), 'call Grandma because The End is looming', 'eat something that isn't a crust'.

So where's my happy ending? Disney built a brand on dreams coming true. Fairy tales always end with this vague sign-off: 'And they all lived happily ever after.' Who did? Where is this place? Who are these people? Lately, an After Eight is as close as I've got to combining 'after' and 'happy'. (Even then there's the risk that someone will leave the empty wrappers in the box, flipping me into an angsty rage.) But if you can't milk some solace from a post-dinner confection, it's surely the end.

There's an idea that we somehow magically gather up all the components – a home, a toothbrush, someone who isn't too much of a bell-end – and then you've made it. You get to gallop into the final furlong, across the finish line and bask in that heavily touted happiness. It's supposed to be a kind of joy that is like easing yourself into a vat of treacly dessert wine while overlooking an ochre sunset and eating a trifle. But what if it ends up more like swigging cider on a park bench?

I wanted to write this book with Matt because it feels like the great vacuum of space between 'I do' and 'The End' needs a little reconsidering. It feels like 'happily ever after' might be the way for a freshly rescued Cinderella, but what if your foot doesn't fit the shoe? Perhaps being 'whisked away' also means microwaving a lukewarm cup of tea so that your chosen person has a hot brew. Maybe being 'swept off your feet' can simply include someone disposing of their toenail offcut in the right bathroom receptacle.

So what is true romance truly like, and do we really need it? What do porn and social media and kids and laundry do to relationships? What's a throuple?

We've followed a pretty well-worn path so far. Now I want to know if there's another route I could have taken.

1

☆ ☆ ☆

One Love

Why do we bother?

Matt

I swear about Anna when she's not in the room. Typically it will be a huffed 'fuckssake' and it tends to happen for the following reasons:

1 I'm doing laundry (because I do 95 per cent of the laundry, and she has lots of clothes).
2 I'm paying bills (and discover that money from the bills account has been used for non-bills activity).
3 I've trodden on her hair tongs again, which have been left on the floor and are probably a fire hazard.

There may be other reasons, but these are the main three. They are not big transgressions. They are not an affair or a secret gambling habit, and they do not merit muttered swearing about someone you're pretty sure you've loved since the day you met them.

And yet the swears come out. Sometimes they're even embellished to become 'doafuckinwash' or 'everyfuckintime'. Partly I think this is because I've mentioned the issues before, using my nice 'hey, honey, by the way' voice. And I've mentioned them so often that each time they now happen has begun to feel like a deliberate slight: that she is silently saying, 'Pipe down, husband, you can't control me.'

The frequency of my muttered swearing increases according to the broader state of our relationship – how often we're laughing, how much sex we're having, the ratio of fun chats to discussions about to-do lists.

These are 'first-world issues', of course. At the time of writing, the UN lists four extreme humanitarian crises in Africa and the Middle East. Wealth inequality in most Western nations is at its worst since before the Second World War. The planet's top scientists have made their 'final call' to avoid a climate catastrophe, and several nuclear-armed nations are getting tetchy. All of these things are more important than who does the laundry in our home.

They're not even the most important things in our relationship. I'm aware of all the good stuff – how she is with our daughters, what she wants for us as a family, and how important it is to me that she laughs.

But these resentments exist, and I wonder how much harm they do. If I'm moved to swear and huff about such things, perhaps they are signs of deeper issues. Perhaps every 'fuckssake' slowly builds, like a drop of water onto a stalagmite, until you're left with something large and unmovable at the heart of your relationship. And it's made me think about my own parents, and how much of an impact your upbringing has on you as a grown-up. If you're from a shouty clan, does it make you the kind of person who squawks in rage whenever your partner forgets the milk? If every issue was solved with a family meeting over herbal tea and dairy-free biscuits, will you be one of those who can muster empathy and calmness in the face of all twattery?

When I was eight years old, my family moved away from our

small flat in Golders Green, north London. It was a place with yellow and orange curtains in giant floral prints and a view of a Tube track. It had a big, brown leatherette sofa that was excellent for jumping on and a sacred place in the corner of the living room for Zebedee, a much-loved (and frequently thrown) two-foot plastic character from *The Magic Roundabout*. I remember that flat mostly as a place of play – of watching *Sesame Street* while sat on the carpet and of crashing toy cars into each other in the hallway.

I have three vivid memories from that time. The first is discovering my younger sister, El, sitting on the kitchen lino and being covered brow-to-chin in chocolate after stealing my Easter eggs. The second is carefully unpeeling the coloured stickers from my Rubik's cube then replacing them in the correct blocks, to fleetingly convince my mum that I was a tiny genius. It was only as she phoned my nan to tell her of this three-foot Einstein in the family that guilt overwhelmed me and I confessed. And the third – unrelated to the second – was El and I finding Mum sat on a tiny chair in our bedroom one afternoon, weeping into her hands.

The place we moved to was a semi-detached house in Sydenham, south London. It had laminate cladding on the living-room walls and a thick purple carpet. The carpet was so deep it held little pockets of Christmas tree needles all year round and would act as a tiny alien forest for my toy soldiers. My dad had a new job that came with a blue Ford Escort, and the suburban dream had been realized.

I remember this house mostly as a place of arguments. There were rows about the carpet and why we couldn't afford to replace it. There were rows about the local area and the 'big school' that

I would attend at age eleven, where a boy had recently been stabbed. There were rows about where things were and who put them there. There may have been a few muttered 'fuckssakes'. It was normal for there to be bickering, and my sister and I would watch, waist-high to the action.

But the biggest arguments came at night. After school and cartoons and tea, El and I would be put to bed, where we'd whisper to each other – me in the top bunk and her below – as we listened for Dad's return from the pub.

Most nights we'd fall asleep to be woken later by raised voices: Mum shouting, Dad dismissive, sometimes shouting back. There was no violence, just the frustrated clatter of domestic rage as hands were banged on tables and doors slammed shut.

Eventually they would give in to weariness, often with Dad heading to the box room or couch. Some nights he'd come into our room and stare at us both as we pretended to sleep and wondered what he was thinking.

And then one night we were woken by blue flashing lights. There was no shouting, but there were new voices. Two policemen stopped by to tell my mother that they had my father at Brixton police station after he had drunkenly crashed his car.

'Well, you can keep him,' she said. 'I don't want him back.'

And that was the marriage done. On a Saturday morning soon after, with me still in my paisley pyjamas, Mum sat me down in the bathroom to explain that we were going to live with her parents, Nan and Pop.

I told her it seemed like the sort of thing that only happened in *EastEnders*. There were tears that day, and probably in the days that followed, but I also remember thinking that it was probably for the best. And if nine-year-old me knew that separation was a good idea, it must have been clear to the grown-ups for a long time.

So was he selfish or just suffocated by domesticity? And was she unreasonable or just unwilling to accept unhappiness?

There must have been signs along the way – little niggles that went unchecked, unhealthy habits that dripped away to build their own stalagmites. Dad died aged sixty-one, which means there's only one person left to ask.

My mum, Paula, is sixty-nine now and lives in Dorset on the south coast of England with my stepfather, Andy. They have a bungalow at the top of a hill and a view of the distant sea from their kitchen sink. We're visiting for a few days around Christmas, and in their cream and dark-blue living room, I set up a camera. She's sitting on their purple couch, and has washed her hair especially.

'There wasn't a lot of love there,' she says. 'Certainly not from him to me,' and we immediately pause to calm wobbly voices. It suddenly seems strange that we haven't talked about any of this before, and I wonder if we ever would have without this book.

'I sometimes ask myself, "Why on earth did we get married in the first place?" but it seemed like a good idea and I thought I loved him and I suppose I thought he loved me.'

They met in 1972, when my mother was twenty-three and living with her parents in north London. My father, Stuart, was five months younger and had left Aberdeen – and the prospect of a life in the shipyards where his own dad worked – a few years before. He had planned to explore the world with a mate but they only made it as far as southern France. The first time he saw a bidet, he thought it was for storing fruit and filled it with water, apples and bananas, much to the confusion of the owner of his digs.

Then the money ran out and, after a few nights on the beach, he hitched back to London and stopped, staying on the couch of a distant relative and earning a little cash by putting out deckchairs in Green Park. He got work at a printers, which eventually led to a job selling advertising space for a magazine publisher called IPC, where my mum was a secretary.

They had their first kiss behind a filing cabinet and she felt a spark of static electricity as their lips came together. Seven months later, she was walking down the aisle.

'I remember actually standing at the altar thinking, "What the hell am I doing here? I don't know this man." But I put that down to wedding nerves. It's very sad now I think about it.'

She talks about his alcoholism, and about him coming home with love bites, and she talks about going into labour with me.

'I was terrified. I didn't know what to expect. I was in a lot of pain, I tried walking around, I tried sitting down, I tried lying down. He went and slept in the spare room because I was disturbing him. He said, "Wake me up when you think you need to go to the hospital." I think that had to be the beginning of the end, to be honest, but I still went on and had another child.'

The more we talk, the more it becomes clear that for her the issues were all around partnership and support. That all those times of rolling over to ignore a wailing baby eventually took their toll.

'I thought, "What a bastard, that he can't help me." You were his child as well, so why was it all left to me? Yes, he did have to get up and go to work the next day, but then I had to look after you all day – and all night apparently – so I could have done with some help, but he wasn't very helpful.'

I ask if there was a single moment when she knew it was over.

'I think it was the build-up. I thought, "I've had it. I can't do it any more",' she says. 'I used to sit on the floor in your bedroom while you were asleep, crying my eyes out because I was so bloody miserable. I was thirty-six and saw myself as a sixty-year-old woman looking back on a completely miserable life, and I thought, "I can't do this. I need to get out." I think that's what made me do it.'

She's now sixteen years into marriage number two. Andy, my stepfather, is a non-drinker. He's slim and quiet and doesn't like spicy food. He spent most of his working life as a quantity surveyor and spends much of it now fixing things: toys for grandchildren, things about the house, overgrown foliage at the miniature railway where he works a few mornings a week. They have well-tended borders in their garden, and life seems calm and content.

'I suppose you know what you're doing more the second time. You know it's not going to be a bed of roses, and there will be times when you think "Why the hell did I do this?" There still are those moments, and I'm sure Andy feels exactly the same, but on the whole, it's good,' she says. 'We've had a few humdingers of rows, we really have. I think now we're both a bit wary of having rows, so I think we both hold back a bit when we feel one brewing. I bottle things up a lot, and then I go out and have a silent scream.'

Silent screaming, we both agree, might not be the best method of dispute resolution, but maybe it's no worse than me quietly swearing about Anna's attitude to domestic life.

I think that, as an adult, you become more aware of the imprint that your parents have left on you, and I have inherited my mum's impatience. Her screams are not always silent, and sometimes come out as strangled noises (imagine a goose stuck in traffic) when her printer doesn't work or a grandchild won't follow teeth-brushing instructions. For me it comes in sharp sighs (imagine a bicycle tyre deflating) when the children are being petulant or the remote control is not where it's supposed to be. But I think I inherited some of her silliness too, and part of the reason I always want to invent stories for my daughters rather than read to them from a book is the lingering memory of the poems that she wrote for us as children – rhyming nonsense about toes that come to life or a cat that can sing.

So what does the happy ending look like to her?

'If you're in a fairy tale, it's where they get married and walk off into the sunset together,' she says. 'But I think it's where you can actually live together without killing each other.'

In which case, Anna and I are doing fine so far.

☆☆☆

So who's been selling us this fairy tale and why is it so appealing that people are ready to run down the aisle to someone they barely know?

It's there from childhood in the first stories we hear and remember, but it's reinforced throughout our adult lives in films and books and music and our quiet, guilty obsession with the love lives of others.

I decide I need to speak to one of the yarn-spinners.

Megan Crane is one of the world's most prolific and successful romance novelists. Working under her own name and the pseudonym Caitlin Crews, she has written eighty-eight books when I speak to her and that figure is likely to be past a hundred by the time you read this. Titles include *Cold Heart, Warm Cowboy*; *Edge of Temptation* and *Undone by the Sultan's Touch*.

She grants me an interview by Skype from her home in southern Oregon, and with my pre-conceived ideas of romantic fiction, I partly expect an American version of the UK's Dame Barbara Cartland: all pink frills and gushing adjectives.

But Crane does not fit the stereotype. She's at her desk in a pale, long-sleeved top, has a tumble of shoulder-length brown-blonde curls and a tiny silver nose stud.

She lives with husband, Jeff (they married in the textbook-romantic island of Maui, Hawaii, in 2008), has a PhD in literature and a succinct explanation for why tales of love remain so popular.

'I've yet to meet a human being who didn't want love,' she says. 'Whatever they might say – to be seen and loved for what they are and have someone think they were wonderful: who wouldn't want that? I think that love is a basic human need.'

Romantic fiction is worth around $1.5 billion a year[1] in book sales in the USA, twice the value of crime fiction, the next best-selling

---

1   'Book genres that make the most money', Mahogany Turner-Francis, Bookstr. com, 6 January 2017.

genre. The appetite for these tales of heaving bosoms and rugged heroes clearly suggests they tap into something, even if we're all a little shy about admitting it.

'We're told that there's something wrong with seeking love – women particularly are looked down upon. Isn't that why Bridget Jones is supposed to be so funny, because she was so desperate to find that? What's desperate about that? Everybody wants to find love.'

It feels to me that this must be as true of men as it is of women. Through my twenties I often wondered if I'd ever find my 'one'. And in those moments I decided that she would be a fair-haired journalist and we'd live in London in a place with original wooden floorboards, being all barefooted and witty. It was a middle-class smug-topia and didn't consider postnatal depression or work-related stress or school runs or swearing at domestic appliances.

I wonder if, partly at least, this ideal affected my thinking when I first met Anna. We met on a training course for the magazine publisher where we both worked. I was supposed to have gone the month before but, being mildly shambolic, had cancelled at the last minute.

It was one of those tiny administrative tweaks that can change a life. I walked into a quiet training room and she was there, glowing like a beacon. So I sat down next to her and immediately fell in love. If I was a cartoon dog, I'd have had a red heart beating out of my chest and my eyes shooting forward on stalks.

I've never felt anything truer, before or since, but I also occasionally think that if I'd been more organized and gone on the course I was supposed to, we might never have met and I would probably have settled down with someone else.

I feel certain I would be less happy, and can't imagine being without her, but it also feels impossible not to be curious: to wonder what I'd see if I was led around like Ebenezer Scrooge to peek at alternative versions of my life.

I once heard it said that people who are afraid of heights are really just afraid of themselves: that sufferers are scared they might be overcome by an urge to pitch themselves off something very high up. I am one of those people. Three steps up a ladder, my head feels light, partly because I think my limbs might betray me. Clifftops and balconies make my heart beat faster. I think this is because I'm curious about the sensation of falling. I wonder how it would feel to have that sensation of absolute tumbling freedom for a few fractions of a second: to have the urgent embrace of cold rushing air and nothing more.

Fortunately, I am clear enough about the effects of landing not to do this. But still, a tiny part of me – perhaps 0.5 per cent of my decision-making lobes – will always wonder.

It's one of the reasons that, despite being an able-bodied forty-two-year-old dad, I do not drive. We didn't have a car when I was a teenager, and I've always lived in cities. But also, that 0.5 per cent in the back of my mind is curious about what it would be like to drive into a lamppost. I can only be 99.5 per cent sure that my arms won't take over at some point and fling me into a large cylinder of steel. I understand it would be painful. I understand that it would be financially unwise and could cause harm to others. But part of me – that nagging 0.5 per cent – wonders if the microseconds before the airbag opened might be *thrilling*.

And it's that part that wonders what it might be like to flee married life. I know that, for all the domestic frustrations of child rearing, if I'm away from my daughters for more than a day then a strange ache starts to develop in my chest and lungs. I know that Anna is – to me, at least – the most remarkable woman I've ever met, and I've never had a closer connection to another human being.

But there's that 0.5 per cent.

Because I could also go tomorrow, couldn't I? Take a little studio apartment and set up a Tinder account. Still fulfil my parental duties but do it from slightly further away, and live somewhere most of the time where the only needs that mattered were my own, and where the bathroom (or, more realistically given London prices, shower/toilet cubicle) only needs one bottle of shampoo.

Or even go further: hand over my card for the joint account, walk to the nearest motorway, stick out a thumb and see where I end up.

These are the familial equivalents of deliberately driving into a lamppost. I know the long-term results may not be nice, but wouldn't there be the tiniest thrill in the meantime?

And perhaps there's something to be said for moving from one happy ending to the next. Because if you keep moving, you never get to the part where you're swearing about hair tongs and laundry.

Other humans can be deeply annoying. They have opinions and needs. They have odd habits and want to do things in ways and at times that inconvenience you. So why do we bother? What if the romance writers are wrong, and humans aren't really meant to be together forever?

Maybe the happiest ending is being alone. The only way to know is to find some men who've tried it.

Anna

My browser history reveals a search for denim Topshop harem pants, a Miffy weaning spoon and a 'bright and airy' studio apartment in East Dulwich on Findaflat.com.

The flat isn't for me, it's for my friend Jessie who has just separated from her husband. But I scroll through the photos of this small, overpriced space and fleetingly wonder what it would be like to leave Matt.

I wonder what it would be like to live without the low-level hum of another adult human. I wonder if I would like just making a cup of tea for myself instead of asking, 'Fancy a cuppa?' I wonder if I'd miss the sex and what my Tinder profile might say. I wonder why I'm wondering these things.

When I was eleven, I remember rifling through *More* magazine with some friends in the toilets of the strict Roman Catholic girls school I went to. The highlight of this well-thumbed rag was the 'position of the fortnight' column detailing sex moves that looked impractical. There was once an illustration of an expressionless woman doing the 'reverse cowgirl' with an expressionless man. This, along with the scene where Tom Cruise touched Rebecca De Mornay's leg in *Risky Business*, was close to what I felt love was. I had a head brace with alternating pink and neon-yellow rubber bands. A poster of Prince William's face was Sellotaped to the inside of my ring binder with a postcard of the actor Edward Furlong from *Terminator 2* laminated on the front to divert attention from my royal ambition.

My only other reference was my parents.

In the years before I turned eleven, we would drive down to the Loire Valley in France in a white Audi 100 that seemed to prompt car sickness at every turn. The car itself looked like the design team had taken inspiration from a bar of Imperial Leather soap. For the eight-hour journey I was strapped into the back with only my sister, Karen, and a battered Groov-e cassette player for company. I would listen to *Now That's What I Call Music! 23* on repeat to distract me from my sibling's presence. It was a cassette compilation that had highlights (Freddie Mercury and Monserrat Caballé's operatic rendition of 'Barcelona' to commemorate the 1992 Olympics) and lowlights (the Tetris music as a club anthem by Doctor Spin).

But that vehicle with questionable aural accompaniment delivered us to our rented gîte in Vendôme year after year and, as soon as my sister and I dumped our tie-dyed rucksacks, memories of my parents, Chris and Lucy, fade for memories of paddling pools, hyperglow T-shirts and Nerds sweets packed with more E-numbers than should have been legal.

On those journeys there were three constants:

1   Phil Collins blasting out of the car speakers, often interfering with my own music (I now struggle to listen to 'Easy Lover' without instantly feeling nauseous).
2   My mum being in charge of map reading in a time before satnav.
3   My dad taking many wrong turns.

A twelve-hour journey with two carsick children, no GPS and few linguistic skills ('It said *droit*, Chris. What is *droit*?') should be a prerequisite for every marriage. It feels like there are tests for everything from maths and general studies to driving and chlamydia and yet there's no regulatory body questioning a union that signs off with 'till death us do part'.

I am now twelve years into a relationship with a man I don't want to be parted from – through death or a sordid Tinder affair – but as I sit here writing, red-eyed after another argument, I do wonder if there should have been some assessment before we drove off without a map. Something to qualify that, even when the road is bumpy and petrol dangerously low, the car is at least pointing in the right direction.

A friend once said that before getting married the vicar at her local church asked her and her fiancé what they wanted out of life. She wanted three kids and a pedigree chocolate-brown Labrador, he wanted one kid and a rescued tabby cat. She wanted to live in the country, he wanted to live in the city. She wanted monogamy, he was intrigued by polyamory. They're still together but sleeping apart because he snores like a freight train and she wriggles like a beached octopus. They *seem* OK.

All I know is that those road trips to France would always be laced with bickering and tense periods where Phil Collins would get louder, but generally my parents were going in the same direction. It's a direction they've been going in for forty-seven years.

What's gone on behind closed doors inspires equal measures of intrigue and aversion. No child wants to think of the more amorous side of their parents' relationship – hugs in the kitchen and pecks on the cheek are enough qualification that all is OK. But as I sit here questioning my own relationship, what I can say is that my mum and dad are Olympic-gold standard teammates. The marital equivalent of Torvill and Dean but with sequins exchanged for M&S V-neck jumpers, and faux smiles swapped for crinkly-eyed laughter.

They've been married 14,235 days longer than Matt and me. As we navigate the quagmire of *Paw Patrol* theme tunes, sleep deprivation, mortgage repayments, grouting and general disillusionment, I never imagined trying to find answers to my amorous questions so close to home. I never imagined asking my parents outside of the confines of that Audi 100, 'Are we (Matt and I) nearly there yet?'

But there's a game my dad plays on my mum. It's pretty basic and involves putting fruit and veg in random places around the house. Most recently we've had a parsnip in the utensils jar, a pineapple on top of the grandfather clock and a heritage carrot in the kettle spout. There was once a slightly less laughable situation with a watermelon falling off the oven hood and nearly knocking Mum out. I'll often hear high-pitched exclamations of 'Oh Chris!' followed by laughter and her appearing, banana in hand, as my dad chortles like Muttley off *Wacky Races*.

'Don't forget the hats,' says my dad when I interview them on the faded cream sofa of our family living room. 'She got very cross when I put her favourite hat on the car antenna. It was Gerry the postman that found it and asked, "What's this, then?"'

While his efforts are unlikely to bag a 'rising star' award at the Edinburgh Comedy Festival, laughter has been the anchor in their relationship, even when there was not much to laugh about. 'No one really talked about it in the seventies and eighties, but we faced two late miscarriages,' my dad says, speaking of the two boys, Paul and Mark, they lost late in pregnancy before having my sister and me.

'I remember sitting on our bed, wondering how we would get through this,' my mum continues, her usual chirpiness momentarily dampened. 'But you have to go on and you cannot start lashing out at the other person when the going gets tough because you are both breaking. You need to learn to break together.'

My mum and dad live in Buckinghamshire, still happily ensconced in our childhood home. It's a red-brick four-bedroomed house with a yew tree out the back that has our deceased rodents buried beneath it. The sofa they're sitting on is the same one where I watched *Risky Business* for the first time with my friend Clare during an early-nineties sleepover. Then, like now, I want to know more about love.

'Anyone who says they are happily married all the time is most unusual and not to be trusted,' says Dad. 'Marriage is a marathon not a sprint.'

My dad is dressed in a pair of unintentionally on-trend Adidas trainers and his favourite navy fleece, which cost £14.99 from a little shop in Dawlish Warren in Devon and he's had to save twice from being donated to charity: 'She [my mum] isn't a fan.' Mum is in a polka-dot jumpsuit that she saw me wearing one day and bought even though she thought it might be 'too edgy'. She's recently ditched the hair dye and gone grey, while my dad's personal style hasn't changed since the invention of the Post-It note in 1974. He wears a St Christopher pendant that he's never taken off and they both check the other has a cup of tea.

They met in a pub called The Cock Inn in Harpenden. He was working as a financial advisor, had a Mini Clubman with dodgy brakes that was 'like driving a sewing machine', and she had flown over from her native Holland to be an au pair for a Dutch actress called Yvonne Vanger. At nineteen, with long bronzed pins and a shock of auburn curls under a big navy floppy hat, my mum and her German friend Ingrid were the talk of the small town.

My dad says, 'One of my friends called Lucy a "low tree nibbler" because of her height, but I also call her Big Bird, Old Dutch Bean and Luce, depending on the mood,' he continues, taking a loud slurp from a mug that reads 'Shoe-aholic'.

She made an instant impression, partly because of that hat.

'His first ever words to me at the pub were: "Ooh, look here, we've got a mushroom",' she says. 'He always has a way of breaking down any awkward moments with a quip. I was saying the other day that I didn't like a presenter on the TV very much and he said, "Well, I'm sure she speaks very highly of you, Luce."'

My dad's first home, bought before he met my mum, cost £3,750 and was called The Shambles, which – according to the *Oxford English Dictionary* – means 'a state of total disorder'. There couldn't be a more ironic place name for a man who dots Is, crosses Ts and enjoys meeting a tax-return deadline. He's a man of complete law-abiding order. 'Everything on his desk is at ninety degrees,' says Mum. 'The hole-punch and his highlighter pens are neatly in line with a two-for-one Odeon voucher and a purple Fimo [the moulding substance] monster you made when you were seven.'

On his windowsill is a photo of my mum looking ethereal and beaming on their wedding day in 1975.

Having been in their company for thirty-eight of their forty-seven years together, I can report that happiness has definitely ebbed and flowed. Yet their benchmark of joint happiness – even when faced with difficult times – has undeniably been set high. (I once believed the only couple happily married were Heidi Klum and Seal – that break-up quashed any hope I had for marital utopia.) But what I've seen is my dad translate his own unsettled upbringing into an incredibly solid family unit.

And so often that's been shown in tiny moments. It was his ability to raise a smile before my exams with a badly drawn cat sketched on a Post-It note that read: 'Good luck, Top Cat'. Or my mum peeling a satsuma, removing the white bits and wrapping it in kitchen paper so she was always 'with me' on a school lunch-break.

Increasingly, I feel as if Matt and I are getting bogged down in what should be domestic bliss – a set-up we thought would lead to that elusive 'happily ever after'. We've had the wedding, we've had the kids, we're doing the jobs but, after chipping hardened porridge off tables and scraping squashed peas off floors, it feels like the spark is fading with every passive-aggressive exchange and that all I have to relight it is a packet of damp matches.

'We would never have made it if we thought marriage was some endless exciting affair,' confides Mum. 'It's really about the small things and enjoying them together. Some of the richest people I know are the poorest in their marriages. I bought some jars of chilli gherkins from Tesco recently and I've never seen him happier.'

She counters this with: 'He has never changed a loo roll, though.'

But my dad has never failed to make her a cup of tea in the morning, either. So it is, perhaps, a long journey (like those long drives to the Loire Valley) with a few bumps in the road along the way.

But is their happy ending really what I want for me and Matt? I don't really like gherkins and I've bookmarked Findaflat.com, so I need to find someone with a bit more scientific authority on matters of the heart. I head upstairs to my childhood bedroom, with Blu Tack still imprinted on the walls where posters of the now Duke of Cambridge once loomed, open my laptop and search for 'love'.

Alongside 'Love Rat', 'Love Ring' and many other intriguing associations with the word, I find 'The Love Lab'.

Run by the world-renowned relationship psychologist John Gottman, author of *The Relationship Cure: A Five-step Guide to Strengthening your Marriage, Family and Friendships*, this Washington University laboratory opened up the science behind 'happily ever after'. It saw 130 newlyweds in the first throes of love stay over in a B&B setting to have their behaviour monitored by Gottman – truly romantic times. But he established a few helpful patterns that I've seen play out in my mum and dad's relationship.

Gottman says that partners would make requests for connection – what he calls 'bids'.

For example: one partner is a bird watcher and notices a stunning goldfinch fly across the garden. He or she might say to his or her partner, 'Look at that beautiful bird outside!' This isn't just a comment about a bird, it's a request for a response – a sign of interest or support – hoping they'll connect, however momentarily, over that rare feathery friend.

Exchange the goldfinch here for a Pizza Express voucher and you've got my dad. I remember, one insignificant Monday, an envelope landing on the doormat and him hollering 'Luce' to my mum. He made a bid for her attention, which she happily responded to, leaving the dishwasher door open and toast burning. While I had algebraic equations on my mind, I remember them buzzing about the abundance of dough balls that came with being a loyal consumer. As someone who has worked as a waitress at this chain restaurant, it doesn't surprise me that happiness can also be found in a 20 per cent discount on a Sloppy Giuseppe.

I feel like Matt has tried to get my attention over the last two years – he's tried to point out rabbits in parks, flowers in gardens and has recently carved toast into the shape of a penis – but I sometimes haven't been able to hear him fully through the din of postnatal depression, WhatsApp messages and social-media-induced self-doubt. I remember people speaking about 'the baby blues' and thinking it didn't come close to the numbing weight of that postpartum period. It's a hole I sat in for eight months and, even though I've had professional support, I'm still not sure I've fully emerged from it.

In fact, I don't think we've heard each other properly since our second daughter was born in June 2017.

All I do know is the ratio of tears to laughter has been skewed since that first wonderful infant cry and, despite being together every day, I sometimes feel more alone than ever.

Delving deeper into Gottman's work, I am a little reassured that the mortar that holds couples together is kindness. There are apparently two ways to think about kindness. You can think about it as a fixed trait: either you have it or you don't. Or you could think of kindness as a muscle that needs to be built up. In some people, that muscle is naturally stronger than in others, but it can grow stronger in everyone with exercise. The pertinent question Gottman asks is: are you willing to try?

There was one day in the summer holidays when we were kids, when my mum made the dramatic declaration that she was off. She was clutching a badly packed suitcase with clothes hanging out of it that looked like deflated zombies trying to escape. I was playing with my hamster (the since-perished Bubbles) and I'd never heard their exchanges reach such a crescendo before. So I peeked through a crack in the door, part-scared, part-curious. It was an argument that started with some domestic irritant like congealed dishwasher salts but really the subtext was that my mum missed having a career and she'd grown weary of feeding, wiping, school running, and generally feeling like an au pair – a position she'd left thirty years before.

'There's stubbornness in both of us,' says Dad, 'but kindness trumps that. It's sometimes the difference between giving them the last Jammie Dodger or just scoffing it in the kitchen and pretending there weren't any left.'

My step-grandfather, John, a towering man with a baritone voice, gave his definition of kindness in a reading by Ogden Nash that he chose for our wedding:

To keep your marriage brimming,
With love in the loving cup,
Whenever you're wrong, admit it;
Whenever you're right, shut up.

Since that wedding day, I can definitely highlight where Matt has gone wrong. There's currently a carpet of crumbs adorning the kitchen surfaces and he won't think to sweep those remnants into the bin. I know many wonderful things about this heavily browed bastion of goodwill that I said 'yes' to, but I also know he has never changed the Hoover bag in the twelve years we've been together. Sometimes in my meaner-spirited moments, I consider asking him to do it, knowing he'll struggle to locate the bags, let alone master the exchange. We know how to live.

How this pedantic, miserly woman emerged, I couldn't say. It was definitely not overnight, more in the day-to-day build-up of little things that Matt and I haven't done for each other. Small disappointments that have turned 'I do' into 'Why can't you . . .?'

He's not an inconsiderate man. He's wiped my tears after painful work altercations and built me up again with bum squeezes and cottage pie. He repeated this when we navigated the hopelessness of recurrent miscarriage. He is, despite the curmudgeonly brows, a kind man in the big moments.

When it comes to things like redundancy, loss and injury, we seem to navigate the marital waters with relative aplomb. The adrenaline of potential disaster unites us like a tired Starsky and Hutch (accompanied by a laundry pile that could prove fatal if prodded). It's in those moments that I know he's definitely The One. It's just in the daily grey where I wonder fleetingly if this is it.

I read a book recently called *The Science of Happily Ever After* by Ty Tashiro and this bit stood out: 'Even in relationships where people are frustrated, it's almost always the case that there are positive things going on and people trying to do the right thing. A lot of times, a partner is trying to do the right thing even if it's executed poorly. So appreciate the intent.'

Having used many things (hunger, general disillusionment with the world, losing at Monopoly) as a reason to start an argument with Matt, I have to disagree slightly with Tashiro. Our intentions can sometimes be wonky and laced with sleep deprivation.

But I am proud of this poem I penned for him on 21 November 2006 after we'd had an argument about my flirtatious manner towards other men (and women – I was even-handed) in social situations:

Matt, Matt, you're not a twat,
You get on my norks but so does Postman Pat.
Matt, Matt, you're a hairy man,
When it comes to your chops, I'm your biggest fan.
Matt, Matt, I'm a bit of a bell-end
It was 73 per cent² my fault, The End.

But it's not the end. And if we're constantly striving for some grandiose happy ending, and only being kind in times of trouble,

---

2   On reflection and with a decade to let the dust settle, possibly 94 per cent.

are we missing the flickers of joy along the way? Happiness isn't a constant, it isn't something you're rewarded with on your death bed – 'Congratulations you've reached death without killing each other! Here's a lifetime of joy as you expire!' – it's yours for the taking now. Life's not a box of chocolates necessarily but it can, perhaps, be a jar of piquant pickles.

And then my newly single friend Jessie excitedly sends a photo of her exposed-brick lounge in East Dulwich, and I make the possible mistake of wondering, 'What if?'

2

Going Solo

Are we happier alone?

Matt

You need two things to visit Mount Athos in Greece: a permit from the Pilgrims' Bureau and a pair of testicles.

Technically, perhaps that's three things.

Either way, no woman has set foot upon the mountain for more than 1,000 years. They're not even allowed within 500 metres of the coast.

It is a jagged peninsula, only about forty miles long and a few across, but the terrain means it would take three days to walk end to end.

It's thought to be the world's largest women-free zone and the only female creatures here are birds, stray cats and some of the wolves that prowl the woods and howl after sunset.

The sole permanent human inhabitants are the Eastern Orthodox monks who live in twenty monasteries dotted across the hills and decided a millennium ago that women would be a distraction from their dedication to God. There are some passing labourers who help maintain the place, and a handful of pilgrims who are allowed to visit on three-day permits.

When I first heard of these monks, cloistered away with no concerns about romantic love (or gender-equality regulations), I wondered: could they really be happy? What must it be like to spend every day in quiet contemplation and to be free from the needs of others? I bet they never have small children banging on the toilet door, demanding that they pretend to be a pony.

I leave on a Monday lunchtime, and by 10a.m. the following morning I'm on a small ferry cruising along the peninsula. It can only be approached by sea or along steep donkey paths. The hills rear up from the water, ascending in darkening shades of green before turning graphite grey at the crucifix-topped peak.

Every few miles a monastery can be seen, usually with its own tiny port. Further up the hills, among the vineyards and olive groves or hacked into the cliffs, are *sketes* – the homes of monks who find even monastic life a little too crowded and decide to live as hermits.

There are about thirty men on the ferry. Some are monks, dressed in black gowns, with long black capes hanging down from rimless black hats. Their beards are long and wild and their hair is tied back in small knots at the nape of the neck, like low-slung hipster man-buns.

The rest are pilgrims dressed for casual practicality – jeans or tracksuits, trainers and leather jackets. When we disembark, we look like we're left-behinds hoping for a day's casual labouring. Most of the men are in their forties and fifties and speak in Russian or Greek.

I'm 97 per cent atheist. That 3 per cent of doubt isn't because I think there might be a God – at least, not the traditional divine creator with a big beard – but because it's kind of impossible to completely disprove the existence of anything and I'm willing to accept that I might be wrong.

We got married in a church and christened both of our daughters, which is pretty hypocritical. But Anna's family had a connection to the church and I was happy to go along. I'd have married her in a leaky barn if it meant saying 'I do'. And on a very shallow level, it was a beautiful, crumbling, eleventh-century building sitting in a field of golden rapeseed. I bought into the aesthetics. Also, it was Church of England, which seems to me to be a religion for atheists who don't want to cause a fuss.

But the Eastern Orthodox Catholic Church requires a little more dedication. The monks pray daily from 4a.m. to 7.30a.m., from 11a.m. to 2.30p.m. and from 5p.m. to 6.30p.m. Pilgrims attend the services in exchange for 'Holy Land food' (bread, olives, bean stews, sometimes fish) and a night in a shared dorm. No praying means no eating, so over the next few days, I hear a lot of prayers.

And the services are gently mesmeric. The Orthodox and Roman Catholic churches split in 1054 in a row about who did what in Jerusalem a thousand years before (including a ding-dong about the recipe for bread used in the Last Supper, and whether it had yeast in it). Today, Roman Catholicism focuses on Jesus the man, while the Orthodox Church focuses on Jesus as a divine entity. It makes for a much more mystical vibe.

There is chanting, incantation and incense burning, and the monks look as if little has changed in 2,000 years. In comparison, the neat hair and white collar of a typical British priest looks wildly modern.

I spend about eight hours a day in dark churches at a few different monasteries, listening to services in an ancient form of Greek.

These places are dimly lit, with dusty bars of light creeping in through thick wooden shutters.

I've always been curious about those with faith, and the process of these services – the physical stillness, the steady chanting by the monks – is oddly therapeutic, if a little trippy.

In my daily life, it's rare for me to be alone with my thoughts. There is always money to be earned, a domestic task to be done, a child with needs or a sports page to urgently scroll through. The closest I come to meditation is standing on the morning Tube with no Wi-Fi and blankly staring at adverts for zinc supplements.

Being here is enforced time in your own head. But the only visions that come to me are my daughters. I think of our toddler and the way her lips form an 'O' when she puffs out her cheeks like a guppy fish. Or how she does an enthusiastic 'Raaaar!' when I read her *Ten Little Dinosaurs*. Or how our eldest, now in her first year at school, has begun adding 'darlin'' at the end of sentences, as if she's an East End barmaid. Or the goofy faces she pulls when she decides, unprompted and at random, to shout 'Let's go crazy!' and throw her limbs around and gurn.

But I think less about Anna and wonder, quietly, if our children suck our love away and that as a result there's a bit less left for each other. When I do think of her, I wonder if telling her this would be an entry-level error in How to Have a Happy Marriage 101.

In each monastery, I say a quiet 'hello' whenever I pass a monk, but it's typically met with a brusque smile and nod. Turns out, men who have fled the world for a life of contemplation are not that chatty.

Eventually, I find a monk to speak to at the Vatopedi monastery.

After lunch, all the monks and pilgrims gather in a leafy central courtyard. They stand close together when they speak and sometimes gently hold hands. One might hold the cuff of the other. It's light and affectionate. Even for those who have foregone love and sex, there seems to be a basic human need for physical contact.

Abbot Ephraim is the big boss, and a crowd builds around him, with pilgrims jostling for the chance to kiss his hand while monks nudge aside the overly persistent. In their flowing black gowns they look like ecclesiastical bouncers protecting a diminutive pop star.

I see a skinny monk with red flame tattoos rising up his neck, just visible between his high collar and scraggly beard. I'm curious about his previous life and explain why I'm there. He sounds like he may be from the US Midwest and looks to be mid-thirties, but he tells me that he must go and pray, and so directs me to Father Theonas.

Father Theonas is Greek-Australian and still has a faint Aussie accent despite living on Mount Athos since 1983. He tells me I need a blessing from Abbot Ephraim and calls upon Father Matthew, a grey-haired American with a Friar Tuck belly, before claiming he too must rush away.

I'm being passed about like a tea towel among reluctant dishwashers and there's nervousness in all these interactions. I'm suddenly aware of the hierarchy among these men. Their lives are governed by strict rules and I wonder if there is some shame attached to getting things wrong.

After a few minutes, Father Matthew's tug on the abbot's cuff gets attention. He translates my request into Greek. The abbot is about eighty, six inches shorter than me and has thin white hair floating out from his hat. He takes my hand and pulls me down, putting his left palm behind my neck, pulling my head to the level of his stomach. The top of my head is an inch from his navel, and I wonder if this is a typical greeting or if he's taken a special shine to me.

He gives a few sharp pats to the back of my skull, lets me up and smiles. Father Matthew translates.

'You are not Orthodox, so you cannot understand true happiness,' he says. 'This is the one true faith and without that understanding there will be something missing from your book.'

I tell him that's why I've come to ask questions. He smiles and asks how many children I have. When I reply, 'two daughters', Ephraim shakes his head, before addressing Father Matthew. They speak for a while and finally Matthew turns back to me.

'The abbot says you should have five children,' which seems rich from a man who's unlikely to have ever changed a nappy. I'd like to see how his spiritual serenity stands up to the eighth rendition of 'Baby Shark'.

(I also later discover that Abbot Ephraim was briefly imprisoned – and later acquitted – for his part in the 'holy exchange' land deal between the church and the government that cost Greek taxpayers an estimated €100 million.)

'But he gives his blessing for you to interview a monk.' Eventually, Father Matthew agrees to be that monk.

We sit outside the monastery on a low wall overlooking newly planted grape vines. The sun is warm for spring and we both squint at its brightness. I want to know what convinces men to come here and give up the modern world and the possibility of a life with someone.

'We have former atheists, people who have been in prison, we have people who had problems with drink and drugs. It's a menagerie of different backgrounds and spiritual journeys and there's no rhyme or reason to it,' he says.

But he has a very clear idea of what 'happy ever after' looks like.

'The source of all our unhappiness is the desire to want to be our own gods,' he says. 'If I want to be happy, I have to stop doing things the way that I think they ought to be done and try my best to do things the way that I believe God wants them done. When we surrender to the will of God, we see how He makes things happen. Things become good.'

I hear the same from the few other monks willing to speak to me – just believe and all will be well. Do God's will and you'll be happy. It may be true, but it seems too simple – like a spiritual pyramid scheme where you're guaranteed success if you just believe hard enough. And I don't.

Towards the end of the day, I fall into conversation with a pilgrim called Panos. He is a sound engineer and an enthusiastic reader of Greek philosophy. For an hour we sit in the courtyard and talk about relationships, responsibility and whether monks have wet dreams. But mostly he talks about the philosopher Heraclitus.

Panos tells me: 'He said that "No man ever steps in the same river twice, for it's not the same river and he's not the same man." It means you can return to exactly the same place but your experience will be different because you will have changed. People try to stand in the river and fight the water to make it like it was, but they should go with flow. Let the river take you forward and steer the new course.'

I'm not very good at meaningful conversations. The moment a chat hints at depth, my instinct is to lower the tone, preferably with a joke about bodily functions. But Panos is a more considered man than me, and as I sit in the dappled light of a monastery courtyard, his borrowed analogy makes some sense. Maybe Anna and I are sitting in a river, scrapping like angry beavers to get back upstream. But things can never be like they were when we first met, because we are different people now. Instead of trying to recreate a carefree yesterday, perhaps we should be steering our way downstream to wherever we want to go next.

I worry that this sounds like a piece of motivational embroidery – the kind of life philosophy that can be stitched on a cushion – but for all that I've heard from holy men, the most meaningful insight may have come from Panos the sound engineer, who has essentially told me that if we're going to make it to the happy ending, we need to stop looking back and start looking forwards.

It seems to me that the monks are happy – they tend to stay for years and, for all the twitchiness about talking to me, they mostly smile serenely when they speak to each other.

But I'm always a little suspicious of religious men – particularly those with no families – who push more breeding as the ultimate happiness. It's basically a slow recruitment drive: more babies means more disciples and more people to buy into their version of God. And it always seems to be men who make these rules and invent the hierarchies to protect them. And it's mostly men who find new ways to shut themselves away from the world (although big shout-out to any nuns who may be reading).

Perhaps I could be happy here, if I gave up everything else, but that feels like quitting.

So I decide I need to hear from someone who understands how the deliberately single life works if you're not willing to banish yourself to a monastery surrounded by wild wolves. And perhaps the most qualified person is a woman on the picture-postcard central California coast.

Back in mainland Greece, I call Dr Bella DePaulo. She is sixty-five and has been deliberately single for more than four decades. She is also a sociologist with a PhD from Harvard and has written extensively about the modern single experience.

Speaking from her home in the idyllically named Summerland, a few miles along from Santa Barbara, she tells me that, 'I did the romantic relations thing. I have no dating horror stories. I'd think, "This guy makes me smile," but every time the relationship ended, I was so relieved and happy to go back to my single life.'

She decided in her twenties that romantic partnerships were not for her and has been studying happy singledom ever since.

'We remain tied to marital mythology. It's very attractive. It says, "Look, all you need to do is find this one magical person and marry them, and all of your dreams will come true",' she says.

The reality, though, can be a little disappointing. DePaulo gathered data from thousands of US college students who were asked to rate their expected happiness before and after marriage, on a scale of one to ten.

The average scores showed a huge spike from a miserable pre-marriage 3.25 to an ecstatic post-nuptial 8.25.

She then plotted data gathered from thousands of people who actually were married. That's the dotted line, here:

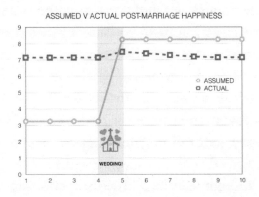

These coupled-up souls started at a steady 7.25, creeping up to 7.5 around the wedding day, and then slowly slipping back down to

7.25. Based on this, your wedding day may be the happiest of your life, but it barely makes a blip in the bland seven-out-of-ten that is human existence. My own wedding day was mostly a blur of prolific sweating, feeling a bit freaked out that everyone was staring at me, and being a bit angry about having to stand in a field to pose for the kind of cheesy images that come with the picture frame at Argos while my mates were all drinking booze that we'd paid for. I was very happy to be marrying Anna, but the day itself was a rare old faff.

And a life of devoted singledom has more merits than might be assumed. 'Studies show that single people have more friends than married people do, and they do more to maintain their relationships with their friends, siblings, parents and neighbours. It's really the single people who are knitting communities together, quite in contrast to the stereotype,' DePaulo says.

'The kinds of stories we tell are so focused on deficits – "Oh, you poor single person, aren't you missing out?" – but we've gotta flip that and realize that single people are living lives that are full and complete and meaningful, and have some things that coupled people miss.'

I can see how this might be true. I only really see my closest buddies every few months or, in some cases, years. We gather to drink, exchange very brief updates on jobs and family, and spend the rest of the time discussing sport or verbally abusing each other.

But I also suspect that the single (or at least unmarried) life works better for women than for men, and there's plenty of proof of this. The Longevity Project, an eighty-year US study, found that straight married men live longer than their single or divorced brethren. It suggests that straight marriage calms men down a bit, and that without the love of a good woman, they tend to drink more and eat less well.

I find my diet degenerates into a cycle of sugary cereals and mayo-slathered sandwiches the moment Anna and I are apart for the night. I'm writing this in a tiny Airbnb in Thessaloniki, and since waking up six hours ago have fed myself a packet of processed cheese, three-quarters of a loaf of white bread, and six instant coffees. I'm not even ashamed, and intend to finish the bread before catching the flight home.

But marrying doesn't bring the same health benefits for women – The Longevity Project found that living solo actually improves female longevity, and it's not the only study to do so.

London School of Economics scientist Paul Dolan did extensive research into the American Time Use Survey, comparing happiness levels among the married, divorced, unmarried and separated.

'The healthiest and happiest population subgroup are women who never married or had children,' he said recently. 'You see a single woman of forty, who has never had children – "Bless, that's a shame, isn't it? Maybe one day you'll meet the right guy and that'll change." No, maybe she'll meet the wrong guy and that'll change. Maybe she'll meet a guy who makes her less happy and healthy, and die sooner.'

One theory is that married women's health deteriorates because marriage drives them to drink.

A nine-year University of Cincinnati study of 5,305 men and women from Wisconsin found that married women drank more because they took on their husbands' boozing habits. Men, however, tended to see less of their flabby-faced beer buddies and drank less than if they were single.

There's certainly some truth here for us. The other Monday we were still a little hungover after going to a wedding on the Saturday. There wasn't much food in the house, so once the kids were down we made cheese on toast. I asked Anna if she wanted wine but she said no. Then I poured myself a large glass of 'congratulations, you've finished Monday', and the sight of it turned her 'no' into a 'go on, then'.

Combined with all these stats, it's making me wonder if Anna might live a longer life if I move into the shed and stay there.

These trends are not confined to hetero pairs, either. There's much less research on same-sex couples because marriage equality is pretty new in most countries where it exists. But an Aalborg University study, based on data about 6.5 million Danes, found that married gay men lived longer than single gay men. Their sample size was too small to draw any solid conclusions about gay women.

Whatever the set-up, it seems that, left to themselves (and without the hierarchies of monkdom to keep them in check), men's health goes downhill while women's flourishes.

All of this brings me back to memories of my dad's decline. In the years after the divorce, he edged away from us pretty quickly. The child-maintenance payments to my mother stopped after a few months. The Sunday visits – when my sister and I, aged ten and eight, would sit awkwardly in suburban Italian restaurants as he smoked between courses – petered out a bit later. His drinking continued. He moved in with a barmaid from his local pub for a while and he worked less. After a couple of years he moved back to Aberdeen and when his father died, he moved in with his widowed mother, to her tiny one-bedroom flat, sleeping on a sofa bed.

By the time I got to uni, we were only speaking every few months on the phone but he made less and less sense. He asked when my birthday was and what I did at school. When my grandmother went into a hospice, her neat little flat fell into decay. By the time she passed away, he was living in a private pub for one, with overflowing ashtrays and stains down the walls.

Our conversations became less coherent. He would only call when very drunk, and made little more than slurring noises. If I managed to catch him mid-morning, between waking up and his second or third drink, he might make a little more sense.

I saw him in person twice in the last ten years of his life, and the last of those was with Anna and my sister, El, who wanted to introduce him to her eighteen-month-old daughter, his first (and then only) grandchild. In the flat the stains were deeper, there was grime across the kitchen and spilled tobacco on the floor. In the corner was an old tape deck surrounded by cassettes of Dylan, Joni Mitchell, Springsteen and all the great American singer-song-writers. My sister held her daughter off the floor and we made polite conversation while my dad drank white wine from a coffee mug.

His old school friend, who I had known since childhood, came by with a present for my niece and we contrived an excuse to walk to the local shop. Dad hollered down the stairs for more wine as we left.

'It's been like that for a while,' Dad's friend said. 'I think he gets up about mid-morning, potters about for a bit then starts on the wine and listening to his music. Then he goes until two or three in the morning. He knows he should stop, but he doesn't want to. It's not usually as clean as it is now. He'll have tidied up because you were coming.'

Six months later he died alone, sitting at the bottom of the communal concrete stairs in that low-rise block. His heart had failed at sixty-one. A neighbour found him and said he looked at peace. When I went to clear out the flat, the gas fire was still burning and cassettes carpeted the floor.

☆☆☆

I like sitting on benches and staring at trees. I consider pacing around while muttering to myself to be a good way to spend time. I enjoy drinking tea and wondering what to do. These things are incompatible with children and a partner who regularly wants to discuss feelings, so I sometimes engineer errands to escape them.

I take the long way round to the corner shop to fetch milk. I feel my shoulders release when I flee the house for work on a Monday morning. But when I'm apart from Anna and the girls, I daydream about their faces. I'm struck by an urgent need to know how they are and what they're doing. I wonder if the girls are happy and if Anna is safe. I can't be without them, but I also, secretly, sometimes really want to escape.

I hope this is normal, and I'm encouraged that my urge to flee is always fleeting and temporary.

Because people need people. The monks have their god but they also have each other. The growing movement of global singles have friends and communities of their own. My dad decided to have no one and in the end I think it killed him.

I have Anna, and I always want it to be Anna, but there's been a bit of a slow drift between us for a while, and I wonder, in moments of doubt, how people who have decided that they do want someone can be sure they've really found the right one.

Partly, I think that's the era we live in: ours is a time when with a few taps of your phone you can change your partner as easily as your taxi booking. I need to know if love in a time of Tinder makes it harder to be happy.

Anna

I'm sitting next to Matt at my friend's wedding and the bride's sister, Kate, comes over and sits next to us. She's a surgeon, looks like Natalie Portman and drunkenly asks if we know anyone with a big cock. My friend Aimee suggests her friend Justin. I clumsily ask why Justin isn't married and Kate jokingly slurs: 'You judgemental crow in your average sexless marriage, asking why someone is single. Brilliant people are single. I am single.'

She is right, even if being equally judgemental. I apologise and then ask how Aimee knows about Justin's penis. (It was a loose friends-with-benefits agreement in the late nineties.) Kate assures us she's happy with sloppy seconds and stumbles away, leaving me to question if my marriage is average. And if I am a crow.

My pre-teen years were lived for the Discovery Channel, which had me fascinated by sedentary marine life. In the village where I grew up, there were 241 residents, a bus stop, and a pub run by a landlord who was once fined £250 for drink riding – his horse knew the way home even when he didn't.

David Attenborough was my escape. Sea anemones might not be the obvious poster critter for true love but I remember watching one crawl onto a hermit crab's shell and hitch a ride across the seabed. Together they were unstoppable. The anemone would fend off hungry octopuses, using its barbed tentacles, while the crab would bat away starfish and fire-worms that loved nothing more than nibbling on sea anemones for breakfast. They were like the deep-sea equivalent of Ennis and Jack in *Brokeback Mountain* but without the steamy tent scene. They were Thelma and Louise but without the fatal ending.

There's a term for this ecological union: symbiosis. Two different species teaming up and each offering something the other is lacking. I am also a fan of the goby fish, a sea-dweller that resembles an angry, floating cigar and stands guard outside the near-blind snapping shrimp's sandy home. In exchange for this 24/7 protection, the shrimp opens its door to the goby fish and they snuggle up for the night.

Increasingly, I'm the snapping shrimp. Matt is the goby fish. And ever since those days in front of the Discovery Channel, in that secluded village that felt a long way from any kind of excitement, I've always hated the idea of being alone.

I have always been in a relationship through my adult life, and if things are coming to an end, there's always been someone – at times, anyone, including a failed Formula Three driver who called me 'Mupps' (short for Muppet) – ready to carry the baton to the next stage of my romantic life. I'm a pack animal, someone who laps up the chatter by the water cooler, and while I enjoy my own company, I prefer Netflix and chilling – sometimes in a negligee, mostly in a onesie – with someone, anyone else.

Before Matt, there was Mike, with a period of precisely forty-two days between them. Six weeks after Mike and I split up, we sat together by the Thames on a bench made for one and a half people as I explained that I had met Matt and was moving to Dubai. Matt and I had been on three dates when he was offered a job in the United Arab Emirates and asked me at 3a.m., after a few Whisky Mac nightcaps, to come with him. Hungover the next morning and both too British to go back on our inebriated declarations, we awkwardly booked our flights.

It had felt right to tell my ex in person instead of allowing the Facebook whispers to flow. In turn, he had started dating a twenty-one-year-old Swedish model he'd met through the flat-share pages of Gumtree. She enjoyed camping (the very activity that dampened our union on a rainy trip to Scafell Pike where I'd forgotten a vital peg). I'm not going to lie, I was winded by The Scandinavian – after some invasive stalking, bordering on digital trespass, I found a photo and she looked like seventies sex symbol Britt Ekland on aesthetic steroids. But there had been hardly time to draw breath between our four-year relationship ending and mine and Matt's beginning. Most Wizz Air flights would struggle with that kind of turnaround.

So if I'm committed to commitment, and have only been single for a few months in the last twenty-one years, perhaps it's time to hear from some people who are a little more comfortable in their own skin. I begin with a naked man.

I first met relationship coach Ben Bidwell when I interviewed him on Heart radio, where I work. He's known professionally as The Naked Professor (this title has not been accredited by a university) and came in – pecker dangling beneath the studio lights – to talk about stripping back 'the masks of masculinity' while slipping out of his kecks. He has a reassuringly gentle manner for someone swinging their bits about willy-nilly.

He's six foot six tall and chiselled to David Gandy perfection. But he's also made the conscious – and, some might argue, cruel – decision to remain single for the foreseeable future. I want to speak to him because he's one of the few people I've met who talks about feelings within five minutes of meeting someone. While Matt's in Mount Athos with celibate monks, I'm in a cafe interviewing a man who prefers to work naked (although he's fully trousered when we meet this time).

He tells me to stop being so self-deprecating.

'You can just say you love someone, you don't have to play it down and go for the comedy line all the time. Sometimes people do just need to hear, "I love you".'

So, I wonder, why has he decided to swerve relationships?

The first reason is physical. Despite a prolific twenties in which he slept with 'quite a few people', Ben has never had an orgasm through sex. Along with 4 per cent of the male populace, he suffers from delayed ejaculation, which for him means he can bang away but the swimmers are never released. (He can, however, relieve himself.)

'By the age of thirty I had a few failed relationships, where it had been a problem, and I'm kind of just thinking, "I want to have proper sex in a relationship, like how it should be." So I'm going to wait for that. For as long as it takes,' he adds. 'I know who she is. I've manifested her. She's Brazilian, a free thinker, she's spiritual and she's the opposite of everything I was chasing when I was twenty-two. She's definitely out there and I'm not going to settle for anything less.'

Those seem like quite specific criteria and I wish him the best of luck. But I don't think you can spend your life waiting for an ideal version of what you want, because it usually doesn't exist. I'm not sure I manifested Matt. I never could have imagined those Spock-like eyebrows, for example.

But I definitely don't want to lose him. In the same way that I think most of my friends probably don't want me to die. We had our first big row a few weeks into our relationship, when he found out I was living in a flat-share with someone I'd slept with a few years previously. He had reason to be disgruntled but I'd never quite found the moment to say, 'Yeah, so the guy who let you use his shaving gel this morning has seen my bits.' Matt is an honest man, someone I would entrust with my most dispiriting secrets. When he found out I hadn't told him about this frisson so close to home, he hoisted those heavy brows into a frown and it felt like he might draw a line on 'us'.

I left his place sobbing in a black cab and remember rain coming down like a climatic recognition of my spirit. The cabbie, whose name was Geoff, made the mistake of asking in a voice that reminded me of my grandad's, 'Are you OK?'

It's always a risky game, asking someone snot-bubbling into your upholstery if they are OK. Especially when you could be listening to Classic FM and letting your thoughts gently seep into the traffic-laden road.

I told him everything. It was like opening a bottle of cheap Prosecco that's been jostled about in the boot of a car. The vinegary foam kept gushing out and landing on Geoff's kindly ear. I explained that I'd not deliberately lied to Matt but had feared him rescinding his lobster-like grip if I'd offered up this vital intel. After listening to my forty-two-minute diatribe on the potholes I'd chiselled into our relationship, Geoff concluded with, 'Mate, you love him, he clearly loves you. He's just a bit pissed off. Give him a bit of time to simmer down and you'll be OK.'

He then swiftly pulled a U-turn saying, 'Let's get you back there,' and took me to Matt's flat to make amends, refusing to take payment for the return journey as I continued snot-bubbling with a little more optimism. Geoff, if you are reading this, I owe you for sullying your upholstery but also for cementing my relationship. I owe you for the purest happiness I've experienced with another human, even if it's not constant or eternal.

But we're not living in a romcom, and Geoff's moderation skills are sorely missed. It's painful to write this knowing Matt will read it, but when he goes away with work I do feel less stressed, perhaps lighter – possibly happier. I spend the first hour putting all his things into drawers and The Bowl – a vessel that carries all the irksome accoutrements he leaves everywhere, including receipts, coppers and rolled-up flyers for Chicken Run, a local eatery that neither of us have yet visited. Then I change the sheets, remove his two pillows and create a boudoir for one that wouldn't be out of place in *Homes & Gardens* magazine. I erase his existence (which is not hard, considering he just has three shirts, a pot of hair wax and a bit of loose change knocking about).

When I'm alone, there's no expectation, no room for disappointment – no swearing as Tupperware tumbles from a cupboard, no tuts as my hair straighteners sit in his path. There's less pressure to be something I'm not. I'm sometimes messy, occasionally stressy, and I'm a spiller and a crier. Matt is none of these things. I love him more than complex carbohydrates but I also don't want to bring him down – and, in turn, myself – with shambolic stacking and relentless nattering. I want him to be happy and I fleetingly think that means being away from me.

Some of my friends call him a lone wolf; others have said he's an island, a man who often speaks about transforming the run-down shed at the bottom of our tiny garden into a study, which he might sit in as some form of self-imposed exile. I said to him recently that if nuclear Armageddon was upon us, he'd still thrive in the barren landscape, alone and happy, like an ant with an in-built radar for crumbs of cheddar cheese. Whereas I'd be skittering about, looking for someone – anyone – to exist with, eschewing basic needs in favour of a chat.

But would he really be OK alone? Would I? I'm curious if we're just slipping into stereotyped roles for a straight man and woman: him in need of a cave to hide in, her in need of a nest to share.

I get in touch with Professor Emily Grundy, director of social and economic research at the University of Essex. She's done extensive work on familial relationships and I'm hoping she has some answers.

She tells me that women in straight relationships suffer more stress compared to single women. 'There's evidence that women spend longer on domestic tasks than men and also do more emotional work,' she says as I nod solemnly, remembering that we need to send out party invites for our daughter's birthday.

According to the Office for National Statistics, women do almost 60 per cent more of the unpaid work, on average, than men. Even in Sweden – that bastion of equality where 'latte papas' in funky knits choose full-time fatherhood at no apparent cost to their sense of masculinity – women are averaging forty-five more daily minutes of chores.

'Being single removes that vast weight,' says Grundy.

I feel that weight. It is vast. Matt may put a few more washes on than me but I think sometimes he overlooks the frenzied tidying, sorting, wiping and polishing that can be ignored for being unnecessary. Clean clothes are needed whereas made beds are not – even if he enjoys slipping into neat sheets at night.

Given all the weight that falls on female shoulders, it's maybe not surprising that Grundy also found in a Mintel report[1] that 61 per cent of women felt satisfied going it alone whereas only 49 per cent of men felt the same.

'There's a new initiative with Age Concern called "Men in Sheds",' she continues. 'It's solely set up for single older men who can't socialise in the same way women seem to. They lose a partner or break up with a partner and they slowly stop connecting with people. They would prefer living in a solitary shed over going out and meeting others.'

---

1   'Single Lifestyles UK', Mintel, 2017.

Perhaps Matt wouldn't thrive so readily in a nuclear apocalypse, after all. Maybe I could live off licking abandoned Nutella jars and talking to myself. I definitely know Matt has joked about 'moving into the shed' on a number of occasions.

Grundy wobbles Matt's independent pillars a little further: 'Women tend to be better at having alternative social networks and other confidantes whereas men tend to rely quite heavily on their wives for that and have fewer other social ties so they are less happy alone. Men are not as good going solo.'

Matt prides himself on his sparse communication with the close friends he grew up with. Weddings and births are noted but generally it's a couple of pints a year and that's a wrap.

I, by contrast, am feverishly tending to close – and relatively unknown – humans on WhatsApp. I'm in a group called 'Mummy Sharks' that I have no idea how I got invited into but I'm congratulating strangers on the first steps of their offspring with enthusiastic foot-and-heart emojis. At the very least I could have a massive house-warming party – one where everyone has to head home at 11p.m. because of the babysitter or an early conference call.

But if I were to break free, I do wonder about sex. My recently single friend Bex ('Sex Bex', as our friends have christened her through her Tinder exploits) said: 'The minute we [she and her husband] broke up I wanted sex with everyone, anywhere, anytime, anyhow. I was a proper horn-bag.'

Keen to chat to someone who qualifies Professor Grundy's research (and to hear an alternative to horn-bag singledom), I put in a call to a woman who my friend Elena describes as 'happily married to herself'.

Saamirah Lawrence is a twenty-four-year-old virgin with a soft manner and a velvety voice who tells me she has no desire to find The One. 'I think the last time I was with someone I was in a cinema when I was eighteen and he wanted to snog at a really good bit in the film. That was it for me, really, because I just wanted to watch the film. I left and have been single since.'

The biggest frustration for Saamirah is other people's attitudes to her single status: the well-intentioned mates saying 'Let me set you up with my friend' or the restaurant manager asking 'When will the other party be arriving?' Society is still set up for a coupled-up existence.

'I am the happiest I've ever been and that's because I know how my body works and I have incredible friends. I'm sexually satisfied – I don't need someone touching me up, I can do that myself – and I have a family. It just doesn't look like yours,' she says.

I hang up the phone to Saamirah and have an uncomfortable flashback to my first boyfriend trying to cup my right breast during a showing of *Jurassic Park*. Rampaging velociraptors are not the ideal backdrop for cack-handed lust.

I'm entirely convinced that Saamirah is content. But she's also twenty-four, and your outlook shifts a bit over time. Someone whose happiness has taken a swerve later in life is Bethany Grace Howe, a transgender doctoral student at the University of Oregon's School of Journalism and Communication, who speaks openly about transitioning at forty-seven.

Still mildly hungover after the wedding and pondering my crow-like existence, I put in several calls to her but get nothing back. I go on a Facebook-stalking exercise and start to feel like a restraining order might be imminent. Maybe Bethany really does want to be alone. I see in one Huffington Post interview that she likes *Dumb and Dumber*, which is up there for me too. I chuck a quote from the film on Facebook messenger as one last attempt and settle in to watch her YouTube videos with a bag of Haribo.

She's softly spoken and yet every word has impact. In her video entitled 'When the Storyteller Becomes the Story', she's wearing a hat with rainbow Mickey Mouse ears, a matching dress and has a tattoo of the world on her right arm. 'Control your narrative,' she advises at every turn. She speaks in depth of her fears of loneliness after transitioning.

She says: 'I gave up on the idea of ever dating again: sort of like knowing I'll never own a Ferrari or have Angelina Jolie slip me her phone number. Some people call that negative. I call it being realistic. Does this mean I want to spend the rest of my life single? No. Am I looking forward to sleeping solo in my king-sized bed for eternity? Absolutely not. Do I want to still pay for two passengers when I'm the only one in my cabin on a cruise ship? An emphatic no: I can still only eat for one at the buffet. (Although I do try to make up for it.)'

After watching numerous clips of her speak about transitioning, I have to talk to her. I've inhaled eight fizzy cola bottles and five strawberry hearts that give me the sugar rush to give it one last go. I send a GIF of Harry and Lloyd from *Dumb and Dumber* in orange and blue suits saying, 'So you're telling me there's a chance.' This will either 1) grab her attention and get me an interview, or 2) get me blocked.

The stars align, she accepts my friend request and messages:

'Well, you've piqued my interest . . . That's always a good start. And it's funny: I probably get ten to fifteen Facebook friend requests a day, and I turn down most of them. I'll admit, though, I don't get too many from the UK, so my gut said, "Yes".'

(While this is a platonic and professional bid for attention, it makes me think that maybe the key to online dating lies in relentlessness and a well-selected GIF.)

I put in a call and we repeat *Dumb and Dumber* quotes to break the ice, and after a few niceties she answers my question about her relationship hopes: 'I want what everybody else wants and what so many people have. Love is special, and perhaps American poet Emily Dickinson put it best: "Unable are the loved to die, for love is immortality".'

(Most of Dickinson's friends and family passed away before her and she died pretty much alone, but the sentiment is there.)

Bethany Grace, who was born Barton Grover and used to be a high school teacher before doing her PhD in journalism, continues: 'What I don't want, however, is someone to think I'm wonderful just because I'm transgender – or in spite of it. Being transgender is only one facet of my life. I was a father and a scholar before I decided to transition, and if you ask me to define myself, those two items still come first. I am not a curiosity to be experienced, nor someone to be pitied.'

After speaking for five minutes I'm finding her candidness with a virtual stranger unsettling and brilliant in equal measure. If the end of the world was nigh, I decide Bethany is someone I'd want to sip puddle water with.

She continues in her soft Oregonian tones: '"I'm sure there's someone out there for you," they say. "You never know," they say. Well, no, I don't – but I can figure it out. I've done the math. My odds of finding a lifelong relationship are 1 in 400. Or, to put it another way, according to *Forbes* magazine, the average person has a better chance of marrying a millionaire (1 in 215) than I have of marrying anyone.'

This is where I realize the significance of that *Dumb and Dumber* quote ('So you're telling me there's a chance') and quietly congratulate myself for excellent GIF selection.

She continues: 'But I don't see anyone I know hanging their hopes for happiness for a bed partner on meeting a benefactor. To quote Bill Murray, we are who we are, "and that's the fact, Jack" – or, in this case, Jane. And yet, things happen all the time that defy the odds; I was once hit by a bus moving at twenty miles per hour. I should be dead and I'm still here. Perhaps happiness with someone is possible, too. For, as another wise – and "dumber" – person once said: "So you're telling me there's a chance."'

We finish the call reminiscing about Harry and Lloyd's canary, Petey, whose head fell off and was Sellotaped back on. It has us laughing like two old dears who have knocked back a little too much of Grandpa's cough medicine. This easy laughter makes me realize I haven't done that with Matt for a while.

He did make my daughter laugh recently, though. He made up an unhinged – and painfully middle-class – song called 'Baba Ganoush'. He did this high-pitched voice that had her laughing until she couldn't breathe. It was weird but I like weird Matt.

Bethany fills me with a renewed optimism. She makes me realize how blasé I have become about even finding Matt. Who am I to be quibbling about toast crumbs when he's a willing 'Papa horsey' – an equine that galumphs around the lounge with our kids on board. Why am I bemoaning all that he isn't when it's clear he's so much. It's easy to forget that the odds of finding The One, or even someone, aren't always stacked in your favour.

One person who doesn't want to take any more chances, though, is Matt's sister (and mother of two), El.

When I first met El, I was almost more certain of my love for her than for Matt. She says it straight and immediately warned me that Matt 'doesn't talk about feelings' but countered with 'he's actually a good person.'

She runs her own beauty business and has a daughter aged nine and a son aged six, and has raised them mostly on her own.

We're down visiting Matt's mum in Lyme Regis, and while my kids and El's treat Matt like a very creaky and slightly weather-beaten climbing frame out in the garden, I quiz El about the benefits of being single.

She leans back with a cuppa and says, 'I struggle a little bit with the idea of literally being with one person for the rest of your life. Like, really? I just think that's not realistic. Maybe it's just me and I've become grumpy, I don't know, but people get on my nerves. I don't know if I could actually share my house with anyone again. Like, if I clean up and go out and they're at home, I'm going to come home and they're just . . . my house will be . . . like, just . . . messed!'

She seems to see similar benefits to going it alone as me – mostly, not having a partner who is incapable of changing a toilet roll and who leaves coppers everywhere. I'm curious if she always saw herself being single or if it's an idea that has grown on her over time.

'I was never that kid who wanted to get married and draw wedding dresses and plan a wedding and all that. I just wasn't like that. I did always just want to be a mum, though.'

Her main regret about previous relationships is not getting out soon enough.

'I think I've just not really known how to get out, because people say, "ooh, you need to just give it a try" and "keep doing this" and "you're not always going to get on", but I think I grew a backbone when I was pregnant with my first.'

Eventually, she separated from her partner and realized that she and the kids were much happier alone. There have been a couple of minor relationships since.

'I was seeing this guy at the end of last year for a couple of months. He was normal, as in he had a job, a nice house, never been to prison, not a drug addict, no mummy issues,' she says. 'But I was bored. I was excited to know what a normal relationship is like, but I was just bored.'

I ask if she ever feels that she really needs anyone. It's something I question myself. I'm pretty independent and financially stable so my reason for being with someone is truly down to companionship, which almost adds an additional layer of pressure – in that, we've chosen to be this dissatisfied.

'Maybe on bin day. Sunday night's the only time I think maybe I'd like a boyfriend. Could I have a relationship with a cleaner and someone who's really good at ironing?'

It's the first time we've really spoken like this, despite knowing each other for nearly twelve years, and the main thing I'm learning is that she just isn't willing to accept something that isn't right for her and her kids. The subtext to our chat is: why settle for average?

'Someone needs to have a lot to offer to be invited into our little circle because it's always just been me and the kids, so they're going to have to be pretty amazing.'

I wonder is that's an unfair expectation of marriage or if I've set the bar lower as the years have eroded the hope of those early oxytocin-fuelled days. What I do know is that I feel defensive of the little circle Matt and I have created together. Even if to a drunken party guest it's seen as 'average'. (I'll tackle the 'sexless crow' bit later on.)

That wedding ignited something. It's like when someone slags off your mum and you see red mist, even though you were just bemoaning her yourself an hour before. It made me realize that what we have isn't exciting, exhilarating or extraordinary, but it's ours – for better or worse.

But, at the same time, in this brave, new, terrifying online world, I wonder if we'd have even found each other at all. If we'd have swiped right, let alone said 'I do'. I want to know. What *are* the chances?

I need to speak to Sex Bex.

3

Swipe Right

How do you spot a keeper?

Anna

Losing Matt is something that gives me deep-rooted, can't-breath-at-night fear. Not solely because I love him, but due to the horror stories I hear of online dating from recently divorced friends.

I'm on a night out with Sex Bex in a sweaty club on Brick Lane and she explains what Tinder is like aged forty-two and living in the sticks: 'In rural Nottinghamshire it's men standing next to their Kawasaki motorbikes who look like rapists and murderers. Paul from S Club 7 was on there once and he didn't swipe me – it was the same week he eBayed his BRIT award. There' are also a couple of married dads on there who I see daily on the school run.'

Mine. Field.

Sex Bex lets me flick through her possible suitors. I'm intrigued to know who (or what – there's a Tinder profile for some weedkiller) is out there. Am I with the right 'one' when there are many others readily available at my fingertips?

My first – and only – foray into online dating was on a website called Dating Direct back in 2002, where I forgot to put the age limit for my potential suitors. I was open for love and seeking men between eighteen and ninety-nine years of age. Within minutes I had a flood of responses, which was brilliant for morale, but with most of them no longer having all their teeth, it was a little dispiriting on closer inspection. One particularly stood out, from an older gentleman called Jon in Herne Bay, who led with: 'I have looked into a penis reduction.'

That's not even the worst. My sister told me about the influencer Lolo @itslololoves, who has a form of muscular dystrophy and uses a wheelchair. She had a guy on Tinder respond with: 'I know what to do to make you walk again.'

Lolo countered, 'It's as if their dick is the magical healer,' on a recent Instagram post.

Way before Tinder, though, my friend Jeremy was wading through unsuitable suitors on Match.com: ten minutes into a pub date with one, she said that she'd forgotten to turn the oven off and had to go home. To be fair to her, Jeremy had made the grave online dating mistake of uploading a profile photo of him post-holiday, tanned and Adonis-like, when the reality was – and he would be the first to admit it – a little more pale ale with a side of Scampi Fries.

The things I've taken from my brief dalliance in the online dating world are threefold:

1 Do not misrepresent the goods. There's no point offering a Fortnum & Mason Victoria sponge when the reality is more bargain-bin Battenberg. Just be honest. Beauty is in the eye of the beholder and building someone up for an aesthetic fall is unlikely to lead to getting laid.

2 Think before you write. A personal favourite was from a guy called Paul on OK Cupid who wrote under 'most private thing I'm willing to admit': 'I'm so sick of being friend-zoned. Ladies, if you are looking for a REAL MAN who will value you for your heart and

not your body, your knight in shining armour awaits. No fatties pls ☺'

3 Don't try to be too funny in your profile. A guy going by the name @IWontMurderYou went with this: 'I'm a fun-loving guy and a self-starter who has absolutely no interest in committing murder. I'm looking for love, companionship, or just that one lovely evening (and rest assured that that one lovely evening will end with you back at your house safe and sound!). Let me take you into my magical world of not murdering anyone, ever, for any reason.'

So it's a dating assault course out there and I know this because my sister, Karen, dabbled on Tinder for a few months before meeting her now wife, Helen. One Argentinian guy called Rodrigo showered her in praise, going as far as to say what a lovely earlobe she had. I was living vicariously through her and suggesting emoji sequences to send to possible suitors. (Never follow the phallic aubergine with the volcano emoji. Instead of stimulating conversation, it indicates you want to blow up his penis.)

But dating apps aren't just playing digital cupid, they're cash cows. According to Marketdata, the dating industry is a £2.3 billion empire with an estimated 40 million singles looking for love at the tap of a screen. Tinder alone sees more than a billion swipes recorded on the app every single day.

If I were to leave Matt – which I am 93 per cent sure I don't want to do – I'd need to speak to someone who can help me navigate this profitable romantic underworld.

Connell Barrett is an LA-based 'dating coach' who charges the equivalent of £2,450 for a six-week online dating makeover that helps his clients write responses to their potential digital dalliances.

'I'm Yoda and I consider my clients young Luke Skywalkers,' he tells me within thirty seconds of picking up the phone. I've found my guy. I *think*. (His service feels a tad morally dubious – I mostly fell for Matt over our fruity text and email exchanges, and faking those would have felt pretty deceptive.)

'Part of my job as a dating coach is to help my clients create dating profiles that sort of knock a woman out of her swiping hypnosis and say, "Hey, look at that great guy,"' says Barrett, speaking to me as if I'm a lovelorn client. 'With online dating, the secret sauce is to break her from her swiping pattern, because Tinder and Bumble can become like an endless video game.'

'Secret sauce' makes me feel a little queasy, and the idea that there's a magical formula that can ignite love feels a bit dodgy. So, other than offering up emotional condiments, how is Barrett actually helping people? How could he help me if I were to nosedive into this world?

He firstly tells people to ditch the dimly lit photos and gurning selfies and replace them with brighter pictures that say something about their personality. 'Most men post these very generic dating profiles that say all the same things, like "I like long walks on the beach" or they post their résumé,' says Barrett. 'Even worse, they'll just be standing there holding a big fish from a fishing trip. Don't follow the crowd. Crack a joke. Put your favourite Beatles quote in there.'

As someone with a deep suspicion of inspirational quotes, I need another opinion. I call up Barrett's rival in the online dating-coach

world, Alyssa Dineen, founder of Style My Profile. She's not as
bombastic as Barrett and speaks at a slightly softer decibel. 'I have
clients in their seventies who are really into Tinder,' she says. 'And
they're having success.'

Dineen's pet peeves are photos of people wearing sunglasses.
Eye contact, on- and off-line, seems to be a good way of convincing
someone you aren't an axe murderer. She's also big on getting rid
of the gym selfies that Sex Bex has had to contend with over the
last few months.

'It's a big problem,' she says solemnly. 'Especially with my male
clients.'

And does she pen responses for her clients too? 'Yes, I am
speaking for them, but it's really innocuous stuff,' she says. 'Like
"Where'd you go to school?" and "Do you have pets?" So I'll never
say anything that's not true to them. And they can watch me do
it. So they're learning that it's OK to be warm, it's OK to be flirty.'

If I'd received a message from Matt (that wasn't him) about my
first pet (the deceased Bubbles the hamster), I'm just not sure we'd
have made it out of the starting blocks.

☆☆☆

Matt was first brought to my attention by my friend BJ (a once-
amusing nickname she's since tired of), who simply said: 'Have
you seen that guy smoking outside? I think he's from the second
floor.' We were working at Haymarket Publishing in Hammersmith
at the time and Matt was a reporter on *Human Resources* magazine,
which meant he wore smart shoes and carried a Dictaphone like

it was a sixth digit. The truth is, I hadn't noticed him but I trusted BJ's opinion because she was the sort of friend who once held my hair when I was being sick in an O'Neill's pub (and she'd also experimented with glow-in-the-dark anal beads, which made her the most authoritative person I knew on matters of love and lust).

A couple of weeks later, Matt and I were sent on a copyright law course together. All I remember from the day is ordering fish and chips for lunch at a Wetherspoon pub and Matt offering up his umbrella when it started to rain on the way back. The umbrella was a little wind-blown and one of the vital spokes was missing but the man holding it was calming, interesting and interested – a rare quality in a human.

A few weeks later, I signed up to walk to the North Pole with two friends for charity. We called ourselves The Blue Tits and had T-shirts made with that Great British bird slapped on each mammary. It was a classy affair and we were raising money for the charity Right To Play, which delivers toys to developing countries. I put a message on the company intranet, asking people to sponsor the expedition.

Within seven minutes I received this email:

Hi Anna,

I was on the copyright course with you, and have just been to the Arctic with the Marines for a story. We did quite a bit on cold-weather survival techniques and ice-breaking drills. I'd be happy to chat if you want to know more?

Matt

Unsure whether ice-breaking drills had a hidden subtext, I drew counsel from a friend, Tim, who knew Matt from the journalism course they graduated from. 'No, he's genuinely into ice-breaking drills, I wouldn't read much into it,' he said. Tim, at six foot three tall and with a brooding demeanour, was used to having the office fawn over him and, looking back, perhaps didn't like this heavy-browed infiltration from the second floor. 'He's an OK guy, but I wouldn't say that's a date.'

Armed with many questions about ice picks, thermal wear and concern over polar ice caps melting, I met Matt for an after-work drink at The Dove, one of London's oldest pubs, which overlooks the emerald-green Hammersmith Bridge. The oak-panelled vibe was in sync with Matt – he almost merged into the backdrop so united were human and environment. Huddled together in a small corner, it became immediately clear that he knew little of ice-breaking drills and certainly had no interest in speaking about the Russian flag that lies under the terrestrial North Pole. (I'd googled 'Arctic facts' to look like a more informed Blue Tit.)

Within five minutes I knew I wanted to stay ensconced in that nook for a very long time. So enamoured was I at this point, I went straight into my panic story about an orangutan called Clive who lived at Monkey World in Dorset. I remember telling Matt I saw Clive urinate in the enclosure and that suddenly there were hollers of 'Daddy, I want to touch the wee-wee' from a young boy behind me. The more the dad explained that wasn't possible, the louder the child hollered: 'I WANT TO TOUCH THE WEE-WEE.' I was drunkenly repeating this sentence to the man I knew I wanted to marry. He laughed, even though I'd hit too much of a crescendo with the final 'WEE'.

I'm not sure I'd have led with that story on Tinder.

But thinking about Sex Bex's Tinder profile, I do have a moment of wondering if I could have been with someone else. The online *Sliding Doors* equivalent, where I end up with another mildly curmudgeonly suitor on another journalistic course at another time. Had Tinder been around when we first clapped eyes on each other, would Matt and I have swiped right or simply left?

Someone who I hope might have some answers is James Rhine, the forty-three-year-old star of Netflix's *Love Me Tinder* docu-series. I speak to the actor, model, former US *Big Brother* contestant and 'Sexiest Man in Reality TV 2006' over the phone from his Las Vegas office. He's the marketing director of various hotspots including clubs LIQUID Pool and JEWEL Nightclub (which all sound like they'd fit in well in my native Milton Keynes and might have a strict 'no trainers' policy).

Love Me Tinder can only be described as a detailed insight into the mind of a randy, prolific dater. It's something that's close to those Discovery Channel programmes I used to watch as a child but exchanges the goby fish for a fading reality-TV star and throws in a bit of ghosting for good measure.

'If you aren't having fun in life, then you're doing it wrong,' Rhine says, asking me to hold for a second while he closes the door and takes a sip of his BANG Energy drink ahead of a workout. He's speaking to me like he has the answer to my romantic problems. I'm wary. I don't necessarily want advice from a man who once carried a journal of his dating conquests around like a set of door keys. I am intrigued, though.

'I spent most of my thirties dating women online and I think I got to a point where I was keen to speak to people instead of swiping,' he says. Between slurps of BANG, he tells me he couldn't ever watch the Netflix series back.

Midway through *Love Me Tinder*, the then-forty-year-old James tells his mates that a woman he ghosted sent him an angry text about his lack of contact. 'She is kind of sensitive,' he says to camera, shrugging off the woman's distress. In his quieter moments, Rhine flicks through Tinder and Bumble like someone seeking out a new fridge. At one point, he recounts the field notes he's made from dating different twenty-two-year-old women over a period of fifteen years: 'Peculiarly eager to eat out your asshole now,' he observes of twenty-two-year-olds today.

I've never eaten an asshole out, and I don't think I want to. A quick google offers 'Twenty Tips About Eating Ass From People Who Just Simply Love It' on a blog called Pizza Bottle. The 'trombone technique' sounds like it's quite something.

My friend Jess – who once got conjunctivitis after a guy from Tinder came in her eye – has waded through the online-dating waters for five years.

We meet for a drink at an old, brown-panelled London pub called The Walrus and The Carpenter. It's early evening and full of City workers noisily knocking back alcoholic personality enhancers. She tells me that, 'If I had to pick any favourite time for dating, it was definitely the early 2000s. The internet was self-selecting because not everyone had a computer . . . But today, I know a lot of guys who have told me they flick through pictures on Tinder while sitting on the loo. Imagine being "chosen" by your partner as he does a poo.'

And these squat-and-swipers are not alone. One survey[1] of active Tinder users – people who are actually swiping right – found that less than 30 per cent had ever been on a date with someone from the app. Many weren't even looking: 45 per cent said they just used it for 'confidence-boosting procrastination'. It's become an empty game we play on our phones – the millennial equivalent of Snake but without the sense of achievement.

Perhaps we've become flooded with choice and we're struggling to make decisions. I feel overwhelmed by Netflix and can only imagine the pondering that would take place over a potential shag. It's all down to something called the 'paradox of choice'.

The theory was demonstrated in an experiment by Columbia University professors in 2000 (later highlighted famously in Barry Schwartz's 2004 book *The Paradox of Choice*). The researchers offered supermarket shoppers six jam samples on one table, and twenty-four jam samples on another. The results showed that 20 per cent more customers were drawn to the table with more choices but only 3 per cent of those people actually bought jam; at the table with just six jams, 30 per cent of shoppers did. While 'an extensive array of options can at first seem highly appealing to consumers,' concluded the researchers, it might actually reduce their subsequent motivation to buy the product. Hence the 'paradox' of choice.

---

1   'Is Tinder a Match for Millennials?' Mike Brown, LendEDU.com, 22 March 2017.

By that logic, digital dating is a conveyor belt of jam jars, with an unlimited variety and a bottomless supply. In short, more swipe can mean less action.

But back to James and the all-you-can-eat buffet approach.

'I don't think I really saw what I was doing as wrong,' he continues. 'I was in this swiping bubble and always had a sense of there being someone better out there than the one I was dating. Humans were reduced to things by those apps. It's like you're in a candy store and you just lose sight of what you like. So you try it all and end up feeling a bit sick.'

This is the fear I share with Sex Bex. How can I become digital candy at thirty-eight with two children, a possible bunion and chat that revolves around fidget spinners? But, equally, is this fear of the dating abyss reason enough to stay with someone you sometimes want to flick extremely hard on the forehead?

When pressed on why he starts ignoring women instead of directly telling them that he's no longer interested, James admits, 'I just don't want to feel their feelings.'

I was expecting him to say 'hurt their feelings' or show some whiff of empathy but no, it's his own emotional alienation at play. Slightly worryingly, this is something close to what Matt has said to me when trying to explain why he doesn't want to talk or decode an argument we've just had. His standard response is: 'Sometimes there really is nothing going on in there. Sometimes I just don't want to talk about the feelings.'

I don't think Matt and James are similar (other than being men who have all their own teeth) but I do wonder if there are small parallels in how they've been emotionally wired.

To provide a counterpoint to this modern-day rogue (James not Matt), I got in touch with the co-director of *Love Me Tinder*, Ronna Gradus, over Skype. She tells me, almost wearily, 'I think hopefully it's helpful to see that at the end of the day, he's not triumphant.'

And he doesn't seem happy in her films; his serial ghosting, shagging and swiping exploits haven't amounted to much. 'Hopefully in the end, for some women, that will be helpful to see, or to think about: "Oh, OK, that guy who totally was a jerk to me, at the end of the day, was he even happy?"' she explains. 'Maybe not.'

But even the romantic villains of this world can find their happy ending, it seems. Almost as an afterthought, James tells me he is now married: 'Stephany [his now wife] and I met through a mutual friend in a Las Vegas bar, whereas I'd gone out with hundreds of girls before who I'd just liked a photo of and dumped after two dates because there was no connection. The show helped me work out what I wanted. It was like therapy. I want the marriage, the kids, the mortgage. I want Stephany. Who would have thought I'd meet someone after all that?'

Who, indeed?

A few days later Sex Bex sends me a screen grab of a recent Tinder message. It's from a guy called Graham who lives in the Wirral. He sent her a photo of his penis in a gold kitten heel. (Google 'your dick looks great in those shoes' – it's a thing.) I don't think I'm ready to swipe left or right just yet. To save any awkwardness at the school gates, at the very least. Or being murdered. Or seeing a dick in a shoe. One thing I am sure of at this juncture is that, if I'm going to see anyone's penis in on-trend footwear, I want it to be Matt's penis.

This slew of dick pics has taken the sheen off the allure of online dating for me. Yes, there are plenty of fish out there, but there are a lot of sea cucumbers floating about too – something that's easily forgotten when you're huffing at your life lobster.

I still think Matt is my 'one'. But how do we keep swimming when domesticity feels like such a weighty anchor?

Matt

To understand Tinder, you first need to consider pigeon-guided missiles. These might sound like a hare-brained invention from *Dastardly and Muttley,* but they were regrettably real and the work behind them has, partly at least, influenced anyone who has ever felt a manic twitch of thumb over screen.

In the Second World War – before GPS, laser guiding or drones – military types would drop bombs from high up and hope for the best, or stick them in missiles and point them in roughly the right direction. As a result, in 1941 it was estimated that just 22 per cent of Allied bombs landed within five miles of their target.[2] The problem was worse at sea, where enemy ships were always moving.

So the US Navy turned to Professor B.F. Skinner, and he gave them a pigeon-guided missile. (I like to imagine a Dick Dastardly-style cackle at this point, but Skinner seems to have been a very serious man.) For a few years, he had been looking at something called 'operant conditioning' – the idea that animals can learn through rewards and punishments. He felt that suitably trained pigeons could peck directions to guide a missile to its target. So he built a nose cone with three compartments and put one pigeon in each. When pointed roughly towards a target, lenses in the nose cone would project an image of that target to a screen in front of each of the feathered navigators. As they pecked the target images, the missile would gently change course.

Remarkably, it worked in its first test, which had a big downside for the pigeons. But as radar developed, Project Pigeon was scrapped. His experiments continued, however, and by the summer of 1947 he was making progress with a device called Skinner's Box. More pigeons were involved, but this time they were getting fed rather than blown up.

Skinner's pigeons were put on a diet until they dropped to 75 per cent of their usual weight. Suitably hungry, they were put into feeding cages for a few minutes each day. These cages had timers that released a seed at five-second intervals. In most cases, the pigeons immediately developed weird tics. One would spin around twice then wait for the seed to fall. Another would stick its head into a far corner of the cage. A third 'developed a "tossing" response,' according to Skinner, 'as if placing its head beneath an invisible bar and lifting it repeatedly'. These twitches had no bearing on whether the food was delivered, but the pigeons did them anyway. They became as addicted to the actions as to the reward itself.

Several decades later, Jonathan Badeen, CSO of Tinder, revealed to journalist Nancy Jo Sales that these experiments were part of the inspiration for him to invent the 'swipe right' mechanism.

While there are many differences between hungry pigeons and

horny humans (feathers being rare on the latter), they both respond to something called 'variable ratio rewards'. This is the idea that you can create addictive behaviour (whether that's spinning around in a cage, paying money into a slot machine or repeatedly swiping right) by varying the reward that people get (and when they'll get it). If you're not sure when the seed will drop, or the one-armed bandit will pay out, or Tinder will provide a match – but you know that eventually these things will happen and you will enjoy them – then you keep spinning, paying or swiping.

Essentially, we're all as dumb as pigeons and just as easily led. I have summarized this in the Pigeon Parallel Theory.

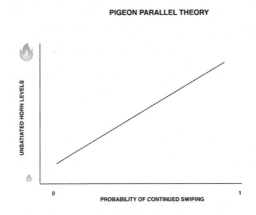

PIGEON PARALLEL THEORY

It's a simple thesis and has not been peer-reviewed. But the more in need you feel (measured on the vertical axis of Unsatiated Horn) the more likely you are to keep swiping because you know, eventually, that something will match.

So if we know dating apps are addictive by design, I wonder

what impact that has once you're in a relationship. Even if we're not actively searching on dating apps, the social media that we use every day has a similar effect. Scrolling in the hope of a reward (whether that's a LOLcat or a new picture of friends) feeds the same impulses as swiping on a dating app.

I have occasionally found myself peeking into the lives of ex-girlfriends after seeing them tagged in mutual friends' photos. It is a guilty curiosity: I want to know how they look now, what they do, who they are with. Mostly I put this down to nostalgia about that phase of my life. I don't ever wish it had been them instead of Anna, but I do wonder if such idle scrolling does a little harm by opening up the imagination to other, unlived lives.

In England and Wales, more than 100,000 couples each year find that 'till death us do part' actually seems like quite a long time and so decide to divorce.[3] Facebook is cited in about a third of these cases[4]: people caught trawling through the lives of exes or getting tagged in places that they weren't supposed to be. About one in three Brits admits to searching through dating apps while in relationships.[5]

Given all this digital cruising of sexually enticing strangers on dating apps and social media, my suspicion is that it's harder than ever to be satisfied with what you've got.

---

3   Office for National Statistics data.

4   According to Lake Legal and Stowe Family Law ('Facebook now crops up in a third of divorce cases over cheating and old flames', Mirror.co.uk, 20 January 2015).

5   'Nearly a third of Brits admit to using a dating app while in a relationship', slatergordon.co.uk, 6 September 2017.

So I speak to Dr Zoe Strimpel, a journalist and historian of relationships in modern Britain. Her wry grin and bouncing red curls can often be seen on the by-lines of UK newspapers, where she has been writing about love and dating for more than a decade.

'There are some studies that suggest that there is a kind of restless "can I do better?" with dating apps that you think you have to check,' she says. 'But I think that when you get to your late twenties and thirties people are so grateful to come off the treadmill that as soon as they're in a relationship they just think, "thank God" and get rid of the app.'

As with anything new, it's hard to know what the real impacts will be on daters today because there isn't yet enough long-term evidence.

'There is a lot of research now coming out about apps – and, whatever you want to say, you'll find a study to support it,' she warns me. 'Unfortunately that is just the nature of present research: there hasn't been enough time to come out with definitives.'

For her part, Strimpel does see positives from our new app-happy dating rituals, though. 'If you're in a relationship that feels stulti-fying or undermining or you feel trapped, it is an interesting and profound psychological outlet to know that all you need to do is touch an app. It can remind people that there is choice if their relationships are making them miserable.'

But while that choice can be good for those looking to get out of unhappy relationships, can it also be bad for those looking to get into something more committed, I wonder?

In recent years, Esther Perel has become perhaps the world's best-known relationships psychotherapist. Her bestselling books include

Mating in Captivity and *The State of Affairs*. Born in Belgium to survivors of the Nazi concentration camps, she retains a heavy Franco-Belgian accent despite decades living in the USA, and has an energetic directness that has engaged millions in her TED Talks and other events. Speaking on a recent *Recode Decode* podcast, she said, 'What we do know is, if I have a choice between two people it's rather limiting. If I have a choice between six or ten or fifteen people, that's a lot better. When I have a choice of 1,000 people, it's crippling.'

It's the same anxiety that might leave you slightly baffled when you get presented with a ninety-seven-option food menu, but with matters of the heart there's the opportunity to 'try before you buy' (which might not be well received at your local takeaway).

The result, says Perel, is that people 'simmer' their dates.

'So we meet on occasion, but I'm simmering a few others as well. I'm with you just enough so I don't feel lonely and not so much that I forgo my freedom.'

All of which sounds a little bleak to me – like settling for the minimum possible human connection that will allow you to share small talk, a meal and bodily fluids.

'I have rarely heard people tell me it's phenomenal or that it feels great. But they can't say it's degrading either,' says Perel. 'It's half-full: it's fast food, and fast food feeds you but leaves you with a bad taste.'

But I also wonder if the reverse is true – that digital dating can mean connections get too deep too fast. I turn to Vienna, Austria, and Sigmund Freud University. One of the academics there, Dr Christiane Eichenberg, recently looked at online dating and discovered the case of 'Patient M', a thirty-two-year-old woman who fell in love with an older man she met online. Their relationship developed in daily WhatsApp chats that racked up thousands of increasingly loving messages, and she shared pictures of her (younger, slimmer) self. Over several months it became clear to her that he was her dream man: she had never in her adult life felt such emotional intimacy. Despite never being in the same room, they became engaged to marry.

Eventually, and after much hesitancy, they met. She immediately realized that her image of him was mostly 'idealizations that had little to do with the real person'. She also, of course, hadn't been that honest in how she'd presented herself. Their relationship ended soon after.

But for all the digital sparks that fizzle out, when real-life connections live up to the digital version, things move pretty fast, Eichenberg tells me: 'We know that being online, for example, accelerates self-disclosure, and this acceleration continues – "online couples" marry faster, and have kids sooner.'

About one-third of new relationships now start online, so there must be some real connections being formed.

But one YouGov survey[6] recently found that 17 per cent of people on dating apps are there to cheat on their partners. And, Eichenberg tells me, apps mean that 'affairs are easier to "handle" and to keep secret. The affair does not have to come from the same social environment that your partner moves in, and the communication can be organized more easily.'

If cheaters gonna cheat, dating apps certainly make it easier.

---

6   YouGov Omnibus, 30 January 2019.

✩✩✩

My first love was a girl called Charlotte. I was about five and when we took a bath together I wanted to wrap myself around her as soon as we got out: to make myself a boy-towel and be covered in her soapsuds. Then there was Penelope Pitstop on *Wacky Races*, whose southern drawl and figure-hugging catsuits made me wonder if a boy could ever marry a cartoon. Later came Kim Cattrall in *Mannequin*, a film that made my blood feel lighter as I wondered what I might wear to woo her should she ever stop by our unremarkable suburb with a slightly creepy interest in twelve-year-old boys.

There were grown-up relationships that ended once they required more effort than choosing somewhere nice to eat. There were some flings that were never meant to get very far.

And then came Anna.

Dating apps were still new when we met, and considered a last resort – to be tried somewhere after joining a gym, speed dating, and holding up a sign reading 'please SOMEONE love me' when the lights went up at your local Yates.

I had always taken a traditional British approach: find someone at work or college or the pub who you like, get drunk, briefly forget what a flawed and laughable human you are, have sex, and if the whole process isn't desperately humiliating, maybe you start going out.

It didn't bring the world of wonder that dating apps offer, but it did mean that if your hopeful lean-in-with-meaningful-eye-contact only led to a palm in the face, the chances were you'd both be too banjaxed to remember. It was a simpler time.

So when I first saw Anna, I didn't ask her out, but waited for weeks in dumb hope. She worked in a different building, on a different magazine, and there was almost no chance of our jobs bringing us together after our random first meeting on a company training course.

I changed my route to work, getting off the Tube a stop earlier so I could walk past her office. Every day my pace slowed as I passed the entrance, hoping for a chance meeting. But it never came, and weeks passed with me sat at my desk, gazing into the middle distance when I was supposed to be hustling for interviews with leaders of industry. I was like a schoolboy with a crush. I drifted into daydreams in a way that hadn't happened since Penelope Pitstop made me feel funny in the pyjamas.

Eventually she sent a group email, asking for sponsorship for a charity trek to the North Pole. It was the kind of thing that worthy and determined people do, which normally really annoys me because I am rarely either of those things. But this seemed like a chance to present myself as a better person. So I emailed and suggested we meet up.

There had been months between our first and second conversations with not so much as an emoji exchanged in the interim. When you invest so much hope in meeting in the first place, it's hard to casually cast that connection aside.

But that was fourteen years ago. The average duration of a marriage at divorce is twelve years.[7] We've been married for nine, and I'm not really sure what conclusions Anna's going to come

---

to when she writes about those nine years. She might reveal things in her pages that I never imagined and don't want to hear. She might find things in mine that change how she views me.

Because whenever we write about our lives, we tend to bicker. I bristle at any things I think are inaccurate or that portray me unfairly. She bristles in return when I suggest changing those things. Our last book saw some of the most tense arguments I think we've ever had – both of us desperate to do a good job and nervous how it would all come together. But we've decided to be honest because, for a book like this, I'm not sure how else you could be.

Esther Perel says that, 'There is no "the one". There is "a one" that you meet at some point, with whom you're going to write a story, but you could've written another. The beauty today is that we can write two or three stories over the course of our life.'

I think she's right. But I also think that my other stories have already been written.

Other people will always seem attractive and interesting when you don't need to share a tumble dryer with them, but the giddy promise offered up by dating apps seems to lead to disappointment more often than not.

I don't want to write any new stories, I just want to make sure that this one has a happy ending.

But there have been a few domestic changes recently that may have made that a little more difficult.

4

☆ ☆ ☆

Home Front

How do people live together?

Matt

At the back of our terraced home we have a small garden. Over the year, different colours bloom like a slow-bursting fireworks display.

We bought the house from two sisters who had just inherited it from their elderly mother and it felt a little like stepping into a 1970s interiors catalogue. There was lots of brown and the carpets were thick.

We hacked into it with cheap tools and dumb hope, tarting it up as our finances, bank loans and my handyman 'skills' allowed.

It was an odd process, ripping out the evidence of all those decades before – the lino flooring presumably laid by the long-passed husband, the interior wall he'd put up at the back of the bathroom to create a space for his home-brewing kits. You're desperate to take ownership for yourself, but it comes with little pangs of guilt. I wondered how many family dinners had been prepared at the kitchen counter that we were casually throwing in a skip.

But we left the garden mostly as it was. All around the perimeter were mature plants and little trees – ivy and rosebushes and broccoli-green loveliness – that had been planted decades ago. This outdoor space quickly became my domain. In the first week, I dug up what looked like a spring onion and chopped it into a cheese sandwich. It had a dull flavour that I felt must be how real spring onions tasted. For almost four minutes I sat on the grass and munched my sandwich, revelling in my ability to live off the land and eschew industrial farming and its mass-produced spring onions, which were almost certainly genetically modified or that somehow exploited migrant labourers or were shot full of cat hormones.

I then doubled over with sharp cramps, and a rapid google on my phone revealed I'd eaten a baby daffodil bulb. I spent the next hour locked in the still-functioning outdoor toilet.

Horticulturally, then, I am inept. But one of our inherited plants has held me in quiet wonder since we moved in. It's a Japanese camellia (thanks, FlowerChecker app), about ten feet tall with waxy, deep-green leaves that form a fat ball starting halfway up the trunk. Over spring and summer it fires out hundreds of bright pink blooms with heads so heavy that they only last on the branches for a few days before falling to the ground.

When this happens, I pluck the fattest ones and lay them in the centre of the kitchen table for Anna and our girls. Our eldest will pander to me and say it looks lovely. Anna will usually move it because it's in the way. The toddler is more likely to eat it than consider the delicate nature of beauty.

But I do these things for two reasons. First, I think my wife should have flowers and that my daughters should see me do nice things for her. And second, I feel like the soil is mine. It is outdoors and requires tools. It is a place where life and death can be dispatched at the end of a mucky trowel. I am master of the soil and I am doing this to provide something for my womenfolk.

In quiet moments I stand and stare at plants that I do not recognize, squinting into the wind like I'm an ancient yeoman with skin like old chamois leather. Despite my gardening gormlessness, every time I get mud on my fingers I feel manly and it feels good.

What doesn't feel quite so manly is earning less money than my wife.

For our first twelve years together, I was the primary wedge-winner, picking up between 25 and 100 per cent more than Anna. We started out as journalists at a similar level but, while she doggedly pursued jobs in the intern-heavy and underpaid world of women's magazines because she was following her dream (the loser!), I was much more willing to sacrifice personal satisfaction for dirty cash.

I put my freelance rates up every time I got a new client. I took duller work that paid better. When I had staff jobs, I pushed for more money. My attitude was 'I'll do it, but give me more.' Her attitude was 'it's so kind of you to have me.'

And while I encouraged her to ask for more, and grizzled about the gender pay gap and how she was undervalued, I also liked being the main money-maker. We both paid into a joint account for bills. I had more left over, and it meant I covered holidays and nights out and topped up the bills account whenever it was needed. I considered everything we earned to be equally 'our' money, but I liked being the one that got a card out at the end of a meal. I was freelance for most of that time, and if I hit a certain target in a month, I would take Anna out for a fancy dinner, swinging my spuds around like Tony Soprano.

But a couple of years ago that began to change. I had a spell in a staff job that was useful for getting a mortgage but fairly detrimental to my sanity. A year in, they had some money issues and I got a small pay-off to go away. It was a relief, and I went back to freelancing.

But Anna had recently quit her job for something less well paid after her boss refused to allow her some flexibility in her schedule. Seeing how precarious our income was, she redoubled her efforts on something she had started a few months before – a parenting platform called Mother Pukka.

Over a few years it bloomed into a business and saw her get a job presenting a national radio show. It also meant that, for the first time in our relationship, her work was more important to the family finances than mine. If we had a clash of commitments, it became her work that got prioritized and me who shifted meetings around to collect a sticky infant. We still talk of it as 'our' money, and I'm still most likely to keep an eye on how it's used, but I no longer get to play the benevolent patriarch. I am proud of what she's done, but also secretly wish it was me who had done it. (Apart from the moments where she posts Instagram stories of herself in changing rooms, trying on peculiar outfits – I'm not sure I could pull that off.)

It makes me wonder what other mates in similar situations feel, so I get in touch with Jack. He's a thirty-three-year-old Londoner and married to Gemma, a thirty-four-year-old Scot and MD of a creative agency. We've all been friends for about a decade and she's one of those terrible people who is both successful and driven and has absolutely no shame about it. She earns almost twice what Jack does as a photographers' agent.

'It just doesn't bother me whatsoever,' he says. 'She's got a very different ambition and competitive edge to her, which will always mean that she'll earn more.'

His mother earned more than his father for most of their careers, he tells me, and while career is important to him, he's always had a bit more focus on the value of his time.

'I think it should be spoken about more and more, because women generally are better,' he laughs. I warn him that if that ever gets out, the patriarchy might crumble.

'They carry the baby for nine months then they can kind of bring it up on their own – although it's a joint effort and I do lots of that as well – but it's no wonder that they're better at a lot of places of work. They're just good. There is a certain type of man that would still probably feel less of a man for earning less than his wife or partner, and it probably comes down to being a bit scared. Maybe they're just a bit thick.'

But this earning shift is becoming increasingly common, and it seems that most men are not as comfortable with it as Jack. In the US, in 29 per cent of straight marriages where both partners bring home some corn, the wife out-earns the husband.[1] In the UK, women also do the financial heavy-lifting in about one-third of straight relationships.[2] So our situation is not unique. But it's also not without issues.

There is some part of me that still thinks I should be striding

---

1   Bureau of Labor Statistics, 2015.

2   'Who's Breadwinning in Europe? A comparative analysis of maternal bread-winning in Great Britain and Germany', IPPR.org, 20 October 2015.

home, slapping bacon on the table and then settling into an armchair with a single malt while she puts the kids to bed. I don't entertain these thoughts for long, partly because I quite like putting the kids to bed (at least the story-reading part – bath-time is a tsunami of angst), and partly because I know that it doesn't really matter who earns most as long as we're earning enough. But the idea that 'the man earns the money' has been well drilled into me over the years. It was the case in every grown-up relationship I saw as a kid, whether in the family or on TV, and it remains the case for most of my peers today. And it still lingers in the wider world too. So much so that, when women earn more than men, both parties tend to lie about it, according to the US Census Bureau.[3] They compared what people told the nationwide population survey about their income and what employers told the tax services (this figure being more accurate). In relationships where women earned more, men bumped up their claimed earnings by 2.9 percentage points. It seems our age-old tendency to overestimate our peckers also applies to our pay packets. But women downgraded their earnings by 1.5 percentage points too. The researchers concluded that those couples wanted to present themselves in a more 'socially desirable manner' and that women might sometimes be a little embarrassed about their underperforming men.

This is backed up by a 2017 study by Harvard Business School,[4] which found that women in high-powered jobs whose husbands

---

3   'Manning up and womaning down: How husbands and wives report their earnings when she earns more', US Census Bureau, 6 June 2018.

4   'Women and Gender', *Harvard Business Review*, 18 January 2019.

earned less were, 'more likely to experience feelings of resentfulness or embarrassment, feeling that their status was decreased by their husbands' lower status'.

So it does seem that, when the financial roles switch, female discomfort and the fragile male ego can combine to create a marital grump. And that might partly be to do with something a little more primal than social embarrassment. Women, according to a study published in *Personality and Social Psychology Bulletin*, are more attracted to old-school blokes who demonstrate a bit of what is known as 'benevolent sexism'.[5]

While 'hostile sexism' is easy to spot ('calm down, love', 'women can't park,' 'back off, Dave, she must be on the blob'), benevolent sexism (conveniently shortened to BS) tends to put females on a pedestal to be provided for by men, such is the saintly virtue and frailty of womankind. 'BS men' tend to dismiss women's rights and legal freedoms, but elements of benevolent sexism can seem quite nice when you're on the receiving end. Frankly, I'm quite taken with the idea of someone buying me dinner and telling me I have lovely hair.

The report's authors, Pelin Gul (female) and Tom Kupfer (male) gave straight women written profiles about hypothetical partners, and found the benevolent sexists were seen as warmer, more attractive and more likely to protect them than the fully woke, non-BS alternative. This was true even among women who were classified as 'high feminists'. Gul and Kupfer reckoned that 'many women –

---

5   'Benevolent Sexism and Mate Preferences', Pelin Gul and Tom R. Kupfer, *Personality and Social Psychology Bulletin*, 29 June 2018.

even those who desire egalitarian relationships – want a man to be chivalrous, by, for example, paying for dates and opening doors'.

None of this is anything that I've considered before. I'm not entirely sure I believe that when a woman earns more a marriage is less happy, but I can see how it might happen. At beers with an old uni friend recently, we were discussing a mutual pal whose wife had just sold her business, and wondering how much she might have collected. He joked about our friend 'asking her for pocket money' and confessed he 'would hate knowing my wife earned more than me'.

It all makes me wonder if gay couples have the same issues. My suspicion is that without a lifetime of fairy tales telling you who should be doing what, it's easier to go about your day without a worry (other than answering all of those straight couples demanding to know who takes out the bins). There's lots of research that suggests domestic labour tends to be more even in same-sex couples, with a slight shift when kids arrive.

Abbie Goldberg of Clark University in Massachusetts has been studying these questions for more than thirteen years, and reckons that, without the traditional roles to fall back on, things tend to be based a bit more on what you're actually good at. But even so, 'same-sex couples wrestle with the same dynamics as heterosexuals. Things are humming along and then you have a baby or adopt a child, and all of a sudden there's an uncountable amount of work,' she tells me. 'Big disparities in earnings most often occurred in the gay male couples I studied, not the lesbian couples – female partners tend to have more similar incomes,' she says. Typically, whoever earned more worked more, and whoever earned less did a bit more of the domestic stuff.

'Although an outsider might be tempted to see those arrangements through a gendered lens, couples did not see it that way. They saw their arrangement as fitting their family needs,' she says.

But views about what makes a man 'a man' might be shifting, according to one of the most admired researchers on the subject. Dr Eric Anderson is a professor at the University of Winchester and an expert on modern masculinity. He explains to me that, 'The 1980s was the apex of masculine ugliness and people are most prone to that sort of social conditioning in their adolescence. So those who had their adolescence in the eighties – that's my age, I'm fifty-one – they grew up with extreme homophobia and violence: be tough, be a man, all that sort of discourse. And then by the mid-1990s, around ten years later, they grew up going, "Wait a minute, I don't have to be like that." They didn't think "There's a fag, let's beat him up." Then you go on ten years, you're into the millennials and they tend to view hyper-macho posturing as preposterous.'

Most of that eighties machismo was a reaction to AIDS, says Anderson.

'We had what I call extreme homo-hysteria, which is not just the dislike of gay people but the knowledge that gay people exist in your world, in your families, in your churches, in your social spaces and this belief that one in ten people are gay and we fucking hate them and "I don't want to be thought gay because that would be the worst thing imaginable."'

Cue a mini-generation of men desperate to prove their straightness by being hyper-macho (which, ironically, can be a little camp).

'You essentially do four things. You hyper-sexualize women, you express extreme homophobia, you keep your emotional status under control and don't cry, and you engage in physical violence with other men, through contact sport or fighting. You do everything you can to prove you're not a "fag". And then as the hatred towards homosexuality wanes, guys go, "Oh, I don't have to be emotionally stoic, I can be an emo, because who cares if people think I'm gay."'

And as a result, straight men are cuddling more. Anderson recently did a study with forty male students at a British university.[6] Of those, thirty-seven said they had cuddled their mates. That's not just a burly bear hug on greeting – it's a proper 'settle down for a bit of spooning or nuzzle into an arm nook until everything feels all right again.' All except one had shared a bed with a male friend. One interviewee told Anderson, 'I love a quick cuddle, just so you remember your friends are about and are there for you.'

My adolescence came after that eighties homophobia peak, and being 'gay-friendly' as a young straight man in the late nineties was an easy banner to wave to prove how right-on and open-minded you were, yet I barely mustered a fist bump of acknowledgement with male friends when I was the age of Anderson's interviewees.

And we were certainly guilty of hyper-sexualization of women. We had a 'shagging league' where we would each dutifully report our highest-scoring 'achievement' with a girl. It was oafish bravado at the height of lad culture, and I was 'a different man' then, of

---

6   'Cuddling and Spooning: Heteromasculinity and Homosocial Tactility among Student-athletes', Eric Anderson and Mark McCormack, *Men and Masculinites*, 12 March 2014.

course, but a stock question whenever one of us started a new relationship was the slightly sneering, 'Would you cry if she died?' The implication was that, if the answer was yes, you were a love-struck little sap. But actually, you're supposed to cry when people die. Crying is a part of being human. Since having two daughters, I am almost permanently on the verge of blubbing, and any news story about a family tragedy or cartoon about a lost pet gets my eyeballs tingling.

The emotional stoicism that Anderson mentions feels a little familiar, too. Anna gives me a steady flow of her thoughts and feelings every evening – and there are *so many* feelings – but whenever she prods to know what I'm thinking, I hold it back. I've genuinely convinced myself that my emotional range runs 'hungry', 'horny' or 'fine' and that there's nothing else to reveal. While those probably are my most stable states, there is also something more.

But on those rare occasions where we have big rows that run into the night – the kind with angry sighs and rolling eyes (there would probably be slammed doors, but that's tricky when you've gone for open-plan living areas) – much of the problem is that I don't know what to say. I stare ahead and shut down, unable to articulate whatever the emotional core might be for my side of the huffing. Every time I do it, I think of my dad whenever we challenged him about his drinking – it was like the lights went out in his eyes as he locked up.

There's a quote I discovered recently, by the Kenyan novelist Mukoma Wa Ngugi. Speaking to QZ.com, he said: 'As men we are emotionally stunted and hence unable to have full empathy for others. So, as a man with an eight-year-old daughter, how do I bring her up in such a way that she has full emotional expression if I do not have it?'

It made me wonder if he had worked out any answers. He's now an English professor in the steepled and leafy grandeur of Cornell University in upstate New York, and I track him down to ask.

'Usually it's the wife who does the emotional heavy-lifting, while men provide advice if their spouse comes to them with an emotional problem,' he tells me, painting a remarkably accurate picture of most of my evenings with Anna. 'It is something I struggle with myself quite a bit – all our lives we have been brought up to be masculine, and society respects and rewards us for it, our male friends reinforce it. Maybe we should first listen and learn from our partners – that is, to be vulnerable to them.'

But I'm not sure I can do vulnerable for the woman I want to see me as a hero. And maybe that's a problem. I'm a dad of two daughters, and I bookmark stories of inspiring women for them to watch on YouTube (current favourites are Kelly Holmes winning the 800m and 1500m golds at Athens 2004, and NASA's Sunita Williams giving a tour of the International Space Station). They never actually sit through these, because they are not videos of singing cartoon animals, but I like the principle. Besides, I know that their most important female role model is the woman who gestated them. When a boy from our eldest's class came over for a play date recently, and the two of them discussed what their parents do, our daughter said in a matter-of-fact manner, 'My mum's a boss,' and it filled me with the kind of dumb pride I haven't felt since I came second in an egg-and-spoon race in 1985.

I am proud watching my eldest climb trees while dressed in a Batman hoody and a tutu, and I direct my youngest to the dinosaurs and trucks as much as the bits of pink plastic that turn up each Christmas. I'm proud that my wife has given evidence to parliamentary committees about making work fairer for parents, and that she went through forty hours of interviews to get her radio job.

But I don't give away much of my emotional inner self, and I still wonder if I might be happier if our set-up was a little more traditional. There are days when I feel submerged in domesticity – like I'm at the bottom of a pond and unable to kick for the surface. Like when the girls squabble and tumble, and whole days are lost servicing their needs for nourishment and comfort, all the while trying to stay patient and playful and remain aware that the most minor moments can lodge in their young memories to cloud a whole period of childhood.

In these days of shifting gender roles, being a feminist husband feels like a lot of work and I'm not sure I'm putting the effort in. I might speak up about mansplaining at work, or call out (rare) elements of oafish laddism on nights out with mates (also rare), but I also think that just 'not being sexist' is probably enough, which makes me wonder if I might be quite an idle ally.

So I ask an expert. Dr Barbara Risman is a distinguished professor at the University of Illinois in Chicago and in the late nineties coined the phrase 'gender vertigo' – the idea that when our roles change very quickly, people become uncomfortable.

I speak to Dr Risman over Skype, as she perches on the end of the bed in a brown hotel room while on a tour of the US to promote her latest book, *Where the Millennials Will Take Us: A New Generation Wrestles with the Gender Structure.*

She tells me that, 'We're all more comfortable when we know how we're supposed to behave ourselves and what we should expect from other people when we get up in the morning. The more routine life is, the easier it is. The less cognitive work it takes. With social change, including changes around gender, people become confused.'

That confusion can be seen every day, on issues from the gender pay gap to protests about school uniforms and which toilet transgender people should use.

At its ugliest, it bubbles away beneath angry but anonymous avatars in the 'manosphere', which roughly divides as follows:

MGTOW (men going their own way): 'women are money-grabbing and deceptive and should be avoided for your own safety'.

INCEL (involuntary celibates): 'women are all sluts who refuse to sleep with us'.

PUA (pick-up artists): 'women will sleep with you if you follow this one simple trick'.

MRA (men's rights activists): 'men are oppressed and feminism must be stopped'.

At the less damaging end, this confusion leaves men and women wondering if they're doing enough to be fair to themselves and to others. I'm keen to know what Dr Risman thinks of our set-up and whether there can be such a thing as a feminist marriage.

I run her through the state of ours to see what she thinks. It can roughly be summarized as below:

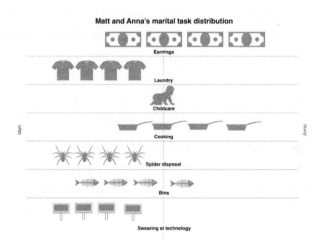

While Anna now brings in more money, we could both probably just about independently support the kids and ourselves if we had to (and did without extravagances like eating three times a day). Childcare is pretty even. Anna cooks a bit more but may not actually know where the washing machine is. I tackle traditional blokey things like arachnid catch-and-release, taking out the bins and swearing impotently at the Wi-Fi router.

I run the professor through this rough breakdown and am suddenly aware that I may have given too much detail.

'That sounds very egalitarian to me,' she says, a little like she's congratulating a child for not spilling apple juice all over their trousers. 'But I don't think it's about exact number of hours, and I don't even think it's about relative earnings. I think it's about each person being able to take care of themselves economically if they should need to, because the inability to be economically independent is what really cripples someone from being able to make life choices.'

And in that, I am reassured about relinquishing the financial trousers: at least I know that Anna is sticking around because she wants to.

'For me, equality in one's partnership – whether one's partner is the same or opposite sex – is a prerequisite for happiness,' says Risman. 'But happiness is really far more ephemeral than that. "Happily ever after", I think, is about enjoying each other's company, about having a satisfactory physical relationship, about being intellectually stimulating to one another, enjoying conversation, being part of a community where you enjoy a social life as a couple. Equality is just a prerequisite.'

It feels to me like Anna and I are equal, even if that new-found equality is taking some adjustment. But those other bits – those bits about enjoying each other's company – they need some work. Mostly that's because of some tiny interlopers.

Anna

I'm in the kitchen, one eye on the kids watching *Peppa Pig* and one eye on my phone, trying to find a 'Spider Girl' costume for our eldest daughter's sixth birthday. The kids bundle in, squawking about who gets to hold the remote control (some arguments filter through the generations) as Matt comes down the stairs. I hear a muffled 'fffffkkkkksssake'. I pad into the lounge and see him staring at the floor. It's a mulch of water and organic maize snacks.

He looks at the phone in my hand and his eyes flicker with mild frustration and I go into the kitchen to fetch a tea towel, muttering 'it's just a bit of water', which is a lie because it's actually closer to glue.

I tell him I don't want to live like this.

He tells me I'm overreacting.

I tell him I can handle big arguments but not the day-to-day frustrations, the steady drip of snark and disappointment.

He tells me I'm making the small frustrations into a big argument.

I tell him the 'fffffkkkkksssake' makes it into an argument.

He says the 'fffffkkkkksssake' is nothing.

I say it's something.

He says he can't hear this anymore.

I don't remember when these small kinks in the marital armour started appearing, but they definitely weren't there when we first lived together.

☆☆☆

It was ninety-seven days after Matt and I had our first date that we started searching for our first flat together in Dubai, a city that resembles a sweaty Milton Keynes. There was dust on everything and, in my homesick state, the place reminded me of *The Walking Dead* but without the excitement of a potential zombie mauling.

Even when my grandma called up to say my cousin's husband

had been caught in a porn film, my spirits couldn't be lifted. It transpired that he hadn't taken the lead role in *Ass Ventura* or *Dawson's Crack*, as initially feared, but simply been caught by his wife watching YouPorn. But even this extraordinary sequence of familial Chinese whispers couldn't nudge me out of the fug of living in a place that prided itself on having the biggest mall in the world, and suddenly realizing that I was co-habiting with someone forever.

Moving in with Matt in less time than it takes for someone to get a dental appointment should have been exciting. I was ready, even though his close friend and former flatmate Joe had warned me of Matt's drunken sleep-walking (on one occasion he mistook the sofa for a toilet: 'Just lifted the sofa cushion, took a piss and put it back down,' Joe said).

I had spent most of my childhood moving the Sylvanian hedgehog family in and out of their caravan, so I felt prepared for this defining life moment. 'We're moving in together!' is something I'd squeaked to a troop of girlfriends while playing Dream Phone – a game that hooked you up with imaginary boys called Chad who 'wanted to go to the mall for pizza', via a nineties pink mobile phone. But I'd lived with boyfriends before and, despite the odd broken mirror and tussle over my hair straighteners nearly setting the house alight, it was a mutually beneficial arrangement. This felt different, though. This wasn't simply something that 'financially makes sense' in my mind: this was it. So how did it get to the stage where he's swearing at crumbs on the floor like they're burglars coming through the window?

I suspect I can't be the only one who hooked up in a whirlwind and finds themselves wondering about it years later. Keen to know how others deal with this, I arrange to speak to comedian Chris Ramsey and his wife Rosie, the co-creators of the podcast *Shagged. Married. Annoyed.* Their very funny show spills the domestic beans on everything from towel-sharing to post-coital flatulence.

We meet at the British Podcast Awards, where I'm presenting 'Best Sports Podcast' (ironic, since I last moved at speed in 2015). It is my first professional experience of opening an envelope, and I manage to read out the right name because I'm a broadcaster and that's Key Stage 1.

We meet in the 'green room' backstage. When I first got pointed towards a 'green room', I thought I had truly made it, and was about to enter a world of *Graham Norton Show* glamour, with beautiful and witty people sipping champagne. Turns out they're mostly windowless cupboards with a bowl of crisps and cold coffee. I cosy up to Chris and Rosie on a worn sofa with a tie-dyed rug thrown over it.

Like Matt and me, Chris and Rosie went big early: in their case, getting engaged within six months and moving in together fairly sharpish. 'She wasn't even pregnant,' Chris says as Rosie serves him brutal side-eye and a quick nudge to the ribs. They've now been together for seven years and Chris reminisces about their first argument after moving in together: 'I was like, "for fuck's sake".' Parallels with Matt, there. 'So I got in the car, and I drove off and I was like, "Where do people go when they've stormed out?" I've never done this. I thought, "Hmm. I can't go to the pub. I have the car." I just came back home and sat in the drive.'

'You were sat out there for a while,' says Rosie. 'You really made your point.' She nudges him and he looks at her like she's an ice cream on a hot day. Despite building a podcast on relative discord, it seems to me they're not that annoyed, really.

'It's about taking the good with the bad,' continues Chris. 'She's got this one dish where she oven-roasts loads of veg then blitzes it all into a sauce for the pasta. Better than any restaurant. But you look around the kitchen afterwards and it's like the FBI has raided us. Like they're looking for Pablo Escobar's fucking stash.'

This reminds me of a book I recently read: Rachel Sussman's rather ominously titled *The Breakup Bible*. A few pages in, she says: 'The reality of living together won't match up with expectations in so many ways. You will fight – it's just what happens when your personal space diminishes.'

But I wonder if that's always the case or if there are some grunting gender stereotypes at work in these fights. In a world that's only slowly bulldozing the clunking narrative of 'man brings home bacon' and 'woman cooks bacon', what happens when you're not one of each?

I hop on an easyJet flight to Amsterdam to stay with my sister Karen, her wife Helen and their springer spaniel Dolly (Parton). I've always imagined that living with another woman would offer a dreamlike existence of shared wardrobes and emotional maturity.

Armed with a packet of stroopwafels and a vat of Chocomel – a drink that makes me proud to be half-Dutch – we get down to it. She says that day-to-day living has been much easier with a woman than in her previous relationships with men. Karen came out at twenty-eight, although she doesn't refer to it as 'coming out' but 'falling in love with a woman'. She says, 'We just get on with it. We communicate much better and we both take the bins out.'

(Why are the bins such a barometer of happiness? Maybe it's time to bin the bins and live like savages.)

Karen continues: 'It was getting married where people struggled. Like, who is going to wear the trousers? Who will wear the wedding dress? Who is the man in the relationship, who is the woman? We decided we might go half-and-half so people didn't have to worry. Saying that out loud, I can imagine a market for it on Etsy.'

Both Karen and Helen work, they both cook, they both walk the dog and there's no ingrained societal expectation about who should do what. It's all hands on deck (which sometimes autocorrects to 'dick'). I mention this over dinner, Karen doesn't laugh. Dolly looks up at me with doleful eyes. They're all wearied by penises, it would seem.

We've always had a deeply competitive relationship – with spikiness peaking around games of Monopoly – but after five days living with them, they do seem less weighed down by who does what with the bacon.

There's a piece of research I find, from the University of Queensland, where Francisco Perales and Janeen Baxter questioned more than 25,000 people in the UK and 9,000 in Australia about contentment in relationships. Their main point? My sister has won relationship roulette.

'Individuals in same-sex couples (particularly lesbian women) generally are more equitable in the ways in which they allocate domestic work, including childcare. Straight couples often reaffirm their gender roles in relationships, which can lead to an unfair division of labour,' they say.

Matt is an excellent life partner but when he puts a wash on it's like he's Emily Davison jumping in front of the King's horse to demand votes for women. There's a slight reluctance to do domestic tasks, which perhaps comes from the weight of 'this is not a man's job' that society has flung our way. In essence it feels like he's doing me a favour when he just needs a clean shirt.

It's near midnight in Karen and Helen's canal-side apartment. I sift through more research papers like a moth to a brightening bulb and turn up this gem from an Open University report on 5,000 people[7]:

'Heterosexual parents are the group least likely to be there for each other, to make "couple time", to pursue shared interests, to say "I love you" and to talk openly to one another.'

In summary: as heterosexual parent people, we're a bit more fucked than everyone else. The stereotypes carved out by our fore-fathers (and mothers) mean Matt and I are more likely to divorce than my sister and Helen. I inform my sister she's 'won' and she reminds me I still owe her €20 for Dad's birthday present.

But I think it's deeper than shifting gender roles. We wrote in some detail in our first book about our experiences with five miscarriages, and – however lucky we feel now to have our two

---

7   'Enduring Love? Couple relationships in the 21st century', Jacqui Gabb, Martina Klett-Davies, Janet Fink and Manuela Thomae, Open University, November 2013.

daughters – those memories linger. The first pregnancy was an 'accident' a few weeks into our relationship and before we moved to Dubai. Memories of Matt's eyes as the nurse asked if he wanted to see the cardboard kidney dish housing our lifeless embryonic sac – when I'd only recently found out his middle name – are hard to shift. I've said before that I remember feeling like I married Matt under those harsh hospital lights. It brought us together much faster and more deeply than I think we otherwise would have been.

Yet the impact of those five lives lost still lingers with me and still makes me angry, and anger can manifest itself in odd ways, whether that's a huff about his sock balls or my defensiveness when he 'fffffkkkkksssakes'.

Either way, big issues start filtering into smaller everyday gripes because they often get ignored. Matt is a man who jokingly – and frustratingly – describes his way of handling emotion thus: 'I just breathe it in and shit it out.' The toilet is his Zen temple.

The reality is he's a man who feels a lot. 'He's a softie deep down,' his mum once whispered to me in our early days together. But he communicates very little because he grew up in a world where boys don't cry. On our wedding day I mainly remember staring at his eyes, hoping some salty happiness would flow. I saw a tear but it was swiftly swept away. So if there's one thing I am desperate to understand, it's why he can't release the emotional floodgates in the same way I can.

And he's not the only man who acts this way. According to the German Society of Ophthalmology, women shed tears on average between thirty and sixty-four times a year (or about once a week) whereas men cry just six to seventeen times (more like once a month).[8] I can count on one hand the number of times Matt has cried in front of me. Until adolescence, however, there is no difference – up until age thirteen, boys and girls turn on the waterworks the same amount. Whether we're blubbing because of joy, sadness or anger, men and women instinctively do it the same, but something around the step into adulthood forces men to turn off the taps. So who or what taught Matt to stop crying?

I call Randy Cornelius, professor of psychology at Vassar College in Poughkeepsie, New York, and an expert on crying. (Quite a dinner-party introduction: 'So what do you do, Randy?' 'I am a crying expert.')

After I explain my fascination with Matt's tear ducts and some brief chat about the weather over there, he offers up this explanation: 'My guess, and the generally accepted explanation, is that sons are discouraged from crying as a larger programme of socialization into masculinity,' says Randy, his rolling American drawl instantly making me feel less teary. But outside of a lecture hall, what does that mean in real life?

'Such socialization involves teaching boys to "tough it out", to refrain from expressing their feelings – except for anger – and, above all, not to appear to be vulnerable. What you can do is make it beyond-a-shadow-of-a-doubt clear you care. Make it clear that you understand it's a confusing time to be a man. Say the words, 'you can cry' and 'you don't need to man up'. He can even use

---

8   'Frauen und Männer weinen anders' ('Women and Men Cry Differently'), 15 October 2009.

the crying emoji if he's feeling sad and can't communicate that in real life!'

But it seems like these are things that we vaguely know, and I want to understand what that feels like for a boy. I email my university friend Simon, who was the only one of my friends with a dry eye after watching *Good Will Hunting* together in a sweaty Reading University hall of residence. His nickname at university was 'Stone Man', such was his stoicism (though it also had weed-related connotations).

Over a pint of lime and soda in Leicester Square's The Moon Under Water, he admits he stopped crying when he was ten. 'I came off my bike doing wheelies on a gravel pitch. My knee was shredded and there was loads of blood,' he recalls. 'Usually, the sight of my own blood would have started me howling, but I was with my mates, so I just gritted my teeth and swore a lot. I could see the pride on my dad's face when I walked into the living room with blood streaming down my leg and a big smile on my face. I don't remember crying much after that. It was a matter of pride.'

Crying is unique to human beings (although Charles Darwin claimed there was a hippopotamus at London Zoo that blubbed when it was upset). But why does society do its best to repress this instinct in men? And is it healthy for men – for Matt – to suppress feelings? (The 'Swallow and Defecate Method', as we shall coin it.) I feel like I still don't have the answer and so I get in touch with Professor Jay Belsky, director of the Institute for the Study of Children, Families and Social Issues at Birkbeck University. He says that we seem to promote disconnection between what a child feels and what is being expressed, which can lead to emotional stalemate.

'I recall being about eleven or twelve years of age and coming out of a funeral home when my grandmother had died,' he says. 'I found myself thinking about one of the nice times I had spent with her. Thinking about that led me to cry. I had a first cousin who was a good ten years older than me and who came up to me and said, "Jay, don't cry." Upon reflection, I have come to realize that that was some of the stupidest counsel I ever received. If you can't cry when a loved one dies, when can you cry?'

When Matt's father died and we went to Aberdeen for the funeral, it took an hour of silently holding his feet – a yogic process that I learn later is called 'grounding' – in an airless Airbnb for him to shed tears. I believe looking at him then and knowing him better now, he feared opening it all up. His sister, El, cried from the beginning of the easyJet flight up there and spoke to me at length in the pub toilets later about how Matt had to 'man up' when his father left them and that his sometimes steely demeanour was simply protective armour.

This is where I believe things go wrong – Matt and I are not on a battlefield, we are not under attack, we were simply two humans trying to navigate the rocks, pebbles and occasional meteorites that life throws our way. We are not two orcs fighting to the death. In our first book, our editor gave this initial feedback: 'Anna, we need to dial down the emotion a little. And Matt, we need a little more.' While there is definitely room for compromise here, after twelve years together, we still seem unable to move beyond this domestic cycle:

Phase one: Emotional issue arises. This can be anything from one of us ignoring the other in favour of sport pages or Instagram to deep-rooted heartbreak and forgetting a celebratory date. (The latter happened this year. I forgot Matt's birthday until a friend WhatsApped us at 4p.m., saying 'Have a good day mate' with a flashing cake GIF. My heart sank – even more so when Matt seemed unsurprised by the absence of even a morning peck-on-the-cheek or a hastily made card from the kids.)

Phase two: The emotional issue is brushed aside due to a lack of time or one party wishing to not labour the point for fear it will open up other issues. Sometimes it can simply come down to just wanting to watch *Queer Eye* (me) or *Breaking Bad* (him).

Phase three: The issue lurks for a few days and filters into banal domestic tasks, resulting in barbed words around The Cupboard of Doom, the place under the stairs where all our unwanted items go to die: 'Do you need this gym mat? You never use it?' Subtext: I'm angry with you. You hurt me. I know you are feeling rubbish about not going to the gym so probably shouldn't have added that bit. But I don't know how to tell you I am sad.

Phase four: These drips of passive aggression pool together until the floodgates relent and I break down mid-spag bol and demand to know what's wrong in a way that instantly puts Matt on the defensive. The armour is on, the cannons are ready.

Phase five: We talk about everything but The Issue for about an hour – me snot-bubbling, him staring at the fake taxidermized butterfly on the living room wall that he's never really liked – until we realize the small, seemingly unimportant snipes along the way have simply built up into a gaping crevice of miscommunication. Then we kiss, have sex and realize we mainly just missed each other.

But, reflecting on these repeated exchanges, I often feel like a dung beetle rolling its precious orb up a hill and wondering why it's routinely impossible to reach the top.

Sometimes we all just need to ignore the domestic load and better share the emotional load.

Sometimes I want him to be the one to break the seal of passive aggression.

Sometimes I feel like I'm talking to Kevin the Teenager – and no woman wants to be seen as 'Mum' by the person who once touched her up in a Milanese cafe as they sank Dirty Martinis.

Emotional labour means many things but it was a term first used by American sociologist Arlie Russell Hochschild in 1983 in her book *The Managed Heart*. (When I initially read the title, I saw 'mangled heart' and instantly felt an affinity.) She describes it as having to 'induce or suppress feeling in order to sustain the outward countenance that produces the proper state of mind in others'. (The term has recently become more specific to marginalized people who have their identity attacked in some way and have to pretend that they're 'fine'.)

In my relationship with Matt, the emotional labour comes from saying, 'I'm fine' (no one is fine when they utter those words) because I know his preference is to never talk about The Stuff. It feels like the weight of communication lies on my shoulders because his preference would be the Swallow and Defecate Method. I essentially don't want to make him unhappy by talking about things that aren't fun, fornication or food. But harbouring that much gas in your upper digestive tract is never going to end well and that's where I think women get unfairly tarnished with the nagging brush.

I do, however, feel there are times when we could heed marriage counsellor Andrew Wachter's advice: 'Say what you mean but don't say it mean.'

And maybe that's good advice for the world in general. We need to open up, but we need to do it nicely. To say it with the same cheery hope that you might use for telling a story on your first date. But emotional labour aside, there are some dreary practical things that have been nagging at me.

Someone I have confided in over the last year is founder of the Women's Equality Party, Sophie Walker. I meet her at Pizza Pilgrims (the closest I got to the monks in Mount Athos) in London's Soho, keen to crack open the three words that have qualified a lot of my frustration over the last decade: The Domestic Load.

'I think that domestic work is the bit that nobody wants to talk about because it's really, really hard to explain away the fact that men are still not doing it in equal measure.'

Sophie shares the load with her second husband, who is a chief executive. They've been together for twelve years and she believes there's something in doing it second time round that makes you more tuned in to any imbalances.

That includes buying presents for a mutual friend's wedding. It includes buying food when it runs out and it definitely includes crafting a Spider Girl costume out of bin bags and black pipe cleaners.

'When we talk about care, there's lots of political arguments about how women are hard-wired to be empathetic and men have all the pressure to be breadwinners,' Sophie continues. 'But when you talk about sharing the domestic load, it's really hard to get around the fact that men just don't like doing it and they're quite happy for women who also don't like doing it to then nevertheless do it.'

But for all the deep-cleansing I want to do here, it's my friend and NHS psychologist (she's one of the ones that couples corner at dinner parties and drunkenly ask for analysis) Emma Cathers who sums up the frustration I feel in this one sentence: 'My husband will do the shopping and buy milk and bread. He won't think, "Ah, we need toilet roll." He won't think beyond the milk and bread.'

That said, Matt and I have increasingly flipped the 'man brings home the bacon' narrative in recent years. Before we met, my first job was as an administration assistant on *Planning* magazine, where I'd mainly be in charge of filing magazines and buying birthday presents. I remember feeling lucky to have a computer that worked, a phone line and a water cooler to casually linger by. That sense of 'luck' is something that's been woven into every career decision and role I've taken since. My career has been navigated as if there's a pack of savage editorially savvy Rottweilers nipping at my heels, ready to take my free biro away.

So being 'lucky' to me has equalled financial stagnation: never asking for a rise (or asking, being rejected and never pushing it). Unlike Matt, who always asked for more. We have the same experience – we met when we were both reporters on similar magazines – but for the first decade of our relationship he was earning more than me.

But then he lost his job – the day we got the keys to our home, the day we were paying off a mortgage and not paying rent. And my sense of luck transformed to something more primal: a need to keep a roof over our head and fish fingers on the table for our daughter, who was eighteen months old at the time. It gave me the push to start Mother Pukka, and I am now the main bread-winner after years of shuffling a few crumbs onto the table every month.

And I'm not alone. Over the last fifteen years[9] there's been an 80 per cent rise in the number of women out-earning their partners in the UK. On paper we've got a thoroughly modern marriage. There are hordes of examples of men rolling up their sleeves and entering a world of soft-play dates and hollers for 'the green spoon, not the yellow spoon'. Look at Hewlett Packard CEO Carly Fiorina's husband and former Yahoo! boss Marissa Mayer's husband, who is routinely photographed clutching his offspring, looking every inch the new feminist hero. My friend Gemma, who is MD of a creative agency, earns a significant amount more than her husband Jack and at a recent dinner, admitted: 'It hasn't changed anything other than division of parenting – we make choices equally but he does more of the day-to-day childmin. It surprises me that people are surprised.'

But for Matt and me there has been a cost with this fiscal shift. The burden of childcare more often sits with him now. The kids sometimes ask for him in the night, not me. My youngest often reaches for 'Papa' as soon as I scoop her up for a hug. He knows when the kids need their jabs or where to find the Calpol in the underbelly of our medicine cabinet. He is now the primary carer.

---

9   'The Condition of Britain: Strategies for social renewal', IPPR.org, 19 June 2014.

And our relationship has been punctuated with a slight sense of resentment on his part about his expanded load – something the new feminist heroes are not allowed to mutter for fear of losing their titles. One chat recently was peppered with talk of 'ratios' and whether the current balance is fair.

The only way we've navigated the ups and downs of our financial and familial responsibilities is with a routine airing of dirty laundry. Money chat is firmly on the table, and we have a joint account that's 'ours' not mine or his. It's all in. (Although my mum did whisper in my ear to 'keep some back, just in case'.)

I'm at a point where I'm done being made to feel 'lucky' – lucky to have my job, lucky to have a man who will pick up the burden of childcare. I'm lucky to have found him and that's the bottom line.

That night, as I tuck our daughter up under her Spiderman (couldn't find Spider Girl) duvet, I remember something Emma said: 'When I read my daughter fairy tales and it says, "And they lived happily ever after", I always say, "And they lived happily ever after except for a year round about when . . ." I try and make it a bit more realistic because finding The One isn't about eternal happiness, it's about working through the unhappiness.'

Sometimes I do think we're so desperately seeking this elusive happiness, we forget to be happy along the way. We're so fixed on moving to the next house, moving the bed around, moving his loose change into a bowl, moving to a better area, moving upwards and moving onwards, towards this promised land of relationship joy, that we sometimes forget to look at where we are in that moment.

With two children clamouring for our attention, we sometimes even forget to look at each other.

5

☆ ☆ ☆

Oh Baby

Can love survive kids?

Matt

Children are the worst version of humans. They are wilful, inconsiderate and egotistical. They drain you physically, financially and emotionally, leeching from your being from day one. They're a bit like a Lego racing car: it's fun making them, but playing with them can be disappointing.

Parenthood is essentially a coercive relationship, with the parent giving everything to the other party but silently acknowledging that they will never love us the way that we love them.

It's no wonder that these tiny interlopers put strains on previously happy relationships. But are long-term relationships any better without them? Well, according to science, yes. Much better.

Since the late eighties, scores of studies have looked at the impact of kids on their parents' relationship, and they all came to the same conclusion: the impact is bad.

This has been proven from research in the Americas, Asia and Europe. It has been proven across ethnic groups in the US, and for lesbian couples and straight couples. As University of Texas researchers noted when reviewing the combined evidence: 'relationship deterioration after birth appears to be a universal event'.[1]

---

1   'The Effect of the Transition to Parenthood on Relationship Quality: An eight-year prospective study', *Journal of Personality and Social Psychology*, March 2009.

You have children because you are in love, and then they begin to slowly dismantle that love. While the arrival of children can be joyful, any couple who have a kid to 'bring them closer together' would be better off with basket-weaving classes.

Those University of Texas researchers studied 218 newly married couples and found that the relationship got worse for all of them over the first eight years (which is sad), but it got worse twice as fast for the parents as for those without kids (which is sadder).

And it got worse in lots of ways – relationship confidence and satisfaction dropped, negative communication (snarking at each other) increased, as did 'problem intensity'. As any parent will tell you, having a child is an intense problem.

Much other research tells a similar tale. A 2018 study in Australia found that new parents had half as much sex as they did before kids, their whoopee-tally dropping from an average of nineteen bunk-ups a month to ten.[2]

In all the academic papers I've read for this book, there is one truth that seems as undeniable as climate change: having kids hurts your relationship.

I spoke to Lori Schade, an expert on the phenomenon of 'involuntary celibacy' in marriages (more of that in chapter 6). But when we spoke over video link – her from the homely scene in her office in Pleasant Grove, Utah, me from a kitchen table in suburban London – she mentioned that she had seven kids, now mostly grown-up. She was open and engaging but also joyously upfront about the toil that took.

---

2   'Your Sex Life After Kids', Leesa.com, 2018.

'I mean, I just wanted to hurt myself!' she says with an exasperated laugh. 'It is absolutely crazy-making. For me, when I look at raising children, you've got to think long term. Because in the short term it's like hell. I mean there's just *so* much. You're exhausted, your life revolves around them. They just absolutely wear you down.'

Seven does sound like *a lot* of children, I tell her, and all of a sudden the image of our two girls scrapping like tiger cubs seems pretty serene.

'Some of the long-term joy for us is watching our kids get older and post-teenage – because adolescents are not always fun – and then having their own kids. We're finally getting the rewards back, by having grandchildren. And they're fun because they're really not our problem.'

But she also reassures me that, while there isn't much long-term research on the impact on relationships of raising kids all the way through to adulthood, 'usually couples come out in the end feeling a little bit better. My personal experience is that our marriage just feels a lot better since more kids are out of the house. I mean, I'm not gonna lie, it's just really hard no matter how you look at it.'

Knowing that this is someone who is professionally trained to understand the feelings of others – her business is called Compassionate Connections Counseling – makes me feel a little better about my own frustrations.

At the other end of the compassion scale, I turn to my friend Dan. A devoutly single man of forty-one and former cameraman for Playboy TV, he now makes props for TV and film. Most male friendship groups tend to have a vocal and prolific 'shagger', and Dan is ours.

After a long-term relationship ended suddenly when he was in his early twenties, he has been a relentless pursuer of fleeting female company. He's six foot four, well built and suspiciously tanned all year round. He made the brave decision to maintain a ponytail well into his late thirties. He attends sex parties and is disappointed that Tinder has become more focused on dating of late, when 'it was supposed to be like Grindr, a casual sex map. But then it blew up, and everyone wants to be involved, like it's Harry Potter or something.'

He recently told me of a girl who asked him to saw a circle in the seat of a wooden cafe-style chair so that he could tie her to it and provide various pleasures. I can't even picture the mechanics of such a thing, or what would possibly go where, and just hope it was all properly sanded down. His experience of relationships is about as far from mine as it's possible for a contemporary to be, and I'm curious whether he has any interest in raising a family.

'It's like finishing a computer game,' he tells me over beer and pizza in a quiet corner of my local pub. 'You're happy cos it's finished, but sad cos it's over. But no one has ever finished raising a kid and then said, "I wanna play again." That's why I got a PlayStation and not a wife.'

While I wouldn't consider a life partner to be tradable with a games console, I do kind of miss having a PlayStation. I once took Barnet FC to the Champions League final on FIFA. Now I worry about climate change and school catchment areas.

I ask if there's any element of the parenting life that tempts him.

'I enjoy seeing friends in couples who've got it right because it seems everyone in the world wants that. But, for me, there's nothing about it,' he says. 'When you start out, it's all blow jobs and meals and late-night conversations, listening to music, introducing people to new things. That is pretty seductive, right? Potentially ruining that with children is a little bit sad for me.'

From the outside, parenting doesn't look fun, and mostly I think that's because of the grizzling of parents. I find it very easy to discuss the hardships, but trickier to make the positive case. I adore my daughters like pot plants love water, and feel a peculiar emptiness when we're apart for more than a few hours, but if we'd never had them I would not know those feelings and in an alternate reality could quite happily have continued developing a pixelated version of my local football team.

And as many of the child-free realize that parenthood is not quite as life-affirming as the nappy adverts suggest, they are less inclined to join up. In the US and UK, almost one-fifth of women now make it to age forty-four without having a child.[3]

One of these was documentary-maker Therese Shechter, who is best known for the critically acclaimed film *How to Lose Your Virginity*. Originally from Toronto but now based in New York, she is currently working on a film called *My So-Called Selfish Life* about the experience of being voluntarily childless.

'Just like I didn't want to be a doctor and I didn't want to live in South America, I also didn't want to have kids,' she tells me, speaking via Skype from her Brooklyn home. Shechter looks younger than her fifty-seven years, is free of make-up, and smiles easily. 'I told my mother when I was a teenager that I wasn't going

---

3   US Census Bureau and Office for National Statistics data.

to have kids, and that if she wanted grandchildren, my sister would provide them for her.'

Despite that early reluctance, she remembers thinking throughout her twenties and thirties that she would eventually have to give in and drop a nipper or two.

'Other women I have spoken to also felt that way. They assumed, even though they didn't want children, that one day they would have to have them,' she says. 'Then as I got closer to forty, I realized that actually no, I didn't. That was a very liberating moment'.

It makes me wonder how many women who don't want children end up having them anyway.

It's a woefully under-reported phenomenon, with little in the way of meaty research, often because it's so hard to find participants to talk openly. One survey of more than 2,000 German parents found that 19 per cent of mums and 20 per cent of dads would prefer to be without children if, in some parallel universe, they could be child-free.[4] One respondent said, 'I really regret bringing a child into the world,' before adding that 'he's the greatest gift I've ever been given.'

As I dig deeper into the academic libraries, I find a 2015 work by Israeli sociologist Orna Donath of Ben Gurion University. She published interviews with twenty-three women who said they regretted motherhood.[5] In a country with one of the highest fertility rates in the developed world (averaging three children per woman),

---

4   YouGov data, 2016.

5   'Regretting Motherhood: A Sociopolitical Analysis', *Signs Journal of Women in Culture and Society*, December 2015.

it wasn't hard to find participants. One of them told Donath: 'I'd totally forgo having children. It hurts me very much to say that, and they'll never hear that from me . . . I'd forgo them, totally. Without batting an eyelid. And it's difficult for me to say that, because I love them.'

And this, it seems to me, is the true contradiction of becoming a parent – you adore your children, you'd happily give up your own limbs or organs to keep them safe, but you also secretly wonder what might have happened if you'd led a child-free life.

So I ask Shechter why she thought she would need to have children, given that she didn't really want any.

'I didn't have any kind of working model for a happy woman without children. I didn't see it. And I just assumed that my partner, whoever that would be, would want children,' she tells me. 'But I never had a serious enough relationship to get to that point. I really dodged a big bullet.'

Shechter married her husband while in her forties and had a chat about kids as soon as their relationship got serious. 'I told him that I didn't really want kids and I wanted him to know that before things got any more serious. I think he thought that my ovaries had kicked the bucket, and he said, "We could adopt." I said, "No, no – I don't want kids. Like, period." And he said, "Oh, OK." That was the extent of the conversation,' she says. 'I've grown to understand that he would have had kids with someone who wanted them, but would never have dreamed of having kids with someone who didn't. It's really never been an issue.'

So, I wonder, what does the happy ending look like to her?

'I'm not sure I believe in the concept of "happily ever after".

I think it's a little bit of a romantic notion. But I would say that, having gone through my fifty-seven years, I'm really happy. I have a lovely partner, I have a family that I'm close to and love, I do work I really enjoy, I live in a fantastic city and have agency over my life. So all of these things, to me, contribute to my happiness.'

Shechter's attitude is reflected by a lot of the women in her film. They get judged a little, and people trot out the same lines to them – 'you'll regret it later', 'you just haven't met the right person yet' – but ultimately they're making a choice and feel others should be comfortable doing the same. But there are some more extreme child-free philosophies out there too.

In early 2019, Raphael Samuel, a twenty-seven-year-old Mumbai man with a giant fake beard, announced to the world that he was suing his parents because they created him without his consent.

'I have a good relationship with my parents,' he told local media. 'But you cannot deny that they brought me into the world purely for their own pleasure. I was made to bring them happiness. Why should you oblige someone to make their way through the hassle of life: going to school, looking for a job, making a career?'

At the time of writing, Samuel had not found a lawyer willing to represent him, and was planning to train himself for the case. But he did bring the concept of 'antinatalism' to global prominence (or at least got a few people talking about it on Twitter).

Antinatalism is the belief that to have children is morally wrong – that life is cruel, it ends in death, and because humans are the only creatures that understand that, having more is a bit mean. It's kind of like a seven-year-old hollering 'I never asked to be born!' but developed into a philosophy on obscure chat forums.

It may have taken YouTube and a comedy beard to bring it to wider public attention, but it has existed as an idea for hundreds of years. Second-century Christian sect the Encratites felt that, as birth leads to death, the best way to conquer death was to not have any more kids. They were so convincing that they all died out.

There are also those who believe we need to stop breeding for environmental reasons. As the planet gets warmer and more crowded, movements such as BirthStrike – women who are refusing to have children until climate change ends – have begun to gain public attention.

Then there is the 'voluntary human extinction movement', or VHEMT (pronounced 'vehement'). They believe that Earth would be better off without people on it, so we should all stop breeding until we go extinct.

I track down the movement's de facto spokesman, Les U. Knight, who works as a supply teacher in Oregon, in America's lush, green Pacific Northwest. We talk over video link, while he sits at his kitchen table. He is slim, white-haired and avuncular, and behind him are brown laminated kitchen cabinets and shelves stacked with rolls of paper towels, cereal and tinned foods. There are a dozen yellow Post-Its on one cupboard door.

'We are encouraging people to think before they procreate,' he says. 'If people really think about it, there's no reason to.'

I argue that there are many great reasons to have kids – guaranteed elder-care, the heart-liquefying sound of a toddler's giggle, the vanity to think the world needs more of you in it and that your kid might do something amazing.

'It's pretty exploitative to want to create a new human so that they'll be there when you get old,' says Knight. 'And yes, it's possible that if we raise them right they will do some good in the world. But if we used all of that energy to just do the good in the world ourselves we might be better off.'

And of course, we could do that good and still raise our kids to do more of it, but there is a strange dream-transference that happens with children. Once I realized that I would never become an Olympic anything or invent a sock that never got holes in the toes, I began to hope that my daughters might fulfil those dreams for me.

'I haven't yet found a really compelling reason to create one more human,' says Knight. 'We are engineering our involuntary extinction and our voluntary extinction would avoid that. A peaceful phase-out would be really quite humane.'

Knight's been making his case since the seventies and had a vasectomy decades ago, before meeting his partner of twenty years who, he says, agrees with his philosophy. I ask what he wants from the future.

'That everybody has a sense of community, of belonging, whether it's a family or a larger community. And that we know we're a part of the human family and take care of each other. We take care of the environment and all of the other species. That would be a happy ending for me.'

That part, at least, is hard to argue with. But when it really comes down to it, I think most people do want a tiny version of themselves to gurgle at, which is why there are so many of us. And they're prepared to do whatever it takes to have them.

I have friends who have endured the physical, financial and emotional agonies of IVF. I've known gay men who have decided to share their entire lives with female pals so they can create nippers. I know women who've bought Danish sperm at £1,000 a squirt. And there are others who are willing to sacrifice almost everything else in their world to care for a tiny human.

One of these is novelist Laura Jane Williams, who I go to visit at her home in Derby, northern England.

Set back from a B-road in a small village outside the city sits a white-fronted, mid-century semi-detached house. It's here that Williams has built a life in preparation for adopting a child and becoming a single mother. It's a cosy home, with cushions piled high on the sofas and tea and biscuits on the coffee table.

In her early twenties, Williams was dumped by her high school sweetheart, who went on to marry her best friend. Heartbreak and anxiety followed and she spent years travelling and nannying, while writing on the side. Eventually, that writing turned into her first book, *Becoming*.

'All I had wanted for ten years was to see my name on the spine of a book, and then it happened. And what they don't tell you about your dreams coming true is that it's brilliant but it's also fucking awful because if your dream comes true, what else do you dream about?'

Her tales of heartache and promiscuity in *Becoming* picked up national press attention, including a profile in the *Sun* headlined 'Around the world in 80 lays', to which her Aunty Barbara said, 'Oh, don't worry about that, duck. I've been around the world in eighty lays. It's just all been with your Uncle David.'

Williams found herself living in London, with a national magazine column, a successful first book and a second on the way.

'I came back from the launch of the second book, *Ice Cream for Breakfast,* and I sobbed and sobbed and sobbed. I said, "I don't understand why I'm working so hard. What's all of this for if I'm not coming home to kiss my kids?" I felt, "Oh, fuck, I really want this." And that was just before my thirty-first birthday.'

She didn't have a partner, and was noticing a pattern in her relationships.

'I was doing a lot of looking after of these twenty-something men,' she says, and she realized that she would often think, 'It's fun or the sex is great but I don't want to be your mother, and your therapist, and your cheerleader. And also I was building a lifestyle, working for myself, and knew I would be able to be at school drop-off at nine and pick-up at three.'

She felt she had a nurturing instinct from her nannying experiences, and also that she wasn't bothered about carrying a child herself.

'It was this perfect storm of ADOPT,' she says. 'Obviously you feel like a fucking nutter and everyone is going, "Oh, babe. You'll find someone, it won't always feel like this." So you do the laptop in bed in the dark. Set it to private. Looking for the filth that is "Can I adopt on my own?"'

And the answer is yes, you can. So she gave up her London life and moved closer to her parents. She's entering the final stages of the approval process, after which she will begin the lengthy process of being matched with a child. There's a bedroom waiting for him or her.

I wonder though if it can really be that simple: that one emotional night can lead you to change everything, or if the maternal urge was always there.

'In my early twenties it was very cool to say, "I'm not gonna have children." But actually I've always worked with children. I was eighteen when I first went to Sri Lanka and worked in an orphanage. I ran a kids' language school in Rome. I ran language camps. Kids have always been in my life and I've always been good with kids.' The first germ of the idea of adopting came during a spell a few years ago when she was working as a security guard at Toys 'R' Us.

'There was an older lady with a three-year-old in the trolley, and I'm bored shitless because I'm paid to stand by a door for eight hours in a polyester T-shirt that made me stink, so I talk to this kid, saying, "Ooh, I love your shoes. Did you put those on yourself? Do they light up?" And this woman turns to me and said, "She won't talk to you. She'll only talk to her sister. I'm a foster mum and we can't foster them together. She only talks when the kids are together but nobody will adopt them together." And I was like, "Me, me, me!" and I think that is the very earliest planting of a seed of wanting to adopt.'

She doesn't know what age her child will be, or what background they'll be coming from, but it's rare for a child to be given up voluntarily. It will follow lengthy court proceedings and reams of evidence of exposure to domestic violence or abuse, be it physical, sexual or emotional. There are social workers for all parties in the process – birth mother, child and potential adopters.

'You can have the best intentions in the world with adoption. A child needs love and a home and you have the capacity to love, and a home to share with a child. But adoption is a process based in loss for everyone,' says Williams. 'In loss for birth mother and birth family. For the child losing their birth family. No matter how I love a potential child there's always gonna be that question of, "Yes, but why didn't my birth mummy love me enough?"'

We talk for an hour, and then I make way as Williams has another appointment with her social worker ahead of her final interview with the adoption board. I wish her luck and head back home.

The lengths to which Williams has gone remind me of that basic urge to care for someone else. Our girls turned six and two recently and I think I've gone through as many developmental stages as they have in the time they've been around. Before we had kids, I was a little ambivalent about the idea. And then the miscarriages began and I knew that I wanted them very much, and that our lives would feel incomplete without them.

Then when our eldest arrived, I was besotted. Having one child to care for between the two of us felt oddly idyllic. Then we moved back to London from Amsterdam and everything became a little more difficult. The costs and the logistics of parenting in the city added a new level of pressure. And eventually, after a couple more miscarriages, we gave her a little sister and I was besotted again.

But that also added to the pressure. Anna went back to work barely a fortnight after giving birth. She wasn't ready and, I think, had postnatal depression. Our youngest wouldn't take the bottle and so for a full year was clawing at her body for food while she tapped away at phone and laptop. Our lives became entirely focused on the needs of our daughters, and I'm still not sure if I did enough.

The only real breather comes from working, when they are at school and nursery. The rest of the time, I am feeding them, or washing them, or helping with homework or being made to pretend to be a 'beautiful donkey'. When I can focus on this, and be patient, it can be beautiful. When I raise my voice to them, guilt sits on my shoulders for hours afterwards as I wonder if I've destined them to a lifetime of troubled relationships with fractious men.

I speak to a man called Andrew G. Marshall, who the internet tells me is Britain's best-known marriage therapist. In his Farringdon office in central London he sits, slim-faced and sharp-eyed. He's in his sixties, with a shaved head and a fixed frown that appears to burrow right into you. It's like he's peering into my chest to mentally dissect all my flaws.

We talk for around forty minutes, and at the end of our conversation, he offers some thoughts on the impact of children.

'The most common mistake people make is one that nobody wants to hear: they worship their children. People write to me and say: "My husband is having an affair, and he's going to leave me and our beautiful children," and I want to say, "Well, if they were ugly, would that be OK?" Because when people say "my beautiful children", what they mean is "these are children that I worship". The number of people who send me messages on Facebook about their marriage being down the toilet, and you look at their avatars, and it's pictures of them with their children – not with their partner or on their own. You think, "Oh, if actually you're representing yourself to the world as a mother or a father, what's that telling your partner? Basically, that they're expendable."'

The answer, he says, is a little readjustment of priorities.

'Put each other first and not the children. It's good for the children as well because being the most powerful person in the house is terrifying for them, although they don't really know it. It's why they're so anxious. If you worship your children, you are going to be undermining them and your marriage.'

And perhaps there is an element of worship with us and the girls. I pretend to be flippant, but I love them in a way that I physically feel like a dizziness across my chest.

For a long time that space was exclusively Anna's. It was a lightness I would feel every time her number came up on my phone. I would feel it when we were in conversation. Now that lightness is more likely to come from seeing my eldest tell a terrible joke, or hearing the cooing noise my youngest does when she discovers something new.

But as much as the girls are heart-explodingly delightful, they can also be teeth-splittingly inconvenient. The little one took a scooter out for the first time the other day. I put on her little red helmet and watched as she stumbled along the pavement, very slowly walking it into lampposts and walls. I felt wonderfully privileged to see it, but it was as frustrating as taking a hedgehog for a walk, because children are terrible at almost everything. They fall over, they spill, they cry. And we put ourselves there at every opportunity to help them, even when it means ignoring the person we made them with.

I think that's a mistake a lot of us make. We become parents and forget about all the other things we were: so of course kids make relationships worse, if we allow that to happen.

Having them is a blessing and something that most humans yearn for at some stage. But the risk is that in that yearning we lose the person we made them – or raise them – with. Usually, the person you raise kids with has been your top priority for years before and you have been theirs. It's a nice feeling to matter to someone more than anyone else does, and one that's worth remembering once kids come along.

So I think Marshall is right. The kids will be fine. I need to start worshipping Anna again.

Anna

My friend Kay and her wife Jules have just ordered twelve vials (or 'straws') of Danish sperm from a man called Jan. It cost £16,500 and they wanted enough so they can freeze some for future possible siblings. On his profile, Jan describes his favourite animal as 'the quokka, a small Australian marsupial that's always really happy.' When asked what he likes about Denmark, he responds: 'I like our selection of snacks.'

He is the perfect match. Well, almost.

'We had added another guy, Gottlieb's, sperm to the shopping cart and were about to pay and it said, "sold out" as we clicked the button,' said Kay, speaking to me in her sun-drenched flat in Brighton. 'I just burst into tears because that was meant to be our family and someone had added to cart sooner. No one prepares you for how competitive it is.'

She equates buying sperm to the frenzy that surrounds Glastonbury tickets. 'If you get a "straw" that has a plus 50 motility [sperm count], which will basically get you pregnant if you breathe near it, it becomes each woman for herself. We paid £16,500 the minute we decided Jan was The One. You have to act fast when online sperm shopping.'

It's a heartbreaking and confusing process. The how, the who, the when – even before you consider the possibility of things not working out. 'You have this godlike status in that you can make all these decisions, but sometimes that can make you feel like you've failed before you've even started,' she says. 'What if we choose the wrong man?'

Kay and I couldn't have taken more different paths to procreation. She identified as straight until she turned twenty-four, kissed a girl and has liked it ever since. They since married and have a mutual appreciation of seventeenth-century pornographic literature, including an intriguing play called *The Farce of Sodom* (the protagonist is called Bolloxinion). Matt and I got married in a rural church and have just invested in a new knife block. They call each other 'love'. Matt ironically calls me 'sweet potato pumpkin pie', which occasionally grates. Matt and I had sex and made a baby. Kay and Jules bought Jan's sperm and will use a turkey baster.

'Do you remember Matt drunkenly offering up his spunk "if we ever needed it"?' asks Kay as her rescue cat Percy weaves in and out of our legs. 'That was a bit of a low for me. Why do guys just think, "Yeah, everyone wants my sperm, right? The more of me out there, the better"?'

I went to see Kay because she's the happiest person I know and has an ability to make others feel that. Her relationship with Jules is one of the strongest I've come across, which further cements the Open University's research that same-sex couples are generally happier than wearied heteros like us. For all the boys and frogs she's kissed, she's someone who has absolutely found The One in her wife, and I know without any doubt that adding a child to that mix wouldn't steer that train off its steely tracks.

And having lived with me when we were younger, she knows me better than I know myself. At times when I'm questioning if Matt and I are simply two mismatched Lego pieces angrily jammed together, she puts me right.

'You are really difficult to live with,' she concludes.

Kay asks me what Matt and I do together when we're not working or parenting. I have nothing. Maybe it's because we live with two fun sponges who've left our bank, brains and boobs/moobs a little dazed and confused. Perhaps it's down to the eye-throbbing exhaustion where it can feel like the sound of sleeping children counts as success.

Kay doesn't have kids yet, so I suggest we chat further when she's manically shushing a mewling baby while one of her kids uses fistfuls of pesto pasta to paint the kitchen wall.

But over a few drinks, we devise the Gumtree Test: if you're living as a flatmate with your partner (administrative exchanges, passing like ships in the night, financial convenience) then you need to have a fun check.

On the train back to London, I go to book a babysitter for Matt and I, but struggle to think about what to do. What did Matt and I used to *do* together?

Gottman, the guiding spirit of relationship dissatisfaction, holds my hand (virtually) once more. Reassuringly/unreassuringly, his research finds that 67 per cent of couples go through a slump in relationship satisfaction in the first three years of a baby's life. That sounds about right, as Matt and I are grappling with a homework-averse primary-schooler and a risk-hungry toddler.

Gottman's report says: 'Though many couples are over the moon about their new bundle of joy, they also struggle with work–life balance, more loneliness, financial stress, more chores, minimal free time and friendship changes.'

I nod, reassured that there are many others as fleetingly miserable as us out there. I come back to the need for a map at the beginning of this journey. Just something that says: 'You will dislike him as he snores despite the child's hollers. He/she will dislike you as you ask, "Did you pick up milk?" This is normal. You are not alone.' (What doesn't help is Instagram's favourite proverb, 'This too shall pass.' I need specific timings.)

So we know there's a problem, but what's the solution? I want to speak to someone who is knee-deep in kids and has navigated the choppy parental waters with relative success. I email Harry Benson, father of six and the director of the Bristol Community Family Trust, a charity that runs a course for new parents called *Let's Stick Together*. (He's also written a book of the same name about working things out with his wife of twenty years, Kate.) I feel like I can take relationship advice from him a little more easily than from Kay, who doesn't know what it's like having sex with 'Twinkle Twinkle Little Star' buzzing around your head. He responds to my email within three minutes and we're on the phone before I can even sketch out my questions. With hardly the intros done, I blurt out: 'How do I make it work?'

('It' is Matt.)

Very clearly, he says: 'Are you doing any of these things: scoring points, returning a perceived criticism or niggle with your own criticism, thinking the worst, assuming an underlying negative in his action, opting out, disengaging from a discussion or argument or putting him down?'

I have a think.

1 Point scoring: I do this. I've singlehandedly arranged our daughter's birthday. I've done it every year since she landed. She's now six. I counted to six this morning. That's a lot of cocktail sausages and crustless cheese sandwiches. I feel angry about this.

2 Returning perceived criticism with criticism: Yes. Who hasn't said: 'Yeah, but you never [insert thing other person never does]' in the face of criticism? It's an easy volley back into their court.

3 Thinking the worst: I want to find fault. I seek it out instead of thinking the best. I feel dispirited by the moments, years ago, when he didn't help me at night with a restless baby. I feel saddened by the times he hasn't slipped his hand into mine when we're walking together. I've felt rubbish at every meal we've eaten where he seems distracted and disinterested. I've felt alone on the nights when he couldn't share the darkness of postnatal depression. Over time and with the juggernaut of kids, I feel he's lost me a little. Or perhaps I've lost him. When did I start thinking the worst?

4 Opting out: As we have a mild altercation about school forms, I ask him if he wants to leave me. He says he doesn't. But sometimes, very occasionally, I think about leaving him. I don't want

to opt out but I also don't want to live in a cycle of perpetual disappointment.

5 Disengaging from a discussion or argument: I think there are times when we don't need to talk. There are times when I push a discussion because I simply want connection, even if it's ugly and ill-judged. I often want to burst the boil of disconnection, and tend to go at it like a bumbling fool. There are, however, times I think talking makes things better and Matt's demeanour of a teenager being rapped on the knuckles for nicking some fags doesn't help.

6 Putting him down: I joke to friends he's emotionally absent. I pierce dinner conversations with quips about his lone-wolf status. I said recently to a friend, 'He's an emotional husk of a man.'

But how do I fix it?

('It' is me.)

'By recognizing we are doing these things in a relationship,' says Harry. 'You need to see a big STOP sign, and take simple steps to remedy things, like apologising when we try to score points. You can change patterns of behaviour. You can do it.'

I am definitely sorry. I doubt, however, that it could ever be as simple as Benson lays down. But he does then make a good point about us overcomplicating things. He says as we battle sleep deprivation and infant needs, we start to flail: 'The utter exhaustion of new parenthood means that we don't always react to one another as best friends should. Bad habits can develop and become entrenched over time and start to undermine even the best of relationships.' He assures me that, 'Little changes make a big difference. Treat humans well and they will treat you well in return. Mistreat them and they will mistreat you. It only takes one person to start the process.'

That 'fffffkkkkksssake' from Matt hurts because it acts as a reminder that he's thinking the worst of me when he used to think the best. We're maybe just not on each other's side any more and I really want to fix that.

The question is, who is going to be the bigger person? On Harry's recommendation, I phone Matt and apologise for calling him an emotional husk of a man. He wasn't aware I'd said that but agreed it was, perhaps, a little harsh.

Matt put together our daughter's bike for her birthday today, he works hard and he's doing the Couch to 5K running programme because he says, 'Now I've got kids, I have a responsibility to die a bit later.' I definitely fancy him. But since having kids I just miss my mate. The guy who once made me laugh with his grotty gags (which now seem more forced) and the guy who helped piece me back together after losing babies.

☆☆☆

After Matt, my second true love is a man called Mark Smith. My close family members and Matt have accepted this and generally leave us to it as we cocoon ourselves in a hyperactive world that no one else wants in on. When I first met Mark, he looked like an escapee from *X-Factor* boot camp, complete with hair teased to dizzying architectural heights. (As circumstance would have it, he was, in fact, voted off various TV talent contests in the late nineties, and would reminisce about his appearance in *Sugar* magazine, where the journalist cut the fact he was gay and rewrote his answer to the question 'What's your ideal date?' with 'I would love to take a girl up the Eiffel Tower.')

Mark does not want to take a girl up the Eiffel Tower and is now happily married to Greg, a kindly, long-suffering Scottish soul. Mark has been there through my stumbling beginnings of project procreation, and is now entering that world himself.

Soon after moving to Amsterdam, I secured a job on an English-language magazine. My desk was next to Mark's in an old Dutch warehouse and we had a 'shared drive' that was a plastic paper-tray that we would fill with snacks, saying things like: 'I've just put a stroopwafel in the shared drive.'

While working there, I suffered a missed miscarriage. I say 'missed' because the Dutch obstetrician flatly said, 'Don't worry, there was nothing really there to begin with,' as I was told to go home and wait for an amniotic sac to pass. When I asked what to do with the bundle of our cells that were currently being rejected by my womb, she said, 'Flush it down the toilet.'

I called in sick to work. My editor wanted to know why. We had had some run-ins before, over how I felt she treated people (me included), and I spat down the phone that I had suffered a miscarriage. I wanted to scream: 'I'm waiting to flush my unviable foetus down the toilet.'

When I returned to the office, she asked to go on a walk around the block because she had something to tell me. As we ambled through the cobbled streets, she said softly, 'I wanted you to be the first person to know that I am pregnant.'

Despite still bleeding into a pad the size of a hamster cage, the truth is I was on some level happy for her. She did, however, catch me at a time when I thought everyone else was going to pass their fertility test except me.

As a medical side note, doctors at Imperial College London say that four in ten women who have a miscarriage go on to develop post-traumatic stress disorder, characterized by flashbacks and night-mares. The physicality of passing the amniotic sac is something that can come flooding back, vividly, at seemingly random moments, like in a pub toilet or in the baby aisle of the local supermarket.

A few years ago, I interviewed Jessica Farren, lead author of the study and she said, 'We have checks in place for postnatal depres-sion, but we don't have anything in place for the trauma and depression following pregnancy loss. Yet the symptoms that may be triggered can have a profound effect on a woman's everyday life, from her work to her relationships with friends and family.'

In the absence of any medical support, Matt is – and has always been – my rock. It's like the softness and curvature of his armpit is tailored to my head. It's where I feel safe, loved, and it is where I am at my happiest, even when salty tears are seeping into his wiry underarm hair. For all the grand romantic gestures advertisers flog us around Valentine's Day, for all the *Cosmopolitan* articles on 'Eight tips for a hot sex life', I feel the armpit is often an overlooked solution, a quiet cul-de-sac that no one else in the world has a valid parking permit for.

We have had five miscarriages. I still don't know if we've found some vague peace with these losses or if we've just taken the stoic British approach of 'time's a healer'. What I do know is that we hit those lows together and I'm proud of how we've come through the other side. Maybe my mum was right when she said, 'You've got to learn to break together.'

On 21 June at 8.26p.m. my eldest was born at Onze Lieve Vrouwe Gasthuis by C-section, and my world, its relationships and everything I knew about my mind, vagina and soul turned upside down.

Once I was home, Mark came round with a Hello Kitty rattle and a bottle of Prosecco and we sat on the nursery floor, with sweaty cured meats on a plate and my boob flopped out. I was tentatively sipping Prosecco from a pink beaker between feeds while Mark quaffed the rest from a paisley Cath Kidston mug. What I didn't realize in those floor picnics (which we would repeat until I graduated to a cafe) was that Mark was looking at the small mewling form with intrigue and not aversion.

Six years later, we sit in the National Portrait Gallery cafe. We've just been to see a photography exhibition that's fronted by an image of a glamorous ninety-seven-year-old lady in a gold bikini with creped boobs pooling into the metallic fabric. My post-breastfeeding mammaries have never felt more represented in mainstream media. It's 10.15a.m., Mark orders a heavily iced lemon sponge cake and we talk about parenthood.

'Greg and I have never really talked about it [parenthood], and that's because, for me, it would be quite painful to talk about something for which the odds were kind of stacked against us,' he says. 'My dad did actually take Greg aside when we were walking through Bolton Abbey last year on my mum's birthday and said, "When are you going to have a child, then?"'

Mark's dad is a salt-of-the-earth Yorkshireman who, like my own dad, doesn't talk much about his feelings. 'It sort of went from "How's the traffic on the M621?" to "When are you going to have a child, then?"' Mark continues.

While Mark had come to the conclusion he would be happy not having a child – 'I think you can find very fulfilling relationships in all aspects of life, and it takes a while to come to that realization' – he describes a photo that sits in their lounge of Greg holding his godson Joe up in the air like Simba in *The Lion King*.

'I've never seen anybody look so engaged,' he continues. 'Both the baby and Greg are sort of locked on each other. And just seeing him with other people's kids, it was clear that he would be absolutely great at it. But it's a really daunting thing to get your head around: what are the possibilities, how would it happen, what would it look like, how would we afford it, where would we be living, what kind of support would we have?'

Greg's sister read out the poem 'Because We Can' at their Amsterdam wedding in 2017, which is about gay rights and 'having the opportunity to express something so mundane as love'. The privilege of being able to love someone freely and openly is something I've never fully considered as Matt and I trundled down the path of dating, marrying and procreating.

'I interviewed Stephen Fry last year,' continues Mark, 'and I just found myself at the end of the interview saying, "Thank you for everything that you've done for people like me," which means just being unapologetically yourself, and just, well, making things better for other people.'

Mark has made things better for me (he could have made things better for Hear'Say if only they'd had him) and now he will undoubtedly make things better for his own children – the first of whom will have arrived by the time you read this, Greg and Mark having decided to co-parent with a dear friend who also found herself wondering how to make and raise a small human.

'I think it takes a little while for people to get their head around it, and part of that is that there isn't a legal provision for people who are co-parenting in scenarios where there's more than two parents. Because there are going to be three parents in our child's life,' he says. 'There's no legal provision for that anywhere in the world. If anywhere does it, then it's going to be the Netherlands, and as a journalist, I'm going to do my part to move that conversation on. As long as we don't have the legal provision or the language to talk about it, then it's very invalidating.'

The 3:1 ratio is something – as someone with a 2:2 set-up – I can only dream of. But more than anything, our time spent talking about parenthood has mainly centred on his love of Greg.

'I just realize that it's not extravagant love, it's not massively demonstrative, it's nothing that sounds particularly exciting when you try to tell anyone else about it. It's just the knowledge that you've been extremely lucky to find this person who can tolerate you. That is what I think love is, perhaps. Tolerance.'

I wonder if tolerance is something you have as a finite resource and if it's something that erodes with every child's grizzle. Perhaps Matt and I have just overcomplicated things and need to hold on tighter.

One thing I'm learning is that if you're a parent you need to be more than just two people who project-manage effectively and miss each other absolutely. More than two people who help small folks with 'things that go bump in the night' while failing to bump into each other at all.

What did Matt and I actually *do* before having kids?

Each other, mostly.

6

☆ ☆ ☆

Hump Day

Does sex matter?

Matt

Well, this is awkward. No one wants to hear another couple talk about their sex lives – there's something dogging-ish about it, like they're trying to flash your subconscious.

My friends very rarely tell sex tales now because married men don't tell sex stories about their wives, and my single friends think it'd be cruel to gloat. On the rare occasion that I do hear a sex tale from a friend, the surprise insertion of their swinging bits into my mind's eye feels like an intimacy too far.

But to truly consider 'happily ever after', we need to consider real 'happy endings' because lustiness shifts over time, interests change, enthusiasm peaks and troughs.

So what is enough? How do people keep the lust alive? And does it matter if they don't?

It seems to me that the best people to answer these questions might be in a free-love commune in southern Portugal, but more of that later.

First, a little reassurance for those suffering from diminishing sexual returns: you are not alone. We're all having less sex, according to British newspaper the *Observer*, and the sex we're having isn't as good.[1]

---

1   'British Sex Survey', theguardian.com, 28 September 2014.

That's true for smug marrieds, free singles, and everyone in between. The paper quizzed 1,000 Brits in 2008 and then again in 2014, and saw the number of people who rated their sex drive as 'above average' drop by ten percentage points. More people said they were unhappy with the quality of their sex lives too. Maybe it's the lingering woes from the financial crisis of 2008, maybe it's the cost of living, maybe they're too busy watching YouPorn, but in the bleakness of the early twenty-first century, most of us aren't getting enough.

One in four couples in their thirties have a sexless relationship, according to Relate,[2] and it's even more pronounced among the young adults who should be enjoying their rampant years. Some 13 per cent of British millennials are still virgins by age twenty-six, according to University College London.[3] In the US, millennials are 250 per cent more likely to be celibate than Gen Xers were at the same age.[4] This seems like a terrible waste of firm flesh.

Because sex is good for you. Orgasms flood the brain with dopamine to make you happy and oxytocin to help you bond with your partner. The few researchers who have managed to convince their bosses to let them watch people wank in MRI scanners have found that the positive impacts of orgasm are similar for both men and women.

For women, climaxing has a painkilling effect too. In 1984, renowned orgasm researchers Beverly Whipple and Barry Komisaruk

---

2   'Over a quarter of relationships are "sexless"', relate.org.uk, 20 September 2018.

3   'Next Steps', UCL Institute of Education, May 2018.

4   Jean Twenge in 'Why are young people having so little sex?' theatlantic. com, December 2018.

got women to masturbate with one hand, while the other was gently squeezed in a compression device (Bev did that part). They found that pain thresholds doubled nearing orgasm.[5]

But it doesn't take the people in white coats to tell us that sex feels nice. Most of us guess that before we've paid our first tax bill.

Aged about fourteen, I had a paper round that started at 6a.m. and I would generally have to do it with an unfortunate bulge in my shell suit. Not because lugging around copies of the *Daily Mirror* got my juices flowing, but because morning glory was a new phenomenon and I didn't know what to do with it. And, given how I looked, it seemed unlikely anyone else was going to help. I was very spotty and very thin, with skin like week-old margarita pizza. I decided I must be gay, and that girls just knew (remarkably, girls don't want to snog week-old margaritas) so I'd better just get used to the idea. And then one cold February evening, something remarkable happened.

After shivering in the park and getting drunk on two cans of super-strength cider shared with two other friends, we stumbled across three girls on the high road who had been doing similar things. Being fourteen, we all began snogging in the shadows of a disused petrol station.

As I inexpertly mashed faces with a girl I'd met eight minutes before, our vinyl bomber jackets creating a scratchy symphony, I even got the vague sensation that there were breasts under her many layers of clothes.

In a brief pause for breath, I was clamped to the back of her like

---

5   'Functional MRI of the Brain during Orgasm in Women', Barry R. Komisaruk and Beverley Whipple, *Annual Review of Sex Research*, 15 November 2012.

a soppy limpet, inhaling the hairspray that had left her curls fixed to the point of crispiness. She was speaking to her friend about which bus to get home (the 326, hop off at New Barnet Sainsbury's) and reached behind with her right hand to give the junk a squeeze. I almost levitated with joy and gratitude.

It may have been through some very baggy jeans, but contact had been made and hope was restored to my world. My virginity lingered, along with the acne, for a while longer, but that one moment is etched in my mind as perhaps the kindest thing one human has ever done for another.

So if sex is a nice thing, why do we do it less once we've found someone who we could, in theory, do it with all the time?

One big US survey found that 15 per cent of married couples had not had sex with their partner in the last six months.[6] Mostly, they were 'involuntary celibates' – a term used for those unwillingly caught in sexless marriages (but also recently by lonely men on angry corners of the internet).

There are lots of reasons why involuntary celibacy might creep in to a marriage, according to a *Journal of Sex Research* study[7]. Having small kids was a big factor, along with lack of shared interests and diminishing body confidence.

Dr Lori Schade (the seven-kid mother from Utah) has been a marriage counsellor since 1989 and has seen many straight

---

6   General Social Survey, cited in 'When Sex Leaves the Marriage', well.blogs. nytimes.com, 3 June 2009.

7   'Involuntary Celibacy: A Life Course Analysis', *The Journal of Sex Research*, May 2001.

couples who have slipped into sexlessness. Much of the issue comes down to how men and women are socialized, she says.

'I have five boys and two girls, and I couldn't keep my boys from being socialized like typical males, which means: "don't be afraid, don't be sad, don't be a girl". Boys do a really good job disconnecting, but it's cool to be sexual, so a lot of men channel their insecurities into sexuality. They get reassurance because the range of emotions they get to have are: angry, happy and sexual.'

Girls, by contrast, tend to be socialized to be a little more expressive. The result can be a loop of disappointment for everyone involved.

'You've got men who don't really know how to get their emotional needs met because they haven't been taught to. They don't say things like, "I worry that you don't love me any more." For men it's more: "if you'll let me get that close to you physically, I'm OK." And then you've got women who feel, "if I'm not close to you emotionally, I don't want to get close physically."'

I have summarized Schade's thirty years of in-the-field experience in this slightly flippant illustration:

THE DESIRE DISCREPANCY CYCLE OF WOE

BOB

"I have been socialized to have the emotional range of a teapot and need sex to feel loved"

JANET

"I have been socialized to have a full range of emotions and need the feels to want the sex"

It won't apply to all 3.7 billion people on either side of the gender divide (and those in between), but there is something there that I recognize. On those days when Anna and I are drifting a little, the best and most obvious answer seems to me to be a quick bunk-up. But I know that there will have to be an airing of emotional griev-ances first, which – as foreplay goes – ranks somewhere below a verbal algebra test.

So how do couples resolve these issues, I wonder? What can they do to make sure they re-engage with one of life's greatest free experiences?

I contact the Kinsey Institute, named after Alfred Kinsey, the 'father of the sexual revolution'. He's the guy with the bow ties and high-top hair who invented the scale of human sexuality, from hetero to homo. The institute continues his work, and I speak to Dr Justin Lehmiller, a research fellow there, over Skype. His brown hair is in a tidy indie cut and he wears a full beard and dark, scoop-neck T-shirt.

'Some people find it effective to schedule sex, to make sure it happens,' he says. 'When it's on schedule, they try and build up to it. They will text their partner or sext them during the week. It becomes this romantic event for the low-desire partner.'

While this sounds reasonable, there is, I think, something a little depressing about having pre-booked lust: the bumping of bits etched into the calendar somewhere between your nan's birthday and a session at the chiropractor.

'You can try and make it sexy by building up the anticipation and adding in some sexual novelty,' Lehmiller explains, because individual tastes change over time but couples tend to be nervous about telling each other.

I wonder if gay and straight couples have similar issues. Lehmiller tells me that it's an under-researched area but, 'There has long been an assumption that when partners are matched in terms of gender they'll be more likely to be on the same page with respect to sex drive and sexual wants. However, the studies out there don't support this assumption. In fact, desire discrepancies can and do exist in same-sex couples and they tend to have the same negative impact on the relationship.'

Openness about your tastes, and trying out new things – whether that's keeping the lights on or donning a rubber suit – is part of an area of sexual psychology called 'sexual communal strength'. This is the idea that you're willing to sacrifice your own needs for the sake of your partner, he says.

'That's not to say that you want to go without having your needs met, but just that you're willing to prioritize your partner's pleasure and not make it all about you. I think those are some of the key factors for a happily-ever-after relationship,' says Lehmiller.

It's hard to argue with the idea that being a less selfish shag might mean you get more (and better) sex. But so might having more partners.

It's time to step into the field (literally) because perhaps no one does 'sexual communal strength' more enthusiastically than free-loving hippies.

In the late sixties, something became clear about the European student movement: they were good at publishing books, staging protests and looking dashing while smoking cigarettes, but too often passions ran high, love affairs caused friction and they fell into acrimony. They were more likely to take down each other than to tear down capitalism.

Part of the answer, according to a radical German leftist called Dieter Duhm, was free love. If people don't 'own' their partners and everyone is free to follow their impulses, then they're likely to be a lot happier. It's hard to be a grump when you've recently got your rocks off, so perhaps the world could bonk its way to peace.

Over the following decades, he tried to establish communes across Europe: there was a free-love community in the Black Forest, which eventually broke up, then another outside Berlin that still exists today. And finally, in 1995, Duhm and his devotees found a dusty spot in south-west Portugal. They raised the money to buy 350 acres, and five of them pitched tents and went to work trying to create a new kind of society.

They called it 'Tamera', and it's now home to about 170 people. They describe it as a 'peace research and education centre' where they 'work for a global system change'. They've turned a barren land into something lush and green. And they still believe in free love.

I arrive on a wet Monday in April to be met by Frederick. He's fifty-four, tanned, with dusty blonde hair and a lean frame. We've been in contact for a few months and he's offered to show me around during Introduction Week. This is when about forty guests pay to stay in Tamera to learn about ecology, peace work and free love and sexuality.

Originally from Washington, DC, Frederick is a physics graduate who spent years teaching at French universities. He's been a Tameran (which, I realize, makes them sound like aliens) for about eight years. He speaks softly and his years on the continent have given his US accent a central European flavour.

The first thing you notice about Tamera is the greenness. There is life everywhere – towering eucalyptus trees, wild grasses, fruit trees, meadows scattered with daisies and bright gold buttercups. It feels a little Edenic.

Years ago, the community's ecologists created a lake by damming up a low valley so that water run-off gathered in a puddle that just kept growing. They positioned it so the breeze always moves across the water to keep it free from algae and mosquitos, and built tiny trenches all around Tamera to hold water and help life bloom.

Everyone here has a few jobs, and one of Frederick's is in Tamera's solar project. Next to a small outdoor kitchen is a ten-foot-high silver oblong of reflective panels on a frame that is moved with an old bike-chain mechanism. It looks like a giant Frisbee made out of Bacofoil. But these thin reflective sheets have been angled so that they concentrate the sun's rays to a point so hot that it can boil water.

'If we concentrated it any further,' he tells me, 'it would burn through the saucepan before the water heated up.'

They're literally cooking on sunbeams.

The work they do here is also shared with the wider world, from projects in the slums of Kenya to peace campaigns in Columbia.

But Frederick's other role is in Tamera's Love School. This is the place where you learn about the ideas that Duhm developed – with his main partner Sabine Lichtenfels – about free sexuality. Frederick promises to introduce me later to a woman called Ida, who he describes as his 'most intimate lover', and over a communal lunch of lentils, he explains to a curious Introduction Week guest from Italy that Love School is about 'the social context and ethics of love more than the tantric and anatomical. You're not going to learn how to perform clockwise circles on the perineum.'

(I make a mental note to google 'clockwise circles on the perineum'.)

As we walk past fields of vegetables and campsites of tents and caravans, I spot a large mural that includes a rough painting of Rodin's 'The Kiss' and the words 'A person who is in love cannot make bombs'.

It's like the old hippy slogan 'make love, not war' has been developed into a bigger philosophy, but I wonder how it works in practice. Not the sweaty details of the bump 'n' grind, but how do you raise a family in a polyamorous community? How do you tackle the sting of jealousy that must come from seeing your 'most intimate lover' head off to a caravan with someone else?

That evening I speak to Janni Hentrich, one of the first pioneers here, when water came from a well and the toilet was a hole you dug in the ground. We're in the bar they've built – a roomy but simple hut with a wooden floor and large windows. She is in late middle age, has a shoulder-length bob of wild grey hair and an ankle-length vest-dress. Her skin has turned the colour of burnished oak from all the years outside and she speaks with a strong German accent.

I ask if she has mastered the question of jealousy, and she gives a deep, smoker's laugh.

'No one comes here because of the ecological work; they just want to know about love!'

She settles down and explains: 'Of course, I see a woman and think, "What is better on her? Her breasts, her arse, her smile, her eyes?" So you compare. You sometimes think "I'll lose my partner if he falls in love with someone else."'

One of the principles here is that jealousies are discussed openly, often in front of your whole social group. They sit in circles and discuss feelings until things are resolved.

'With free love, of course you still long for a deep, lasting relationship with another person. But how do you keep a love alive without lies? You have to find your truthful path. Is it with one person? Is it with two? Is it without a partner?'

They talk a lot about 'love free from fear' here. And the main fear people have, as they see it, is admitting their feelings for more than one person.

The next morning, I wake with the sun. I'm in the guesthouse, one of the few concrete buildings in Tamera. Some of the original residents have built cabins and there are a few communal spaces built with hay bales and plaster, but local regulations stop any more going up, so most residents live in caravans or tents. Guests for Introduction Week sleep in a large dormitory marquee.

The main kitchen serves simple vegan meals and we all eat together. Tamera grows about 30 per cent of its own food, and Frederick admits to having detailed debates about the ethicality of various types of lentil. From the terrace where we eat breakfast, you can see the lake and hear the birds sing.

I'll have a few meals here over the course of my stay, and am struck by something: people smile a lot. They make direct eye contact and offer honest grins. There are people from all over the world, but Germans are the best represented. I've never looked into so many sincere blue eyes.

And people look healthy: they are slim and clear-skinned and speak in a disarmingly kind manner. I can't decide if that comes from an inner contentment or because when everyone is a potential partner you're always presenting your best self. If you know that every interaction could lead to sex, it must make you a little more polite. Perhaps a free-love policy should be introduced for supermarket queues.

Sex can influence every aspect of your life – the mood you're in, the places you go, who you speak to – and I'm curious about the experience of raising a family here.

Frederick sets me up for a chat with Mariló, a forty-year-old from Spain, and her partner Andy, who is thirty-nine and from Germany. They have a nine-year-old son and have lived in Tamera since 2013.

'We had a nice little house in the countryside in Spain, because we thought "now we have a child we want to have a little nest", like the beautiful happy story that is made up for us all,' says Andy. 'But in the first months, we both felt it was not meant to be. I was a father, I was a worker, I was a partner, I took care of many things. After three months, I had a breakdown and we said, "OK, this is a sign to look for alternatives."'

The pair originally met as Erasmus students, and dabbled with polyamory in their early days together.

'We opened the relationship,' says Mariló. 'It just happened. You go to a party, you meet someone and something happens. Then at some point we started to look for communities.'

I wonder about what tensions polyamory brings to the already fraught dimension that kids add to any relationship.

'Miló and I have different sexual and loving relationships and still we are very close,' says Andy. 'We have been together for fifteen years, and with ups and downs, but we are faithful to each other on this solidarity level. I've had a lover for two years now who I'm quite close with. I don't hide that. Our son is growing up in a system where he does not feel mama and papa are hiding something. He sees me with her, and he actually loves her.'

I wonder how that makes Miló feel.

'When we came here, I was feeling very guilty,' she says, 'because I had been through a process of getting pregnant and transforming my whole system, but I knew in Andy's body, nothing changed. He became a father but he still has the same sexual longings. I felt guilty because I didn't want to offer him sex. I wanted to support him, but how? When we came here and he met the first woman, I felt "wow, great, it's not just me that's responsible for his sexual fulfilment."'

She says that she herself, 'hasn't had so many sexual adventures, but when I've had an impulse for another man, I can follow it.' But she also admits that tension exists. 'I struggle a lot because I'm still conditioned by all the Hollywood movies I've seen in my life and the propaganda system we are bombarded with. I struggle to let it go.'

I spend a lot of time with Frederick during my stay at Tamera. He is unfailingly informed and helpful, always considered in his answers. He also gently flirts with every woman we meet, and I'm intrigued to meet his 'most intimate lover'.

When we do, a new lightness comes across him.

Ida is forty-seven and was born into a Bedouin family in Palestine. She was working as a nurse during the Second Intifada – the intensive Israeli–Palestinian violence at the beginning of this century. She was also pregnant and separated from the father of her unborn child.

'I was treating both suicide bombers and Israeli soldiers,' she says. 'When buses were exploding all over, I made a vow that I will create another life for this child.'

She's one of the most engaging people I've ever spoken to, not just because she has a remarkable story, but because she is so energized and her bright eyes so alive.

Over the years that followed, she and her daughter eventually came to Tamera. She even managed to convince a sharia court judge not to grant custody to her ex-partner when he sued because she was going to live in a polyamorous commune.

There is something remarkably tender about Frederick and Ida and they look at each other with the affection of honeymooners. I ask how they came to be together and she pauses to turn and smile at him.

'I mostly remember this very direct and simple invitation to "meet intimately",' says Frederick, who adopts a mock-appalled look at the memory. 'I had been here a while but I was still very new.'

The sexual invites are not always so direct. For a while Tamera had a 'messenger of love' system, where invitations to sex or a massage or private walk would be sent via one of eight older women, like a playground whisper of 'I fancy your mate'.

And before that, says Ida, 'we would use every meal to ring a bell and say, "I'm attracted to X, and I would like to go with him," or we would have a goodnight round, and everybody would say who they want to spend the night with.'

It sounds like choosing school sports teams, and I can't help imagine one poor soul being left to trudge home alone.

Given the obvious closeness between Frederick and Ida, I find it hard to believe there isn't the slightest twang of hurt when one of them goes off with someone else.

Ida smiles. 'Through the years I had many love stories, and all these love stories are still in the community, still active in some way or another,' she says. 'When I arrived at thirty-five, I was like this celebrity – people were projecting a role onto me as a Muslim woman from Palestine. I would go to bed with somebody, and he would say, "You are my first Arab!" and I would say, "You're not my first German!"' and she bellows a laugh. 'But Frederick is known for flirting and creating love stories with a lot of people, especially the guests, and so we always have stories about him and I have to deal with it.'

For his part, Frederick says he has 'this deep level of trust for a very sexual woman like I have never known before. There's no way for me to want to turn that beautiful, lush, abundant rainforest into a potted plant.'

And in Ida's case, 'happily ever after' has a very clear picture: 'Growing old in this community where I will always have a network of lovers: young, my age and older. I have my beloved partner, Frederick, and others.'

They both argue that monogamy is something that most people

blindly accept as the norm rather than actively choose, and that – given the choice – many more would opt to 'love free from fear'.

'I know many people in happy marriages who have compromised. There's an unspoken agreement that you swallow it and you go on. De-privatizing these things – speaking about them openly – can create trust,' says Frederick. 'It's about not ignoring your impulses, but also asking "What does love need?" Not what *I* need. Not about being competitive with someone. If you know what love needs, then you'll find happiness.'

There does seem something honest about Tamera. I had kind of expected something a little more cultish – perhaps a sinister and charismatic leader telling people what to do. But there's no sense of that. Everything is discussed communally, right down to the ethicality of different brands of lentil. People gently mock the 'old-timers' for their tales of settler hardship, and are open about the place's failings: how it could be more self-sustaining, how things take longer because everything must be discussed with the group. Not everyone buys into the more spiritual elements.

People seem content, despite the hardships of community living, but I'm not sure that polyamory is any more trouble-free than monogamy. It just comes with different troubles.

For an outsider it feels like the electric promise of sex hangs in the air, and I found myself wondering about some women I spoke to: 'If I lived here, might we have something?' On some base level, I think that most people feel that in their real life too, and we all just swallow it down – file it away in a microsecond before it can take hold.

The idea of a world of free love sounds exciting. But if it meant giving up any of what I have with Anna, it wouldn't work for me. In the Love School philosophy, that would mean I'm clinging to ideas of ownership. Maybe that's true. But however much I think – somewhere in the back of my mind – that having a 'network of lovers' sounds like a giddy treat, I know that more than that I want a better connection with the one I have.

The thing that resonated most for me was when Frederick said we shouldn't be competing to have our own needs met, but should ask 'What does love need?' Because in that moment it occurred to me that I am competing with Anna: competing to be the most tired, or the best parent, or the busiest, or sacrificing the most, competing over who is the most let down by the other.

And perhaps there might be something in the 'sexual communal strength' that Lehmiller mentioned. Perhaps we should stop competing with each other and start competing to make each other happy.

I don't want to live in a free-love commune, but that one question of Frederick's has lodged in my brain.

So whenever we're tired or stressed, whenever we're impatient or hungry, or in need of sex or some emotional support, perhaps the best thing for all of us, if we want to be really happy, is to stop thinking 'Here's what I want' and start thinking 'What does love need now?'

Anna

I'm clearing out The Cupboard of Doom. A box with 'Matt's stuff' written across it in Sharpie pen collapses and out fall three items:

a tripod held together by duct tape, a bobbly grey coat (the one he wore when we first met), and an A4 notebook filled with his spidery writing.

I'm alone in the house and it's not abandoned journalistic notes. I know I'm about to invade his privacy. Page one reveals it's Matt's diary from when he travelled the world in 1999, hoping to find himself (along with thousands of other youths who read Alex Garland's novel *The Beach*). It turns out he found lots of women instead.

I read on, intrigued about a sex life before me. Every page references doing it, trying to do it or having just done it. There's one bit where he talks of a woman he's travelled with for a bit who 'definitely fancies me' but he's caught in a moral quandary because the other guy they're travelling with fancies her. They have sex all the same. 'Sealed the deal tonight,' his diary reads.

I don't know what I expect to feel twenty-seven pages into an opus on Matt's conquests. Sadness? Jealousy? Longing for more youthful times when you could just do it in a hostel? Confusingly, I feel horny. I feel like I want to be done in the way he did women back then. I want do-me-now-or-lose-me-forever sex, not cowgirl to doggy followed by a chaser of Sleepytime tea.

I have a bath and think about him in a new light. As soon as the kids are asleep, the kitchen cleared and the buzzing fridge noise fixed, I jump on him. I knee him accidentally in the balls a bit and we clash teeth. He's slightly taken aback and I feel excruciatingly embarrassed. How did we get from banging bits to banging teeth?

When we lived in Amsterdam, in the red-light district, we had a rescue beagle called Douglas who one of us would walk at 7a.m. every morning through the chip-strewn streets. This was often the quietest time in the area, when even the most spangled party-goer had retired. There were usually only a couple of sex workers on the morning shift, the neon-pink glow of their windows breaking early-morning mist near Oude Kerk, the eleventh-century church that sits like an ecclesiastical schlong in the heart of the world's most famous sex hub.

While strolling past S&M boutiques with cheap mannequins swathed in studded, crotchless garments, I'd nod to any of the women working, as if walking my dog through a park and happening upon a kindly stranger. Some would have their doors open, and the conversation would usually run thus:

'Morgen.'

'Morgen, hoe gaat het?'

'Goed.'

It would be repeated most days, because those were the only Dutch words I knew.

One morning, Douglas planted two slightly muddy paws on the lit-up window of 'Hera', a twenty-seven-year-old Surinamese woman in a fuchsia-pink two-piece with matching tulle train. She teetered over in four-inch PVC heels, opened her door, cracked a smile and gave him a scratch between the ears asking, 'Wat is zijn naam?' I apologised for the paw marks, while trying (and failing) to use poo bags to wipe them off her sullied window. From that day on we would occasionally stop and chat to Hera as much as time would allow between her work schedule and Douglas's bowel movements.

A few weeks into these exchanges I started to see a pattern with Hera's regulars. They were mostly suited men, stopping off for a pre-work release. These were not lads on a hedonistic weekend or lonely figures looking for a cuddle. They looked like polished bankers, brisk-walking lawyers, trusted psychotherapists, family men (like Matt) who possibly had cornflakes for breakfast, kissed their kids on the head and drove to work via Hera's window. One parked his car – with crumb-strewn child seats in the back – near our flat before heading in to hand over his €50.

I eventually asked her for an interview and she told me: 'Men are sometimes loneliest in their own relationships. Sex is their connection, it's their *knuffel* [cuddle] and without it, they can look in other places. Maybe porno, or fantasy about women they work with, or it can be me. But for women the *knuffel* is what leads to *de seks* and many men do not see this. I get paid because they [couples] do not see this.'

I decide I want to find out about *de seks* from someone who has the moves and, perhaps, the secret, so I get on another easyJet flight and go back to Amsterdam.

I reassure my sister I won't be grilling her this time. Instead I'll be attending the city's first Hand-job Workshop, led by former sex worker Cora Emens and her gigolo husband. My sister thinks this sounds a bit sexist. I think she's probably right. The penis once more seems to be the centre of attention.

Feeling a bit unenthused about the whole thing (Matt's penis), I cycle through sheets of rain to Mail & Female, a pleasure emporium that boasts the biggest array of female-focused porn in the Netherlands. The female-friendly sex shop hosts monthly erotic technique classes for mostly young professional men and women, who typically gather on a Thursday night and pay €30 for the privilege of perfecting their bedroom skills. Workshops range from Vaginal Massage Level 1 and 2 to a Love Academy for couples seeking more connection under the sheets. All's fair in love and wanking, it seems.

I walk in and put my umbrella next to a mannequin wearing a pair of crotchless leather trousers. There's a sea of multicoloured dildos scattered across the tables.

'You're already wet, I see!' Cora laughs, looking at my dampened appearance.

Emens made her name on RTL4's TV programme *Beter in Bed* and she's married to Shai Shahar, a famous former gigolo who's now a jazz singer. One has to assume they know a thing or two about doing it.

We're offered lukewarm Prosecco, and the couple direct our gaze to a badly drawn picture of a willy on a whiteboard. 'Oral is easier but hand-jobs are equally important,' she says, slathering her dildo with lube and gesturing for the seventeen-strong class to follow suit. We all take this moment to pick up our new toys. Once the childish mumbling has subsided, Emens asks us to hold it as if it's part of our anatomy, to just start having a 'go' with it.

The women range from eighteen to fifty-seven, with some in suits or pencil skirts after a day in the office, or dressed like they're about to hit The Sex Palace, a local swingers club round the corner. Guffaws ensue before Emens, watching us from behind bifocals, asks in a matronly tone for us 'to sit down and listen to teacher'.

'So, we're basically coming at it [the penis] from the wrong angle,' she explains. 'Firstly, we need to see how a guy does it – because, let's face it, he's been perfecting the technique all his life – so we can learn from that and try and adapt our technique.'

The group's concentration is palpable as we pump away, occasionally glancing up towards our mistress for guidance. 'Am I supposed to use the whole thing or just the top?' asks Marjolein, a lawyer for a Dutch bank and, for this moment, a keen student of wanking.

'Contrary to popular belief, the whole penis doesn't need to be in contact with your hand for a man to come,' answers Emens, who studied under esteemed US sex therapist Betty Dodson in New York before setting up Cora Emens' Sex Consultancy twenty years ago. 'Focus on just the tip, making sure you have a firm, two-fingered circular grip and a limp wrist,' she says. 'Swing your hand up and down, building up the speed until he comes on your face or his chest – whatever is your preference.'

Next, she walks us through one of her special techniques: the 'clock', a repeated rotation of a flaccid penis from the twelve o'clock position to the six o'clock position. This allegedly gets the blood pumping, which in turn gives a rock-hard erection and an intense orgasm (you stop the movement once it's erect). If I ignore the lashings of lube and plastic penis eye staring back at me, it feels like I'm winding up an old grandfather clock.

To anyone questioning why we should be studying how to pleasure a man, Emens hits back with: 'This is more than a cheap trick. This is about real, dirty, happy lust. It is about love, giving and receiving – stop over-analysing and learn how to enjoy your body, his body, their bodies – there's a workshop on vaginal stimulation too.'

I make a mental note to tell my sister.

As Cora takes a swig of Prosecco and wipes off her lubricated digits, she points to the anus on her diagram. 'Now that's a whole different lesson.'

I emailed Marjolein a few days afterwards to ask how she got on (she was my partner in the 'yoni' [vagina] challenge that had us pretending to touch ourselves while masturbating a lubricated dildo). She said: 'I went home, forgot what to do and then we couldn't stop laughing when I realized I'd been winding the clock up the wrong way.'

While hand-jobs and blow jobs – 'job' makes it all feel instantly laborious – might have their place, laughter is what turns me on. That's what mine and Matt's relationship was largely formed on. It's a quick-witted response or a cheeky bum squeeze that has me wanting to stare into those mahogany eyes. All I do know after twelve years together is that when we're not laughing, we tend to stop kissing, hugging, talking and ultimately doing. Without *de knuffle*, there is invariably no *seks*.

I'm with him every day, and yet I miss him very much as the majority of our exchanges have switched from titillating to administrative.

Witness these recent texts.

EXCHANGE ONE:
Matt: Aerial man coming between 11 and 2.
Anna: 👍
EXCHANGE TWO:
Matt: Just leave it. I'll do it before 5 if you send me the invoice.

Anna: OK, I'll feed the kids here if you could get a bath going at 6.30p.m.?

Keen to steer our relationship away from a romance cul-de-sac, I want to speak to Cora and Shai outside of the confines of the classroom. I go and visit them in their red-brick Amsterdam house, hoping to find out if they have any tips beyond what to do with the tip.

Their cat clambers over them as they sit side by side under a picture of a man seducing a woman in a 1920s cocktail bar.

They've been together for twenty-three years after meeting on an Amsterdam party bus that was heaving with the city's bright young things. Shai had a woman with pneumatic breasts (aptly called Barbie) on one knee, and Cora walked up and asked, 'Is the other knee free?' They've been together ever since.

I tell them about accidentally kneeing Matt in the balls. Cora and Shai nod like two caring parents who just watched their child fall over in the egg-and-spoon race.

Cora starts: 'You have to make time to feel sexy again. So if that's a bath, two weeks in the Cayman Islands, half an hour with a vibrator, or walking out the door from the children and your partner for five minutes, whatever you do, you need to come into your body again and stop thinking about what you should be,' she says.

But I had a bath. I wore an outfit. I went textbook minxlet.

'How many times are you not having sex because you think you're too fat, too saggy, too tired, too disconnected? It's a waste of time thinking these things. You do not want to be the person who closed off to Mother Nature's greatest pleasure because of a bit of cellulite.'

OK, she's maybe got me there. A few lumps and bumps don't put me off my stride, but since becoming a mother I've definitely struggled to feel sensual. I lost a bit of confidence somewhere around having a baby hauled out of my innards. How can I wet-wipe snot off a onesie or accidentally spurt breast milk onto the bathroom mirror (like a lacklustre fembot) and then look at Matt with 'come hither' eyes? The cruellest trick of nature is that lactating breasts tend to spurt more when you're turned on.

Cora says that we are mothers in our hearts but 'you have to connect with your yoni, your vagina, your vulva: it's as much a part of you as your heart is.'

I'm not convinced. I can't even see my yoni, let alone connect with it.

Shai draws a more base analogy for men: 'How many times are men compared to dogs? "You dawg" or "He's such a dirty dog"? But let's run with it for a second . . . You know how dogs react when you praise them? They wag their tail, they go fetch a newspaper and they want to remain loyal to that person forever more.'

I think back to the last time I said something nice to Matt and nothing comes to mind. I make a mental note to tell him I think his Couch to 5K is paying off. I definitely don't see him as a dog, though, which is reassuring.

Shai continues: 'Men aren't dogs, that's too basic, but I think it is fair to say good sex starts by patting instead of shouting, choosing a different tone, offering a cup of tea and not thinking the worst at every turn. Saying, "You didn't pick up your goddamn underwear" or "You need to listen to me" might be necessary but it's not going to make him feel virile, or you particularly sexy.'

That's all well and good, but the dishes need to be stacked, the children need to go to school and my latest Google search was on post-operative bunion care. It's not a backdrop for fruitiness.

'Nobody has walked into their own home and gone, "That floor is so clean, I've got to fuck you!" or "Show me those tax returns because I want to get turned on!"' says Shai.

I don't know. I find cleanliness and hygiene right up there. I just clearly struggle with the transition from domestic to-dos to doing it. I think back to the women Matt was doing through Asia and beyond, and wonder what they had that I now don't.

Time, mostly: time to work out, time to laugh and joke and play with their hair coquettishly. Time to impress him with their chat. Time to drink for pleasure and not to de-stress.

'But this is where fantasy comes in,' Shai argues. 'If you are more open, then you start by telling him what you want to do, how wild you want to be. Cora's dream is to be with seven guys. I'm not threatened by that, just turned on! It's funny you even call it the "marital bed" – that makes it sound like a jail sentence! You have to escape "The Marital Bed"!'

I don't fantasize about doing seven men but one (in the marital bed) really well.

☆☆☆

Someone I've been keen to speak to about doing it when time is not on your side (and who also believes in 'The Marital Bed') is

Joyce Williams, the eighty-four-year-old blogger who has built a late career on writing about octogenarian sex. Entitled 'Sex at seventy? Sex at eighty? Of course!' her first blog on how it's possible for 'wrinklies' to get down went viral. I interview her over the phone a few days after getting back from Amsterdam.

'Don't turn off the lights – dark is dodgy at eighty and we'd probably fall over climbing into bed. Don't worry about orgasms and instead make the most of the time you have together by cherishing each other on a mutual pleasure journey. After all, touching is much better done by someone who cares what you will feel.'

She points me to a statistic from a study by *Saga* magazine: '65 per cent of over-50s are sexually active, with 46 per cent claiming to have sex once a week and 25 per cent of 75–85 year olds claiming to have had sex within the last twelve months.'

There is hope for Matt and me yet.

So it's definitely not over the minute you're issued with that bus pass. With a youthful bob, a colourful beaded necklace and an impish smile, Joyce does not look eighty-four and she is definitely in that 65 per cent bracket. She continues: 'Sex in your later years is very sensual – much less acrobatics and thrust stuff.'

She gets her pleasure from satin on skin, long lingering mornings spent in bed followed by a joint shower and even Poundland's latest range of sex toys ('hopefully including a slippery oil,' she jokes, 'is there anything nicer than mutual massage as foreplay?'). It once again comes back to time. It seems the more you have together, the more you want to be together.

She admits that this period of life that Matt and I are in is the hardest, though. 'I want you both to know you have so much to look forward to. Right now you haven't the time for each other, you haven't the time to be yourselves, but cling on to each other for dear life, my loves, because it is so worth it on the other side.'

It's the best news I've had since the Toblerone went back to its original shape.

In terms of the practicalities of doing it when you're older, Joyce admits, 'There's a reason we still have the fur rug and the armchair, though we maybe need to borrow the garden kneeling stool to get up again.'

Mornings, she explains, can be long and lingering and, 'Before you know it, you're having to explain to the postman or neighbour that, no, you're not sick, you just needed a lie-in. Then, of course, us oldies need a nap after lunch, don't we?'

Her final tip? 'Steer away from any positions that require you to kneel.'

I feel oddly jealous of Cora, Shai and Joyce, who all seem to have been given an Ordnance Survey map that tells them how to keep the motor rolling, when I'm often too tired to start the car.

Perhaps the short-term fix is getting over yourself to get under? To just do it and stop overthinking it. Good sex, bad sex, ugly sex – it all counts as connection. As Matt put it in his diary, maybe it's time to just 'seal the deal'.

One thing I've found is that thoughts of your partner with someone else can take things from nought to sixty, even if those thoughts are of them fifteen years ago when they were wearing dubious neck beads.

But what if this fantasy world Shai talks of starts invading your reality?

What if your partner's just not that into you because he or she is into someone more X-rated?

7

☆ ☆ ☆

Porn Free

What about the grot?

Matt

There really isn't a perfect answer to the question 'How was your stay at the free-love commune?'

I've come through the door just after midnight, and she's sitting at the kitchen table with our friends Bella and Hersha, with empty plates and full glasses in front of them. I smile and say, 'Well, they're having more fun than the monks.'

This, I realize, may not have been the best response. Anna gives a quick non-smile smile. One that flashes across the face out of duty to what's just been said, but that also reveals something else.

So I think, 'What does love need now?' And I tell her how good it is to be back. I play up the hardships of community living and how everyone lives in leaky caravans. I explain that most of the people I met were over fifty. I make it clear that I was not tempted (even if 0.5 per cent of me was).

And over the next couple of days, I ask myself that question at regular intervals: what does love need me to do right now?

When Anna leaves her cash cards and one of mine on a radiator, causing them to warp and meaning that she has no access to money, I decide that love needs me to not be a dick about it, give her one of mine, and order a replacement for her.

When she's back home later than she said she would be, inconveniencing me in my efforts to get the kids to bed and do some work, I decide that love needs me to not have a tone, but to instead welcome her in with a gentle snog.

Asking myself 'What does love need now?' seems to be working. She's less mardy because I'm less huffy. We're back to every night for a bit. Such a simple equation.

So, I wonder, what does love need me to do about porn?

I first saw a naked woman when I was nine years old. I was in the toilet at school and bright summer light came in through the frosted windows. A boy called Paul had something to show us. We gathered next to the trough with its scented yellow cubes and he uncrumpled a piece of paper.

Three boys shouted 'URRRRR!' in the appalled tone that kids use for everything from people kissing on the telly to the sight of a carrot on their plate. I just stared a little dumbly, trying to work out what was before us.

The woman was naked and on her knees, head down, looking back over her shoulder. Paul told us it was Pepsi from eighties pop duo Pepsi & Shirlie (libel disclaimer: it was not). But I was more confused by the free-flowing fuzz between her legs. It looked alive and I wondered how it got there. I had the vague idea that the man was supposed to thrust in that direction, but wasn't really sure why.

A few years later, my mum, sister, step-dad and I went on a

family holiday to Ibiza to spend a week getting sunburned on plastic furniture. Our hotel had a weathered ping-pong table and two-for-one colas.

I became friends with some older Brummie boys, who dared me to steal the porno playing cards at the local gift shop. Being keen to impress them, I did. The cards were on a shelf next to decorative glass ashtrays and *Isla Bonita* tea towels. With a film of sweat across my forehead, I grabbed the cards, hid them up my 'Loadsamoney'! T-shirt, and edged out the door.

Being an inexpert shoplifter, I then stopped because I was so desperate to show off my swag, but the other boys shouted 'Run!' so we all sprinted down the street, flip-flops slapping on tarmac, and clustered together to sift through the deck.

We saw women with horses, women in threesomes, lots of men with beards and, most memorably, a woman taking hold of a pig's penis and stretching it out like a strawberry lace while the porky porn star stared casually ahead. I basked in the congratulations of my holiday friends.

And then, aged about thirteen, I bought my first magazine. I'd had a growth spurt and could finally reach the top shelf, so I walked into a newsagent, stared very intensely at *AutoTrader*, reached for the first mag that had a bit of flesh on the cover, went up to the counter and sheepishly laid down the money. The newsagent put it in a brown paper bag without a word.

Within those pages was a hushed anatomy lesson, with women of various ages and sizes, all contorted for imaginary access.

I had no formal sex education until GCSE biology classes began two years later, by which time porn had taught me everything about the remarkable possibilities of the human body, but nothing about sex or love in relationships.

Porn was something to be laughed at with friends or viewed guiltily behind a locked door, but as I've grown up and porn has become more prevalent, I've begun to wonder if it's a harmless release or a dark business that colours our outlook forever. And, of course, how it affects happiness in relationships. Can you really be happy with your life lobster when the internet offers an ocean of other creatures willing to do so much more for your gratification?

In the last month in the UK, three-quarters of all men and a little over one-third of women have looked at porn.[1] We watch more porn than YouTube or Netflix videos.[2] Take a look around your office, pub or train carriage. The likelihood is that 75 per cent of the men you see will have recently watched some digital smut.

According to PornHub, 'amateur', 'milf' and 'lesbian' have remained the most popular categories over the last decade, and the average visitor spends a very efficient nine minutes on the site.

I know adult men today who still revel in grot-related tales as much as my teenage contemporaries did. One has a tendency to watch porn on his phone in the work loos and masturbate to 'clear his head' after lunch. One told me he 'keeps a *Razzle* in the Skoda' because he doesn't want to sully the Wi-Fi that supplies his children with cartoons. Technically, I think both might be committing acts that constitute 'outraging public decency'. But they're also honest

---

1   'The Sex Census 2012', relate.org.uk, 2012.

2   Thinkbox data cited in 'Brits are still watching more porn than YouTube or Netflix', businessinsider.com.au, 17 June 2015.

tax-paying men with nice children and steady jobs. Their attitude – much like any peers I've discussed it with – is that what they're doing is as meaningless and unstoppable as a sneeze.

In turbulent and worrisome times, the stress-relieving, endorphin-releasing benefits of masturbation (male or female) can be a convenient route to a brief moment of Zen. Orgasm has been shown to boost the immune system, strengthen muscle tone in the pelvic area and, for women, relieve menstrual cramps.

A US National Cancer Institute study of 29,000 American guys found that those with 'high ejaculation frequency' (that's five to seven times a week) were less likely to get prostate cancer.[3] We know that across age groups and relationship types, UK adults have sex on average between one and three times a week, so there's some catching up to do to hit the weekly target. Men are literally tugging for their lives.

So coming is good. But I wonder if the getting there might be a problem. Anti-porn campaigners have claimed links between porn use and everything from loneliness to criminality, but often all these studies show is a correlation and not a cause. Loneliness may be what turns people to porn in the first place. Burglars probably have some self-indulgent tendencies to begin with, rather than being driven to rob by their taste for 'hot milf action'.

Given that its use is so common, you could prove a correlation between porn and most things. If a study were to prove that porn users are more likely to gratify themselves by eating salted caramel

---

'Ejaculation Frequency and Risk of Prostate Cancer', *European Urology*, December 2016.

chocolate bars, I'd be tempted to believe it. It doesn't mean that a fancy for digital filth is driving their cocoa-bean addiction.

But one thing does seem undeniable: porn does peculiar things to our brains. Since 2011, more than thirty peer-reviewed studies have shown that watching porn has a negative impact on our grey matter.[4] Some showed it can diminish the bit of the brain associated with reward sensitivity. According to one researcher at Berlin's Institute for Human Development, 'regular consumption of pornography more or less wears out your reward system.'[5]

It's been shown to negatively impact 'working memory' too. Working memory is the human equivalent of the RAM on your computer – not the bit that stores away all the important images and childhood joys, but the short-term processing: the stuff you need for problem-solving and decision-making. Masturbation may not make you blind, but too much porn could make you a bit dimmer.

These impacts are worse the younger the mind is: adolescents have been shown to be more susceptible to digital addictions and, as a father of two, I am terrified that for my daughters and their peers, the equivalent of a scrap of an old magazine in the loos is the cavalcade of hardcore porn available online. I don't want that to be how they learn about love and sex. And a survey of 1,500 US kids aged nine to seventeen found that those who watched online porn were more likely to have a poor emotional connection with

---

4   Yourbrainonporn.com, 2014.

5   'Brain Structure and Functional Connectivity Associated With Pornography Consumption', *JAMA Psychiatry*, July 2014.

their caregivers than those who didn't watch it at all or stuck to print.[6]

It may be reactionary to hark back to a golden past, but it seems life may have been simpler when all a young lad had was the lingerie section of the Littlewoods catalogue or a copy of *Knave* that a schoolmate had nicked from his older cousin.

However, there is a 'but' to all of this. Like most of my peers, I sometimes play poker, I drink alcohol and will occasionally watch a violent film. None of these things have made me addicted to gambling, or an alcoholic, or given me an urge to run down the high street waving a butter knife at strangers. Like anything potentially addictive or damaging, there remains an element of choice. Surely, for most rational adult users, porn has little to no negative impact?

I call Dawn Hawkins, vice president at the National Center on Sexual Exploitation in Washington, DC. NCOSE was founded in New York in 1962 by a priest, a rabbi and a pastor (it is unclear if they ever walked into a bar). Under its previous name, Morality in Media, it became one of the biggest anti-porn campaign groups in the US.

One of their arguments against porn is that it affects how users interact with the world and that movements such as #metoo have revealed 'a number of stories of people in high-up positions who are acting in what seems to be a pornographic way against colleagues,' says Hawkins.

Much of the reluctance of social media and tech organizations

---

6   'Exposure to Internet Pornography among Children and Adolescents: A National Survey' *CyberPsychology and Behavior*, October 2005.

to do anything about porn, she believes, is because, 'generally men are in these leadership positions who have been watching this stuff and they don't see any problem with it'.

She gives the example of EBSCO Information Services. It is a research database available to thousands of schools across North America and accessed by children aged five and up.

'There's tons of hardcore pornography, recruitment websites for prostitution, and sugar-daddy dating sign-up forms within these databases,' she says. And because porn is of a low reading level compared to most academic work, much of it was served up to younger kids.

NCOSE began to highlight this, '50 per cent of schools that heard about it would shut down the programme until the company was willing to fix it. But the other 50 per cent had school administrators and principals saying to us and the media, "It doesn't matter, kids can get porn anywhere,"' Hawkins tells me. 'Maybe those individuals have absolutely no idea what mainstream pornography is today, or they're using it and they've bought into these rape myths – these lies that pornography perpetuates: that everyone's doing it, that this is normal.' EBSCO has since made an effort to clear up its databases, she says.

The idea of today's porn being so readily available to kids sets off a churning horror in my belly. As a parent, I feel slightly powerless, given porn's accessibility, and can only hope to delay exposure as long as possible and have open conversations when (or before) that exposure happens.

But my bigger curiosity today is about the impact that porn has on adult relationships.

'Some are arguing that pornography could help you grow closer to your spouse, help you explore your sexuality together,' says Hawkins. 'But there are also tons of people who are hurting because one partner is using pornography. There are tons of forums and online groups with these heartbreaking stories.'

And here I can see a problem. If one partner is saying to the other 'Don't use this, it upsets me,' then it might be pretty heartless to continue. But I also wonder about the relationships where that has never happened, and everyone is quietly going about their self-loving business.

Over the last few years, research into the impact of porn has bloomed, although there's a heavy bias towards straight people watching straight porn. Most found that porn use was almost always 'negatively associated with relationship quality'.

It was slightly better when couples watch porn together, but that also didn't happen very much, porn being something that most people use alone. Tandem grot-watching has always felt a little pointless to me, given that there's a real-life person right next to you. It's a bit like going to the cinema to read a comic.

One report found that married Americans who viewed any porn at all had lower relationship quality compared to abstainers.

As Gail Dines, author of the book *Pornland*, once wrote: 'Anyone who doubts these trends should talk to marriage therapists and divorce lawyers.'

All of which sounds pretty damning. But I'm not sure I completely believe it. I realize this sounds a bit like a climate-change denier on a melting iceberg, but my feeling is that most rational, adult porn use is so meaningless and functional that it does no more spiritual harm than an overdose of Ritz crackers. As a friend once said, 'If you have to go beyond the homepage, you've probably got a problem. Otherwise, carry on. It's called a release for a reason.'

Masturbation is healthy, and for most people will always be a poor second to actual sex. Porn could be removed from the self-loving scenario, but I suspect the average male imagination is just as grubby as anything to be found on poontrain.com.

A thoroughly unscientific survey of mates in one WhatsApp group suggests that the tastes of my peers are pretty vanilla. As one said, 'I want proper sets and actresses. One guy, two at most. Hopefully without seeing his face. But something with lights and a crew.'

And maybe that's the key: the specifics of what's being watched and how it's made. Because not all porn is made equal, and a new wave of female smut-makers is hoping to offer something a little different. Perhaps the best known is Erika Lust, a forty-two-year-old Swede based in Barcelona. When we speak over video link, she's sitting in her cosy-looking apartment. She is natural and frank and speaks as openly as if she were discussing the quickest route through rush-hour traffic.

Lust first discovered porn as a student, she tells me. 'My body was turned on by what I was looking at, but I wasn't entirely satisfied with the images,' she says. 'The more porn I watched, the more it seemed a male-dominated genre. It was about him, and women were used as these beautiful objects. Most of my male friends had a very easy relationship with porn. But most of my female friends, they had similar conflicts to me.'

She began a career in film and TV production, before eventually deciding to make a porno of her own.

'We have so many prejudices when it comes to porn workers. People think that they are promiscuous night people, going out, doing drugs and lots of alcohol and parties and sex orgies. And most of them are just so normal: just great, funny and smart people who have this clear idea that they want to do this because they really like sex and can earn quite a lot of money.'

She entered her first film, *The Good Girl*, in some festivals and it began to garner interest. She started to blog about porn and feminism, and within a few weeks her film had been downloaded millions of times. It's become her full-time job, thanks to Xconfessions, the subscription website where she shares her work. I wonder if she believes any of the stats that show the impact porn can have.

'It can make people feel like shit sometimes – like they are not enough, that they are not good enough at having sex. But at the same time, I also think that porn can be positive for lots of people. Porn can help you to develop your erotic side. I definitely know that, in the process of becoming a mother, everything changed. I think that porn can be an inspiration and help to reconnect with your own sexual being.'

It's something that is reflected in the emails she gets from subscribers, many of which tell her the films have been a great help 'to open up a dialogue about sex' in their relationships.

'I get many emails about BDSM, because it's a power play that so many couples are interested in, but don't know exactly how to fill these roles.'

For her, even as a porn director, it's content that is best enjoyed alone. 'I feel freer in that situation. If I look at it with someone then it's kind of expected you'll do similar things afterwards, and that gets me a little anxious.'

And there's some evidence that porn's impacts have been a little exaggerated. A 2014 study noted that much of the media hype about porn addiction failed to be matched by the research, and that 'a large, lucrative industry has promised treatments for pornography addiction despite this poor evidence.'[7]

But, while the idea of addiction might be overplayed, there does seem to be enough weight behind the idea that porn can harm relationships.

For Hawkins, it's all about informed use. 'We're not trying to ban it or censor it,' she says. 'We want people to be able to make an informed decision.'

She likens it to smoking in the twentieth century, and suggests it might be time for a health warning: 'Now people know the harms, they can choose to smoke or not smoke. It's the same thing we hope for with pornography.'

The research does have me a little worried. I don't think it troubles Anna, or has any impact on our life together, but there is a building body of evidence that regular solo porn use hurts relationships. It won't be going away because, frankly, most humans need to wank, most of us are a little time-poor, and porn makes it simpler than dredging through an internal fantasy bank.

---

7   'The Emperor Has No Clothes: A Review of the "Pornography Addiction" Model', *Current Sexual Health Reports*, June 2014.

But perhaps anyone who's regularly having a peek needs to think a little more carefully about his or her habits, and what it's doing to their partner.

Anna

I do wonder what he looks at. When I get home and see the bedroom curtains are closed after I'd opened them this morning. Maybe he got changed? But I think he's wearing what he had on when he left the house.

And why did a bit of tape appear over the camera on his laptop? Does he think the NSA are spying on us or is he more concerned with covering himself?

I'm no prude. I was the Vice editor at *Time Out Amsterdam*, reporting on sex parties with 'love tunnels' where you walk in and anything – with anyone – goes. (For the record, I was fully dressed, not engaging in sexual activity, and clasping a Dictaphone.) I've interviewed sex workers on their favoured dildo and what they thought of the city's prostitution support group The Red Thread before being turfed out by a burly man who was hoping for PR not probing. I've even commissioned Matt to write a review on Amsterdam's Banana Bar, sending him out on a wet Tuesday night to watch a sex show on his own while clutching a notepad and pen:

Improbably dexterous female genitalia can be seen performing night after night, spitting out an average of 15kg (33lbs) of fruit every evening.

There's always been a lurking sense in all relationships I've had that porn was there, a low-level buzz that I just needed to adjust to. Something that shouldn't be seen or heard; a dirty little secret to keep behind closed doors – even if those doors are in our own home.

'It's just a release' or 'It means nothing' is always the response that my friends and I have heard from partners if the topic is broached. And I've watched porn myself – always with a partner, never alone – so I'm no celestial porn-avenger. I'm just confused by it.

I know when Matt has watched porn because when I come home there's the indentation of his body on our bed – a bed that was perfectly made earlier. The pillows will be propped up, the curtains uneven and, while this all sounds a little Angela Lansbury in *Murder, She Wrote*, I know every inch of those four walls because it's my home and he's my husband. When I see The Signs, I feel varying degrees of this:

1 That I'm not enough. With a post-baby body that has a dough-like consistency in places, knowing Matt is watching someone's stretch-mark-less, toned form going like a yapping flip-over dog makes me feel a bit rubbish. It makes me feel like I won't match up to the buxom protagonist in *American Pussy Pie*.

2 That it's hidden. When I imagine Matt watching porn, I know he's looking at someone I'm not and feeling a sexual connection. It feels, on some level, deceptive. It's one thing having a 'quick wank' but what if that moves offline to dimly lit Soho boudoirs and scantily clad escorts?

3 That it's my fault. When you've been 'opened like a tin can' or your breasts are spouting milk like a leaky tap, sex is the last thing on your mind. Medically it's advised you hold back for at least five weeks post-caesarean, but even beyond that phase, sometimes you just don't feel like it. Matt has seen me hunched in a corner, trying to wrangle a lady pad into my nude-coloured support pants. He's seen me crumble halfway up the stairs when I felt a stitch pop on my C-section scar. He's respectfully put my Anusol back in the bathroom cabinet ahead of friends coming over. He's seen me at my lowest, while milf Jackie Blow will always be on her A-game.

4 That it's turning him off sex.

5 That I'm overreacting.

To try to turn up the dimmer switch a little, I download a twenty-nine-page report called *Pornography Consumption and Satisfaction: A Meta-Analysis* – a treasure trove of hardcore facts and figures that blows apart the 'it's just a wank' theory. This isn't just a loose bit of paper to qualify my feelings, it's a report that pools together fifty previous global studies with over 50,000 people and removes the bias that can creep into smaller studies.

Firstly – and bulldozing the walls of accepted doctrine – the report concludes that watching porn has no negative effect on women's sexual satisfaction in a relationship. This is because women watch porn with their partners, which boosts both their sex lives in tandem.

That makes sense. Matt and I have watched porn together – Erika Lust's *Tinder Taxi* and *Speedos Cleptomaniac* included – and it generally makes the night more erotically charged than if I'm flinging off my paisley pyjamas and flopping onto him, hoping ends meet.

Perhaps an exception to the rule is my friend and colleague, the TV and radio presenter Zoe Hardman, who enjoys watching porn alone and has done since she was twenty-two. I siphon her off after work for a quick chat at the nearby Hampshire Hotel in Leicester Square. It's a marble-floored gaff that makes us speak in hushed tones, which is silly considering most hotels offer grot on demand on the in-room TV.

So when did she first get into it? 'I started with entry-level stuff like girl-on-girl but it has increasingly got a little more X-rated over the years,' she explains. 'I just found it a huge release, I was less stressed. Like some people might have a bath to chill out, I'd watch porn.'

She's always been open with partners about her erotic screen time. But, as much as she enjoyed being able to switch on an orgasm on her laptop, she's recently found it's not been a healthy place to seek sexual solace.

'There was a point a few weeks ago where I was watching a woman shoving a lava lamp up herself and I thought, "Is this really what I want to do with my spare time?" The lamp was switched on and it just, well, made me switch off.'

We both reminisce about owning lava lamps in the late nineties, illuminating Athena posters of buff men cuddling babies. Those lamps got quite hot if left on for too long so that's something else to consider.

But what about her husband? Does he mind her watching porn alone? Or is he too busy watching decorative lighting being put in places that don't see the light of day?

'No, he's not,' she assures me. 'We have the most open relationship and I wouldn't care either way if he was. But it just doesn't do it for him. He's a rugby player and even the lads struggle to understand why he's just not that into porn.'

My slight fear for Zoe is that men tend to be secretive about porn, even if in a loving relationship. Understandably so, because there's no easy way to answer the 'How was your day?' question with: 'Good, thanks, darling. I had a meeting with the MD and watched *Asian Babes Rimming* when I got home.'

They squirrel themselves away, watching porn alone, locked in toilets, hidden upstairs and ensconced in stationery cupboards (I made that one up but imagine it's been done). Matt told me the other day that a mate of a mate of ours wanks in the office toilets daily. Apparently it's one of those toilets where the door and walls run floor to ceiling, so that's OK, then. Though it's made me think twice about shaking anyone's hand at work.

But hand-sanitizing aside, it's the impact on relationships that's key: across all fifty studies, the authors found that porn had 'an overall negative effect on men's real-world sexual and relational satisfaction'.

The money shot: porn is turning men off sex. Why? One essential finding in the report is that misogynistic, body-punishing porn doesn't do it for the majority of men. The punishment of a scantily clad shoplifter by a monstrously hung police officer turns on and repels men in equal measure, leaving them 'emotionally unfulfilled, alienated from their partners, and sexually and relationally dissatisfied'.

What relief is this?

Words I see ricocheting about porn sites qualify this disconnect: 'drilling', 'nailing', 'ramming', 'hammering'. Removed from the visual, it sounds more like a *How To Make A Fence* YouTube video than two (or more) people exchanging bodily fluids in an erotic setting.

And it seems porn viewed alone in the downstairs loo is then invading headspace in the bedroom, which is where I feel disconnected from Matt. I slip into a bed every night wondering if he's mentally slept with other women – women who don't look like me. And women who don't have sex like me, because I am not a fence.

I need to speak to someone who can help me work out if I'm overreacting. I call up Paula Hall, founder of sex and porn addiction clinic The Laurel Centre and author of *Sex Addiction, A Guide For Couples*.

After a bit of awkward chatter about what I think Matt might be watching, she says, 'When faced with the partner who is looking at porn, try to take a step back to think about your own thoughts before you confront them. Is it that you think it's disgusting and has no place in a relationship? Is it that you don't mind but feel excluded? Or is it that you suspect the sexual relationship isn't satisfying your partner and they've decided to find out if porn is more alluring?'

I don't know what I think, really, that's the problem. I know I want Matt to enjoy life and if that means a quick wank here and there, who am I to come between him and his happy-ending-for-one? But I also feel like we have so few shared hobbies, other than silent snacking in front of Netflix, that maybe this could be something we *do* together. I try to instigate watching porn together that night and it turns into another excruciating exchange. I feel like a county-level footballer that's just turned up to play for England.

I don't know what I'm doing and he doesn't really want me on the pitch.

'Porn is a personal thing,' Hall says. 'If it is not for you, then be clear about this. Ultimately a partner who can't hear this and still wants to indulge in heavy usage may not be the partner for you. Equally, don't necessarily exclude experimenting with it together either. As with anything to do with sex, agreeing how far you want to take things is a definite requirement in any healthy relationship, so don't let anyone insist you look at or re-enact the things they've seen if you are not comfortable.'

I think that's where I've been going wrong with all the clumsy advances. I'm acutely aware that I'm coming across like a desperate shrew (not crow) at times, and I think Matt will vouch that's not the case. I've just lost my way a bit. I've lost my confidence a little. Porn feels like something close to a threat now that the foundations of who I am have been wobbled slightly by motherhood.

That night Matt assures me that I am great. He says I don't need to be someone I'm not and that trying to be is slightly alarming. The crotch zip on the bodice I hastily purchased is also fairly chafing.

But maybe I'm one of the lucky ones with a partner who understands how it makes me feel. Matt's from another era of porn to boys growing up online today. Guys in their thirties and forties were mostly raised on magazine and DVD porn. It was difficult to get hold of and was comparatively wholesome compared to what the internet dishes up now.

I need to speak to someone who knows about degenerate wankers.

There are very few people who have seen the bump and grind

of the pornographic world more than Martin Daubney, ex-editor of *Loaded* and now Brexit Party MEP (but that's another story).

After a bit of chat about all the magazines we've worked on that have since folded (*Horticulture Week* still thrives, although I don't want to rub salt in any wounds), Martin is delighted that someone is tackling the emotional impact of porn. He reveals over the phone: 'Writing on porn and sex addiction, I've worked with some of the UK's most seriously dependent porn users. One lad masturbated to porn twenty-eight times a day, even in pub toilets and on buses. Another guy spent £52,000 on escorts he'd met on porn sites. One woman told me she could not have driving lessons with male instructors, as she feared she would try to have sex with them.'

Of course, extreme users are no more representative of all porn users than one alcoholic is of all drinkers. But there's something to be garnered from these examples. Porn is undeniably shaping our offline view of sexual expectation: it's setting men up for a fall.

And that disappointment can translate to erectile dysfunction. Sadly and worryingly, sexual psychotherapists at Nottingham University Hospital have found that British men in their teens and twenties are more likely to have erectile dysfunction than men in their fifties and sixties, and the cause is almost always unchecked access to porn.

Hall confirms: 'Porn can effectively "rewire" the brain's dopamine pleasure centres, meaning – just like a drug – the more porn you watch, the more you need to get the same hit. Think of it like a Big Mac. You know it's comfort eating, you know it's not good for you but you do it anyway. Then vegetables start to look really boring in comparison and all you want is a McDonald's. You need to ask why you want the junk food in the first place. It's really just an easy, lazy substitute for good sex.'

Real sex with real women who don't look like porn stars becomes too pedestrian to do the job. Then there is the nagging anxiety that men won't measure up to ripped, pendulously endowed male porn stars.

There lies the irony: a generation reared on endless free porn and self-educated via its cartoonesque, *Playboy* offerings are finding the best thing in the world – real, loving sex – just doesn't measure up. When faced with the real thing, increasing numbers of Generation Z cannot rise to the occasion.

'For me, that was my "hang on a minute" moment,' continues Martin. 'We were sold the myth that porn would make us master swordsmen. Instead, it's turning increasing numbers of men in their sexual prime into flops. Porn was meant to empower us. But is it enslaving us? And if it is, why aren't more men angry about it?'

I'm angry about it. I'm just not sure who to be angry with.

Maybe the founder of YouPorn.

Maybe I'm angry at the exaggerated squealing-seal sex noises.

Maybe I'm angry that it bothers me.

But I can't be angry in silence, and neither should you be. Because how long can this build before it doesn't just turn us off but breaks us up?

There can be no happy ending with one partner silently swallowing the feeling that they are fancied less than a 2D computer screen. There is no happiness to be found in sensing you are second choice to a galaxy of fantasy flesh. So if you feel that way, speak up. I want him to read these pages and think 'Maybe I need to discuss this with her. Maybe she should have discussed it with me a long time ago. Maybe without it, I'll be so charged at all times that I won't be able to leave her alone.'

So he will read these pages and I will tell him how I feel.

Because love can't last if resentment lingers.

8

✩ ✩ ✩

True Romance

Can love last?

Anna

Matt and I are having an argument in our kitchen about something I can't remember (possibly cats pooing in our garden), which ends with me saying: 'Do you want me to just fuck off?'

I stare at a squashed pea on the floor of our kitchen, unleash great balls of emotional fire – some flickering back to 2009 – and feel lonely. I don't give Matt a chance to draw breath before I say, 'I'll just fuck off, then.'

So I fuck off upstairs, a sort of disappointing halfway house of actually fucking off; fuck-off purgatory. A place where you huffily wait, red-eyed and confused by who you are and why your relationship doesn't look like the well-thumbed Jackie Collins novels dotted about your local GP surgery. A process that is eerily on a par with the time you, aged seven, told your dad that your sister could 'have the fucking My Little Pony' and decided to take yourself to your bedroom to save him doing it.

I sit in this temporary hole of self-punishment, wondering how things escalated from Matt not listening to my question about possible feline defecation.

The truth is, to carry out the fucking-off would require packing of bags, managing of childcare pick-ups and drop-offs, timetabling, a snack inventory and, well, somewhere to go. The Stratford Holiday

Inn isn't financially or emotionally viable long-term, and moving back with my parents at thirty-seven would be The End. Logistically, it's impossible for one of us to simply exit the building without a month's notice. We can huff and we can puff but we would never blow our house down. It's not just us, there's always a tiny 'them' and 'they' will always make us think twice.

So I just sob defeatedly into the Simba toy that my daughter had tucked up on my side of the bed. Until he comes upstairs with a slightly softened – but mildly pained – brow and says, 'I never want you to fuck off,' which is always nice to hear.

So is this the end of love or just a phase it goes through? And if it's the latter, what do people do to get through it? How do people make their love last?

When Matt was living in the Portuguese free-love commune (a sentence I never imagined penning in relation to our marriage), I felt a twinge of jealousy. I imagined him absorbed by deliriously happy, sexually satisfied people who grow their own lentils. When we Skyped he seemed energized, happier and much lighter than when he left, weighed down by my hollers of 'What time is her swimming lesson?' Now I want to be around some people like that.

My friend Elena (who is also friends with Saamirah the virgin) suggests Cathy Keen, her husband Thomas, and their girlfriend Nicole Everett. Cathy and Thomas are married with a eight-year-old son, and Nicole lives with them at weekends. They have a photo on their Instagram page that says The Throuple, mirroring the famous imagery from fashion store The Kooples.

I hop on a bus and head towards their east London home,

wondering if the key to everlasting happiness is as simple as adding more people into the mix.

Their house is rammed with the kind of furniture picked up at flea markets, and which wouldn't look amiss in MOMA. It feels like somewhere The Kooples would inhabit.

I've heard people say 'they've got such great chemistry' when speaking about couples, but after accepting a cup of coffee, here I am sat opposite two people who make me want what they've got. There's a flirtatious, anything-could-happen energy in the air that makes me wonder if this is what Matt felt at the commune. Free love is all around.

Cathy touches Thomas affectionately throughout the first ten minutes of chatting together and I'm erroneously convinced they want a threesome with me. I joke about this and immediately wish I hadn't as they laugh awkwardly, looking a little bit sad for me. (My sister says on the phone that night that it's probably the same frustration she feels when she tells women she's a lesbian and the women assume she fancies them. She doesn't. And they don't, either.)

But when did Cathy and Thomas realize they wanted more than a monogamous relationship?

Cathy starts: 'We'd had a conversation about being open. I wanted it for my own personal, sexual reasons, and my fantasy was to be with more than one guy. And Thomas wanted to experiment in his own space, and to flirt with and get close to other people.'

They can't stop touching. I feel like a third wheel.

Cathy, who works in events for couples dating app Feeld, admits being nervous until they went to a sex party where they were open to others joining them. 'It wasn't a dirty, seedy thing,' she says. 'It felt warm and fuzzy, and almost like we'd transcended the normal party vibes. It was such a long-lasting experience. We came out of that first party and were skipping down the road.'

Then, two years ago, Cathy met Nicole Everett while working in events at an 'ethical house of striptease' in London. When an opportunity came up for a quick drink, Cathy introduced Thomas to Nicole. 'It felt like a chemical reaction,' she says, 'and the sparks went off between them. I've always had this twinge of sexual excitement when I see someone I love with someone else. Nothing was explicitly said about the three of us being together, but I just felt this connection.'

That's where I think I'd struggle. I don't like people touching my stuff. I'm not possessive but I also believe that jealousy will eventually break something along the way. Matt tells me there's even a jealousy circle at the love commune. Why take the risk?

Nicole doesn't live with them permanently, but comes and goes like an ethereal sex (and friendship) nymph who also makes tea. It reminds me of what Amsterdam sex worker Hera said about cuddling more and I can only imagine more arms means more connection. Either way, I could come round to the idea of having another pair of hands for paint jobs and blow jobs alike.

'Cathy and I will never be monogamous,' continues Thomas. 'We have nothing against it, but we've learned it just doesn't work for us. True love is all about being open to other people, to each other's fantasies and this is ours – even if it doesn't fit in with the rest of the world.'

They seem so sure. I want to be that sure.

✰✰✰

It's a fairly overcast Sunday and I've walked out of the house, leaving Matt with the kids. I'm leaving him for five hours to attend a lecture on 'How to Make Love Last' at The School of Life in London's leafy Bloomsbury. It's on the same street as The Marquis Cornwallis, a gastropub that has a blackboard outside offering a 100 per cent Aberdeen Angus beef burger with 'chedar'. I take a photo for Matt because he is a grammar and spelling pedant and would need there to be 'cheddar' on his meat. I forget to send it to him but it's there in my camera roll, along with a photo of a 'chode' (a penis that is as long as it is wide) from a WhatsApp group ironically entitled 'Slaaaaaaaagggggggggggs'.

Despite offering an escape from Sunday hollers of 'I want the Octonauts plate', a relationship school is probably the last place I want to be. I once got seated next to a self-appointed 'love guru' at a wellness event, and she said things like 'I think I just made a happy wee-wee' when the vegetable tempura arrived.

I arrive in the basement classroom four minutes late and am welcomed loudly – 'Come right on in and make yourself comfort- able' (which always has the opposite effect) by lecturer Damian, a charismatic guy with a green tartan shirt and a perfect set of teeth. I wonder if the combination of gnashers to plaid might be the secret to true love, before scanning the room and being surprised by the diverse and attentive intake – one woman (not a journalist, I later learned) had a Dictaphone poised to capture the full 180 minutes.

I'm sat next to Steve, a gay forty-seven-year-old artist who is wearing a leather gilet and has a slightly weathered look that indicates fun times have been had. He's my partner for the first exercise, which kicks off with this question: 'How long can one of your sulks last?'

After an uncomfortable handshake with an accidental grazing of my left breast, Steve says it's half a day, while I admit things can linger for a month 'because I sometimes don't even know what's making me angry'. I feel in a safe space with Steve. Steve looks a bit sad for Matt.

The next question is 'What sort of thing might your partner do that pushes you into a sulk?'

This is where Steve comes into his own: 'So my partner seems to think it's OK to arrange a play date for our son on a Saturday morning without asking me. He then leaves me with the kids and goes to play squash with our mutual friend Darryl.'

I inhale and go straight into Cher Horowitz (of 1995 film *Clueless*) relationship-analysis mode:

'Steve, you have every right to be hacked off,' I empathize, instantly furious at the gall of this man I don't know towards another man I don't know with a context I'm not a party to.

'Do you think? I'm not overreacting?'

'It's rude, Steve, it's inconsiderate.'

While there's nothing to qualify my analysis, he looks momentarily cheered as his feelings of angst are rationalized by a stranger with a sweaty upper lip.

'Matt . . .'

Damian's bell tinkles as we're told to switch partners for the next exercise. This is probably for the best because I was about to chew Steve's ear off about Matt's crotchety Kevin the Teenager demeanour every time I ask if we can talk about matters of the heart. 'He just won't feel the FEELINGS, Steve' is something I'm glad never made it to the table.

Once we've all shuffled about the room, Damian halts our chatter, gesticulates like a seasoned National Opera conductor and has us chant: 'I will not blame you for not already knowing what I want. I am radically imperfect, we all are.'

He then explains that for any relationship to survive long-haul, we need to adopt the role of teacher and student – 'Few people are psychic,' he explains. (I feel like that's an obvious one, really – it was, after all, the go-to dig of my teens: 'Duh, I'm not psychic, Mum.')

Damian then says something that I have recently started saying to my eldest daughter: 'You have to use your words.'

My next partner is a single, six-foot-five male model called David, who has floppy flaxen hair and spray-on pleather trousers – few could carry off this look but he succeeds. Our initial pleasantries lead to this summary: his last girlfriend was a vegan and she got incredibly angry with him for booking a restaurant for her birthday that only had four vegan dishes. Two weeks later, she drunkenly hauled him into McDonald's on the way back from a friend's birthday where she inhaled a Big Mac and refused to acknowledge the irony.

'She was furious at me for questioning her so I never brought anything up about her wonky veganism again.'

They lasted another three months before she called it a day because he was 'too closed off'. I was furious at her. Over the years, I've noticed that friends (or near-strangers in this case) tend to have these default settings when a relationship hits the rocks:

1 To slag off the other person – who isn't in the room to defend themselves or fact-check events.
2 To slag off the other person – who isn't in the room to defend themselves or fact-check events – and offer up tea.
3 To slag off the other person – who isn't in the room to defend themselves or fact-check events – and offer up wine.

Damian's bell tinkles before I can offer up rage and a beverage. We're galloping towards the root of our relationship issues at a rate of knots. While I appreciate speaking about the jumbled thoughts in my head to Matt, I am less comfortable spouting things to a flurry of strangers. I find myself editing my thoughts a little more, thinking before speaking and generally being a much nicer person.

'How are you difficult to live with?' Damian asks.

This I can do. I sit with Anita, a thirty-eight-year-old self-confessed perfectionist and HR manager whose husband Mike (sat the other side of me and now partnered with David) doesn't live up to expectations.

'I don't think he has ever called my mum up for a chat,' she explains, misunderstanding the 'you' element of the question. I nod empathetically, wondering how Mike gets through the day. I'd never expect Matt to call my mum; I wouldn't expect anyone else to listen to the issues she's having with the upstairs shower head, because I came out of her vagina and it is my duty, not his.

My turn: I'm wildly inconsistent. I have a strong business head but a shambolic grasp of finances. My dad still has power of attorney over my bank account from the time I lost all my bank cards after a Koh Phangan full-moon party and woke up on a beach with a dog licking my big toe. I have a lurking sense that there's a Topshop card from 1998 that still needs paying off. I'm reactive and hyper-active. I never put a wash on. I overanalyse feelings and underestimate travel times. I leave crumbs in the butter and undrunk cups of tea on the floor. I have broken five out of our eight wine glasses. I've never unblocked a drain clogged with my hair. I've never let a cross word 'just go'. I'm sometimes (often) nicer to strangers than to Matt. I eat pickled onions straight from the jar and once put myself off sex because of the briny smell on my index finger and thumb. I never listen because I don't like being told. I'm a catch.

(That evening, I read the above to Matt. He looks astonished that it's taken a stranger, a £55 course fee and four hours away from the children to make such acute personal observations. He tells me he actually broke two wine glasses and I broke three, so it wasn't as bad as I was making out. There's a lightness between us that hasn't been there for a very long time. I kiss him under the oven hood as he stirs some scrambled eggs.)

Damian claps loudly and we all return to our seats as he offers around a packet of lady-finger biscuits. He continues his sermon: 'If you are angry with your partner, give it forty-eight hours before addressing the issue because in this time you will either: 1) have found a calmer way to discuss the issue or 2) forgotten the issue entirely.'

Stealthily under the table, I put this snippet out on my Instagram stories and instantly get this back: 'Forty-eight bloody hours . . . I could kill him and hide the body in less time.'

Someone else suggested this: 'We have an argument safeword that resets everything. When you're bickering about stacking the dishwasher right and then twenty minutes later you're ranting about how something nine years ago is still annoying you, you can use the safeword and you both have to stop. Reassess what the issue is, calm down, both apologise and address whatever it is rationally. Nine times out of ten you both realize that it's not worth arguing about and you both just need a cuddle and some nice words.'

Someone else added: 'My safeword would be "dickwad".'

I wonder what mine and Matt's safeword would be. I flit between 'fat beagle' and 'electric blue sloth' (my eBay name from 2006).

The next lesson Damian has for us is about being childish – eschewing the banality of adulthood and allowing each other to be infantile on occasion. He explains that children aren't always sure why they're angry but their parents will always find a kindly excuse or rationalize the tantrum. Usually one of the following:

'I think she's teething.'
'She's probably hungry.'
'He was up all night.'
'He just wants his Boo Boo.'

'Children can be really annoying,' continues Damian, as all the child-ravaged members of the congregation sombrely nod in agreement. 'But we always find a compassionate way to soothe the issue with hugs and kindly deflection from the fact that they are probably just being irrational.'

(I have a moment of self-reflection here, where I recount the times I haven't been compassionate about my youngest daughter sweeping a bowl of Cheerios onto the floor, staring me in the face and dead-panning 'Uh oh.')

So I think Damian's saying that when Matt calls a broken bank-card reader a 'fat fuck', he's just having a moment of childish anger. Sometimes we're just kids in need of a Dairylea Dunker and a hug.

What I came away with from The School of Life – before passing the 'chedar' sign on the return and still forgetting to send Matt the photo – can be summarized (and laminated) thus:

1 We are all wrong. Being right isn't the answer.
2 Look to your childhood for the root of your problems. My parents have been together for forty-seven years, while Matt's separated when he was eight. I'm an open book, he's a closed book. I need editing, he's an editor. Try to understand each other before ripping into the pages.
3 Use your words. Even if they don't come out right. Be open to each other not saying the words right. Come to the argument with compassion and kindness over bullishness and superiority.
4 Nothing is too small. If it matters to you (singular), it should matter to you (plural).
5 Use the forty-eight-hour rule for things hacking you off to save a 24/7 slew of emotion that might simply be down to commuting angst or an irritable digestive tract.
6 Don't huff, tut, stomp, slam or spit. It rarely starts or ends well.

7 Allow each other to be childish sometimes. Tackle adult petulance with the compassion usually reserved for a hollering child. (I reiterate: I lack compassion on occasion with both child and adult, but one must persevere.)

8 Use humour to highlight radical differences. Lighten the mood where you can; be open to being teased where possible. (A slight deviation from this is my friend, the comedian Ellie Taylor, who complained of cramps in her stomach post-birth and her husband chirpily said: 'Maybe they left a few tools in there!')

9 Fantasize about other people without guilt. The human mind can't unsee attractive people; if that's associated with guilt, it will turn into something darker. 'We should be open enough to let our partners fantasize and wise enough not to mind,' assures Damian. He tells me to stop making Matt feel guilty for watching porn if that offers him some fantastical release.

10 We are all difficult to live with.

11 None of the above has worked for us yet. But all of these things convince me that love can last longer than I thought, if you're just willing to put in a little work.

But Damian has missed a huge Duplo block of disgruntlement for me. There's no mention of the 'smart' phone that renders us dribbling cyborgs. There's no mention of the times I've chosen to compare my life to strangers on the internet over looking at what's right in front of me. For all the talk of threesomes and forty-eight-hour cool-off periods, there's no mention of the worst influence lurking between us ☹

Matt

'We need a safeword,' says Anna.

Well, this is promising, I think. What has she learned today?

'For arguments, when one of us is being a dick.'

Oh, I think. Less exciting.

'Is it said by the person being a dick or the one on the receiving end of dickishness? And how will we know who's who?'

'Anyone can say it,' she says, 'when it's time for a time-out'.

We're in the kitchen, which is where most of the arguing tends to happen. My guess is that we have a proper row every four weeks, on average. It's rare that these will involve tears or shouting (there's hardly ever shouting), but they will be biggish and could run for anything from an hour (in most cases) to a couple of days (more common since kids came along and there's less time to put things right). Hackles will be up. Someone will say 'FINE!' in a way that suggests things are not fine.

Recently, I crept to the slightly retrograde assumption that this timing might be linked to her period, and marked the date in my Google calendar. But because we have access to each other's calendars, I gave it a drearily financial codename. It says 'Accounts Due'.

This may make me a bad ally. You may have decided that I'm not an ally at all. But she's definitely a bit meaner to me before she comes on – for all the many valid physiological reasons there are for being mean pre-period – and I think it's wise for me to be a little more sensitive in advance. Both for her sake and my own.

But whatever the cause, these rows are different to the minor niggles that happen more often – those little huffs about life admin that come and go before anyone really notices them. Those ones that are usually fixed with a quick 'sorry' or hug, but are sometimes left to slide by, and might be dripping into a big stalagmite.

So perhaps a safeword is a good idea. We settle on 'fat beagle', after our sadly departed pet.

I hope not to need it, given I'm regularly asking myself 'What does love need now?'

☆☆☆

If you're married, and said your 'I dos' after about 1995, the chances of making it to your fifteen-year anniversary (crystal, so a nice shiny one) are statistically higher than they were for those who married in the seventies and eighties.[1] Go *you*.

That's partly because there was a divorce spike in those decades, as women realized they no longer had to listen to men called Alan telling them how much to spend on groceries. And partly it's because the social pressure to marry in the first place has now diminished, so fewer people wed just to keep their mums happy.

But there is one age group that bucks this trend, and it's the older folk.

In the US, divorces among over-fifties have doubled over the last twenty-five years. In the UK, the same is true for over-sixties.

These silver splitters get through the child-rearing, settle back in their empty nest and, without the hustle of daily parenthood to

---

1   Office of National Statistics data and Statista.com.

keep them distracted, realize they've fallen out of love. All of a sudden, your logistical task-partner is once again expected to be your daily date, and it turns out they're no longer twenty-five or impressed by your taste in West Coast garage rock.

This is my worry for Anna and me. On the days when it's hard – when a small person thinks they're Wat Tyler and stages an uprising about cutlery, or decides that all they want to do is shout 'no!' while kicking me in the shins – I get through by telling myself it will get easier. Tomorrow we will read stories together, I think. In a year or two, they'll both be able to dress themselves, I reassure myself. They will eventually be eighteen and I will be able to evict them, I daydream. Then Anna and I will be just like before. But what if we're not? What if this isn't a blip but a trend?

All of which makes me wonder how love changes over time – physically, chemically and emotionally.

A man called Dr Fred Nour thinks he might have the answer. He is a neurologist with very neat white teeth and wavy hair who wrote a book on the science of true love. The cover has a couple in silhouette on a beach with the sun setting behind them, and briefly reminds me of a 'Visit Florida' towel that survived in my family for longer than any of our pets, despite the fact that none of us has ever been to Florida. I suspect it was accidentally inherited on a trip to the local pool.

But back to Dr Nour. He believes that love is all to do with the chemical make-up of your brain. Speaking to me from his Paris office, he says that 'the most common mistake is believing that romance is true love and expecting the feeling of romance to last for a lifetime. It doesn't.'

Nour argues that there are four stages (the explanations in brackets are my own):

1 Finding a mate (your eyes meet across a crowded room).
2 Falling in romantic love (you're floating on air and at it like dolphins).
3 Falling out of romantic love (you're wondering if you really want to see that face every morning until you die).
4 True love (you decide that you do).

He says that these can be tracked through our chemical reactions to each other, and the romantic-love stage doesn't last very long.

'Romantic love is multiple chemical changes in the brain for the purpose of preparing for a strong, true-love phase. It's associated with a lot of emotion: happiness, excitement, obsession, compulsion, all of that. The biggest misconception in history is the belief that romantic love is love. It's not. It's like believing the pregnancy is the baby.'

MRI studies have shown that the first flush sees a rise in the production of monoamines. This chemical family – which includes 'happy chemical' dopamine – may explain the giddy butterflies and susceptibility to acoustic ballads.

One of the best pieces of research was by anthropologist Helen Fisher. In 2005, her team scanned the brains of 2,500 American college students while they were shown images of people they knew. When students saw a picture of their current love interest, dopamine-rich parts of the brain lit up. Stimulating these 'reward centres' makes us happy. These are the same spots that get uplifted when someone takes amphetamines or cocaine (or watches porn).

A 2012 study in *Science* magazine even noted that unloved fruit flies hit the booze in response to sexual rejection.[2] Male fruit flies that were rebuffed when trying to mate drank four times as much alcohol as peers that got lucky with a lady fly. The theory was that once they were swatted away they needed to hit their reward centres in some other way. So when people say love is a drug, they have a point.

But excess dopamine production is also a common trait among people with schizophrenia, and may be partly responsible for psychosis. So maybe love is a kind of madness too.

This is certainly backed up by other chemical effects in the early stages of love. Levels of the stress hormone cortisol rise, along with epinephrine, which raises sensations of fear. This combination can make us feel jittery and obsessive, and perhaps a little afraid that we might lose what we have. But epinephrine also enhances our recall of emotionally charged events, which, Dr Nour says, helps form those sharp memories of the first kiss or date.

Even now, more than a decade on, I have very clear memories of the early days with Anna. It was a period when iPods were new and Kanye West was emotionally stable, and I spent a lot of time listening to both, generally strutting about like a peacock with freshly flapped plumage. But I was also beset by a kind of soft-headedness. When she called me on my work phone I would fold in on myself at my desk, physically diminished by the sound of her gently husky Home Counties poshness, and terrified that

---

2   'Sexual Deprivation Increases Ethanol Intake in Drosophilia', *Science*, March 2012.

colleagues might notice my cheeks had turned a shade of boiled radish.

I've never been particularly possessive, but I found myself riled whenever she spoke to men I didn't know. I had never pined for another human in my life, but on nights when we were apart, I'd sit in my room in the tiny flat I shared above a north London timber merchant, chain-smoking roll-ups out the window and listening to the mournful strumming of José González on repeat.

But this madness doesn't last long. One University of Pavia study suggests the effects wear off after a year.[3] According to Nour, they might run for two or three years, which is why so many relationships break up after that point.

Yet, for those who last beyond the romance phase and past a period of re-evaluation after the flutters fade, there may be something worth clinging on to for much longer.

'Romance starts very suddenly and intensely, while true love happens gradually,' says Nour, as this is when the oxytocin and vasopressin really kick in. 'Both are equally important. Both are equally powerful. Oxytocin is more in women than men. Vasopressin is more in men than women. But both are present. Both are responsible for the true-love phase, the bonding, the attachment, the altered perception, the ultimate joy and happiness and permanent relationship.'

Slightly worryingly, though, he says that not everyone can make this stage.

---

3   'Raised plasma nerve growth factor levels associated with early-stage romantic love', *Psychoneuroendocrinology*, April 2006.

'Genes affect our ability to love . . . but some people don't have the chemicals,' he says.

Our genetic make-up can affect how the receptors in the brain respond to oxytocin and vasopressin, and those with 'defective receptors' may never fall in love, or may find themselves in a constant cycle of swooning without settling.

'They believe that romance is love, so when romance ends, love ends, and then they move on,' he says. 'Some people are incapable of having true love, but this is relatively rare.'

I'm sceptical here: people can be genetically inclined to alcoholism, or to weight gain, but there are other factors at play. You can choose not to hang out with boozy friends, and you can decide to eat healthily and exercise. Our genetic make-up gives us a broad direction of travel, but we're still sitting at the wheel. My feeling is that there's more choice involved, though there is evidence that this choice can be harder for some than for others. At least in rodents.

When neuroscientists look for models of human mating behaviour, they often turn to prairie voles. These squat little furballs pair for life, share parenting and burrow-building responsibilities and are about as woke to gender issues as it's possible for a small mammal to be. Several studies have shown that paired-up prairie voles have more receptors for oxytocin and vasopressin than their single peers.

But not all voles love equally. Montane voles are bigger than their prairie counterparts and prefer the high altitudes of the mountainous west of the US to the flat bits in the middle. They are also highly promiscuous, and bandy it about like sailors on shore leave.

Dr Thomas Insel, who spent thirteen years as director of the US National Institute of Mental Health, discovered that this can be controlled. When montane voles had their vasopressin receptor gene altered to make them more susceptible to it, they stopped their philandering and became clingier than a teenager with their first crush. When researchers blocked the vasopressin receptors of the homely prairie voles, they kept the urge to cop off, but were much less fussy about who it was with.

So whatever your genetic make-up, and whatever your predisposition to settling down with an Ikea catalogue, it seems clear that a certain mental chemistry is at play.

I have taken Dr Nour's stages of love, and adapted these into an approximate theory of my own:

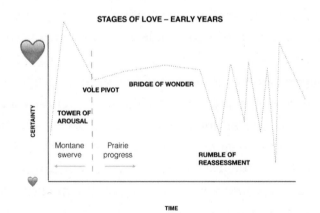

First, comes the tower of arousal: that first flush of wild-eyed emotion. Then, as this wanes and you have a chemical comedown, we hit the vole pivot, where you decide to quit and look for the next peak as fast as a montane vole on a good-hair day or settle into a burrow, happy as a prairie vole.

For those who stay, there's a nice period that follows, which I've called the bridge of wonder – you're comfortable together but not yet bogged down by kids or mortgages or contemplating the essential futility of human existence. It's nice. Maybe you buy furniture.

Then there comes the rumble of reassessment. You've become more aware of the failings of yourself and your partner and are quietly wondering 'Is this it?' You may even take the unwise step of writing a book about it, because you're too emotionally stunted to tell them in person.

That's where we are. But this theory only really covers the first few years, and I'm still not sure what stretches out beyond that.

For some, what stretches beyond is a proper time-out. Simone Bose is a relationship therapist with the charity Relate and has become something of an expert on couples who decide to take a break. We speak by video link and on the wall behind her is a large canvas image of James Dean.

'From my experience people talk about a break – and not a break-up – when the emotions are just too difficult to untangle. Usually it's when there's a negative pattern that is really difficult to break,' she says. 'It gives them a chance to imagine what life might be like if they weren't together, because they have that space.'

She finds that about 60 per cent end up together after a break of a few months (and in better relationships as a result), while the rest go their separate ways.

It works best, she says, 'when there are boundaries. When you know that you are doing it for the best of your relationship because you both care about each other but you're too angry or emotional to be able to have logical discussions.'

It certainly feels a little like that's where Anna and I are – the same frustrations creeping in, the same circular arguments. Maybe the safeword will help, maybe asking 'What does love need now?' will make things happier, but at the moment I do feel a surge of guilty relief whenever one of us has to go away for work and I know that for a couple of hours every evening I will have no one to consider but myself. But then a pang of yearning kicks in after a couple of days, and I think how nice it would be to have Anna by my side again.

There's also a risk that too much time apart slowly kills things off. One of the factors that Nour talks about is the benefit of physical contact – not necessarily sex, but that touch, hugs and other affection can help keep the oxytocin flowing. Bose recommends trial separations of no more than three to six months, with some set rules about contact and meeting up. Any longer and things start to fade too far away.

The idea is interesting but feels quite dramatic. Even when we're apart, we usually exchange messages daily. There's usually a call every night.

But I do wonder what happens if you don't take a break: how often I drift away when I'm at home, lost in reveries or music or TV. There's a risk, I think, that if you don't do something you end up taking a break without going anywhere and all of a sudden years have passed.

A few weeks later I speak to psychiatrist Charlotte Fox Weber. She is blonde-haired and gently glamorous with a slight US accent.

Like Nour, she agrees with the idea that the first flush of love is temporary.

'That giddy lovesick stage lasts for a couple of years. It's often mistaken for deep love. Recovering that kind of infatuation is very, very difficult,' she says. 'Often relationships become "side by side" over time. Where you co-exist, but your lives are more overlapping than deeply connected. The person is so familiar to you that you don't have to bother looking and engaging.'

She suggests going 'nose to nose' instead.

'In the infatuation stage I think there's a lot of nose to nose, where you're intensely looking at each other, listening to each other,' she says, and this is something that can still be rediscovered. 'I'm a big fan of a very simple game where you sit for sixty seconds and observe each other intensely and say nothing. It may seem pointless, and actually a whole minute can seem like a really long time, but it's about not taking for granted that you have memorized that person.'

So a few nights later, we do exactly that. I've just returned from a stag weekend and am feeling emotionally frail. There has been the domestic tsunami of kids' bedtime, I've cooked dinner, Anna's read stories and after we eat, we sit on the sofa to try Fox Weber's staring exercise.

After three seconds, Anna laughs in my face.

'Are we just supposed to sit here?' she asks.

'Yes,' I say.

A few seconds pass and she laughs again.

'But you look so sad,' she says.

'That's because I'm hungover.'

She manages a bit more silence, and I take in her face. It reminds me that perhaps I haven't just stared at her for a while. When I think of her face, I think of it when we first met: when it was framed by her natural curls, instead of straight as she keeps it now. I think of it beneath the green floppy hat she wore on our third date, which got in the way when I tried to kiss her. But her face is the same now: same rosebud lips, same wonky nose from when she walked into a plate-glass window as a student, same blue eyes.

Then she laughs again.

'This is like that game you play as kids, where you're not allowed to laugh. I always laughed straight away.'

An alarm goes off to mark the end of the minute. Then Anna stacks the dishwasher and I order a new electric toothbrush off Amazon. Nice as it was to look at her for a bit, this may require more practice.

But later I find a study that offers a little hope. In 2011, researchers at Stony Brook University in New York put ten women and seven men through MRI scanners.[4] Each of them claimed to be in love with their spouse. They had been married for an average of twenty-one years and were shown a series of pictures: their partner, a close friend, an acquaintance and someone they recognized but didn't really know. The researchers then compared the results to a similar piece of research done in 2005 with people who were newly in love.

Dr Arthur Aron said: 'We found many very clear similarities between those who were in love long-term and those who had just fallen madly in love.'

---

4   'Neural correlates of long-term intense romantic love', *Social Cognitive and Affective Neuroscience*, February 2012.

Some chemicals may fade away, we might lose focus, but in the brain as much as the heart, it seems some kind of love can last a lifetime. It just requires a bit of work.

Perhaps love over the decades goes through three acts, like your average multiplex thriller: Act I is the whirlwind opening, Act II the functional middle and Act III is the conclusion, whatever that might be. And perhaps we're in the middle somewhere, ploughing on through work and kids and bills, looking ahead at the next thing on the to-do list but forgetting to look around at who we're doing that with.

I like what Charlotte Fox Weber had to say: that relationships become side by side over time, when they should be more nose to nose.

Because Anna and I are staring dumbly up a hill at the moment, while some bastard keeps rolling barrels down, leaving us to leap them like a pair of increasingly exhausted Donkey Kongs.

And perhaps there comes a danger that by Act III – with kids gone, working life finished, and a twenty-year resolution to play out – we'll look around and not really know each other any more. We'll have taken each other so much for granted that we'll decide we don't really need each other after all.

But there's time to fix that. If we're those Donkey Kongs, hopping over barrels, there have definitely been stumbles. I'd say we're down one 'life', with two more remaining.

And how quickly they get used up will come down to the one thing that I've been ignoring for too long and that I think is the core to all our problems.

9

Anti Social

Do phones kill love?

Anna

I'm in the room, leaning against the kitchen counter, but I'm not really there. Matt asks me to budge so he can get a tin-opener out of the cutlery drawer and I barely move. He asks me again and I make a point of moving to the living room, where my daughters are playing with a deflated football with the din of *Horrid Henry* in the background. I'm working on my phone: I'm emailing, I'm scrolling, I'm liking, I'm commenting, answering, swiping. I'm engaging.

My daughter asks me for a drink. I tell her 'in a minute'. She then says, 'Sometimes I don't think you like me when you're on your phone.'

It's a jolt. I switch off and I'm in the room. I get up and put my phone in the cutlery drawer. I bring her some water and watch them play but I can't sit still. I'm wondering what's unfurling in that dark, pixelated space.

I ask Matt that night if he thinks it's a problem. He says he thinks it is. He says he wants me back. He says I'm not there and haven't been for a while. He's said that before. Quite a lot.

I do have a problem and it's become *our* problem. The overspill from that small rectangular device floods into our home and over those within it.

But when did this slow drip of disconnection start? I scroll back through 2,457 posts to the beginning.

I downloaded Instagram on 13 September 2014. We'd just moved back from Amsterdam to Acton in London and I decided to try and 'put myself out there', as a friend had suggested, to save me lurking in soft-play areas in search of parental comrades. She promised me it was 'like Tinder-meets-Netmums but without the casual sex or acronyms.'

My first post was a tile that said: 'FRIYAY'. It was an annoying start. It was also just past midnight, so technically Saturday.

My second post was of a 'flatlay' – a bird's-eye view – of a pink plate with some halved grapes and pesto pasta for my daughter. Three likes. This was going to be a long game.

I continued in this pixelated hinterland for four months until I quit my job as senior creative copywriter for a large beauty brand. I had asked if I could start and end my day fifteen minutes earlier to ensure I wasn't landing at nursery late to a child who didn't understand signal failure, leaves on the line or an urgent conference call about lash-boosting mascara.

My flexible working request was denied and so I had to quit. I posted about it to burst a boil of frustration. I had sixty-three followers at the time, but there were 132 comments. My phone suddenly came alight.

With a few avatars behind me, I launched Flex Appeal, a campaign to fight for more flexibility at work for all: parents, those with mental health issues or caring responsibilities, those wanting to live. It was for the woman who wants to tend to her pet iguana on a Wednesday morning, and the dad who wants his daughter to remember his face at the school gates.

I had never campaigned before. I thought an algorithm was a new type of exercise class.

All I knew was it was Friday, not FRIYAY.

The lightness of mine and Matt's early years slowly got overshadowed by the blue glow of an iPhone. I'd sit in bed next to him, messaging words of support to a stranger who had been asked when she was 'leaving' not when she was 'going on maternity leave'. I shed tears for a woman suffering her fourth miscarriage, while missing a WhatsApp message from a friend to tell me she'd lost her baby at nineteen weeks. I was finding myself online, while losing myself – and those around me – in reality.

The more successful Mother Pukka became, and the further afield Flex Appeal went, the lonelier I felt. I became increasingly disconnected from friends, family and even kindly strangers on the bus. I was looking down instead of up.

Social media can be hugely positive. It can bring together people who are lost and in search of a community and I've found some of my closest friends through an app that takes eighteen seconds to download. But increasingly, it was Matt and the girls who suffered, as my focus all went on what happened within the four sides of an Instagram square instead of the four walls of my home.

I was fuelled by anger at the world of work and by the need to earn a living that allowed me to collect my girls from school and nursery. But I was collecting them only to then ignore them and stare into my phone. I was also fuelled, like all social media users, by little hits of dopamine.

Katherine Ormerod is the author of *Why Social Media is Ruining Your Life*. I met her online (sliding into her DMs) a few years ago and I want to speak to her because she's felt equally broken by a messy pixelated world masked by heart emojis, LOLs and avocado toast. I Skype her and she's wearing her pyjamas while clasping a mug of tea. I'm wearing a neon-yellow onesie. It's like a virtual slumber party for the socially fragmented.

She explains about the dopamine hit that's delivered by social media: 'It's a reward cycle: you get a squirt of it every time you get a "like" or a positive response on social media. It's like a hit, similar to the way you feel when you have a drink. The social media "likes" trigger that reward cycle and the more you get it, the more you want it.'

I know the effect but how to break the cycle? Katherine has a rule that no phones are allowed in the bedroom – 'Buy an alarm clock! It will save you so many arguments and so much disconnection. Also log off before 9p.m. to ensure you're looking up – even if at Netflix – together.'

Matt and I try this the next day. I buy us a small alarm clock that sounds like a nuclear bomb warning when it goes off at 7.15a.m. But we wake up to each other and not our phones. It's the first morning I remember turning towards him and not away from him in a while.

When things got bad, I'd hole myself up in the upstairs toilet, hollering 'just a minute' to Matt, so I could answer DMs about everything from pregnancy psychosis – where you hallucinate about a baby you have lost – to where my jumpsuit is from. When things got worse, I'd lie to him about needing to go to the corner shop, and then sit on a bench near our house, scrolling through gossip forums, waiting for something bad to happen.

But I'd originally started Mother Pukka to try and do something good: to try and put something honest out there to counteract all the bronzed bodies and enviable lifestyles that made me feel so bad, because comparing your life to others can be a dangerous game.

Katherine tells me that there is a photo on her Instagram 'where I'm smiling, my outfit is immaculate, and for all intents and purposes, it looks like I'm carefree and happy. Except when that photo was taken my husband had just left me. It was a few weeks before my thirtieth birthday and he was gone overnight with just the shirt on his back. Aside from one brief meeting later to say goodbye to our dog, I never saw him again. We have to stop looking at Instagram as some kind of reality. It's like looking at *Condé Nast Traveller* at times. If you don't want to be reminded of all the places you will never go, unfollow, block, log off, switch off.'

I don't think it's always that simple, because you become invested in people (shout-out to @symmetrybreakfast and their perfectly aligned sausages).

While I don't think I've posted photos that are misleading, I've definitely had close friends, family and even Matt assume I'm fine because I strung a caption together and tapped a button. It can be very easy to see a mother's photos of her child and think she's fine, when that image ('Got a smile today!') could be the cover of a much darker story of how she's really feeling.

Many might say 'it's just an app' but a survey by *Marie Claire* recently found that a quarter of women in their thirties and a fifth in their forties are checking their phones more than 200 times a day, with most heading to Instagram. It can leave people feeling rubbish, especially if you're the person sat next to someone staring into the blue light.

I put out a request (ironically on Instagram) to ask people what impact this pixelated world is having. I received this from dad-of-two, Nathan:

'I know it sounds silly but you almost feel lonely in your own house when your wife is sat three feet away from you. I'm trying to have conversations but her phone is constantly beeping. If we try to watch anything on the television, as soon as there is an advert on the telly she picks her phone up – she's checking Instagram, she's checking her notifications and it's just all the time.'

He said he's resorted to making jokes to his wife, saying it would be easier to get hold of her if he texted or messaged even when she's in the same room. She didn't laugh.

There's even a word for it: 'technoference', the interference smartphones can have in our face-to-face social interactions.

I go head-first into the internet and find a lengthy paper for *Perspectives on Psychological Science* by University of Arizona psychology professor David Sbarra.[1] It's not just dopamine that keeps us hooked, apparently, it's our evolutionary history at play.

'The draw or pull of a smartphone is connected to very old modules in the brain that were critical to our survival. Central to

---

1   'Smartphones and Close Relationships: The Case for an Evolutionary Mismatch', PsyArXiv.com, November 2018.

the ways we connect with others are self-disclosure and respon-
siveness,' Sbarra recently said. 'Look no further than the next person
you see scrolling through Facebook and mindlessly hitting the
"like" button while his kid is trying to tell him a story.'

I am that person. Matt, by contrast, doesn't seem to need people
in the same way. Perhaps this comes back to the root of our issues
pre-iPhone. I need people, he doesn't. I want to talk, he doesn't.
Maybe he does want to talk but I'm just not listening.

Sbarra says that out of 143 married women questioned, more
than 70 per cent reported that mobile phones interfered in their
relationships. It's not 'just an app', then.

The biggest interference for us came on 3 March 2018. I got an
email from *Hello!* magazine, asking if I'd be able to step in for the
singer Rochelle Humes on a 'Star Mum' judging panel. It was an
unpaid gig but it seemed like a good opportunity to get the Flex
Appeal message out there and on a superficial level I wanted to
meet Kate Silverton. (She once lamped former editor of BBC Radio
4's *Today* programme, Rod Liddle, live on air. He later made this
statement: 'I made a stupid comment about the disabled, which
Kate rightly took exception to.')

Minutes after *Hello!* uploaded the photo of the panel to Instagram,
the comments and direct messages started flooding in about the
lack of diversity. My phone was buzzing, taking on a life of its own.
People were (justifiably) angry:

'I loved you so much and this is so disappointing. Unfollowed.'
'I've witnessed your ugly display. You have behaved like an absolute cunt.'

'Any white women here saying she shouldn't be apologizing need to check their privilege. Read *Why I'm No Longer Talking to White People About Race* by Reni Eddo-Lodge.'

I spoke about this recently to Rabya Lomas, who founded the blog She Flourished and coined the hashtag #influenceinclusivity. We had a chat over the phone in between hollers for 'potty' (her daughter) and 'dooce [juice]' (mine). She said: 'I think you have to think of the micro aggressions women of colour have had to face. It's daily, it's relentless; for you, there's always a way out.'

I also picked up the phone to Candice Brathwaite, founder of Make Motherhood Diverse, who added: 'You absolutely had to apologise but sometimes – having experienced backlash myself – it is easy to forget there's a human behind the profile. There were other people who needed to apologise, too.'

The *Sun* ran a story with this headline: '*Hello!* and Next face race storm for choosing "thin, white middle-class celebrities" as Britain's Best Mum judges'.

The *Daily Mail* ran: 'The picture that turned hunt for Britain's Best Mum into a race storm', while the *Evening Standard* went with 'Furious row erupts over *Hello!* and Next all "thin, white, middle-class" judges of Star Mum Awards.'

I spent a week feeling sick, and like people were coming to get me. I answered thousands of DMs and comments and accusations. Most were well-considered opinion, from women from all walks of life. Some were attacks: you're a fake, you're evil, you're out for yourself.

Matt told me to ignore it, but when it happens to you, you can't.

Imagine walking down the street and having a stranger tell you how disappointed they are in your work. It might sting a little but you'd be OK, you might dismiss it. Then the next one says you're a malicious liar and they hate you and you make the world worse. A few are people who have been friendly until then. That's a little harder to ignore. Then imagine there are thousands of these messages on the phone you're addicted to.

I was learning, unlearning and unravelling publicly. But each reply took time and thought and I felt sick with fear that I'd get something wrong.

I vaguely remember my mum coming over and helping out with the kids, while Matt brought my seven-month-old daughter to me whenever she needed breastfeeding. I remember her little bobbing cheeks, softly lit by the blue glow of the phone.

There was a packet of pancake mix sitting on the kitchen counter that I had promised to make with my eldest daughter an hour before everything started. Days later that pancake mix was still sitting on the counter, bookending real-life promises that hadn't been kept.

And then it grew into something else. I fielded spitting rage over entirely made-up stories: that I'd told a mother to 'get an abortion' rather than raise a child in poverty, that I was masterminding an anonymous trolling campaign. People could invent what they wanted, and some were very happy to believe the lies and spread them, leading more people to send me abusive messages. I obsessively checked forums while doing night feeds, praying nothing had been said. It all kept chipping away, and I did this while ignoring the mewling life form staring up at me.

I'd fear stepping outside, so I increasingly didn't. I felt like 'they' might be waiting in the street. Matt would hold me through night-mares – hallucinations of losing my daughter in a supermarket car park, visions of being on a floodlit astro pitch surrounded by dark-ness. It took months but eventually I sought professional help when I let straightening irons bore into the skin of my inner wrist and didn't flinch, willing something to pull me out of it all. This had happened while I was suffering some form of postnatal depres-sion. I was told I had symptoms similar to PTSD.

I try to focus on what it has taught me about women whose experiences I didn't really understand. My experience was rare, and it happened because I am now a tiny bit in the public eye. But it happens to lots of us on a smaller scale every day: little digs, people thinking the worst, fears that you've been misunderstood.

As the first users of social media, we are guinea pigs, and the psychotherapy hasn't yet caught up with the algorithm. But with the guidance of clinical psychologist Emma Hepburn (@thepsy-chologymum), who has been helping me apply cognitive understanding to this strange pixelated wilderness, I've started to slowly look up and see the rubble around me.

The main thing she's taught me is to stop, whenever I pick up my phone, and ask myself where it will lead. Do I really need to check those messages? Sometimes I do, because this is my work. Sometimes I want to, because sharing words and images with people is a basic part of how we communicate and I love looking at pictures of perfectly symmetrical breakfasts. Doggo memes still tickle my funny bone. But I've also started to realize that sometimes I don't.

I've started to see the shape of a man who has been stood in the wings, trying to keep the production going while I'm stood naked on stage, waiting for the reviews. He's been there all along, for better and worse, feeding me my forgotten lines – but I haven't seen him at all.

'Are you OK?' I ask.

'I am OK.'

'Are you sure?'

'I just want you back in the room.'

That evening we ate fish fingers, chips and peas together with our daughters, who sang 'Happy birthday, stinky poo' at a pitch only bats could decipher. It wasn't anyone's birthday.

☆☆☆

I read something recently – ironically on Twitter – while surfing about for any wisdom on love and happiness. It captured something I have probably always known but definitely always ignored. It's a tweet by the comedian Rob Delaney, and it is about the most insightful use of forty-one characters I've ever seen:

The currency of love is focused attention.

Because it really is. It's not dinners or flowers or surprise treats. It's being in the room and offering someone your eyes and mind. It's setting down your phone, or newspaper, or whatever task you're doing and giving yourself to them for a few minutes.

How often have you said 'I've just got to . . .' when actually, you don't? You've just got to look and listen, because they're more important, and the currency of love is focused attention. And if that's the case, I need to admit that I've been offering a pretty terrible exchange rate.

So I will get back in the room. I will put my phone in a box. I will stop and breathe and tell myself that focused attention is the most valuable thing I can give to the three people I love the most.

I try it that night: phone up on a bookshelf as soon as I get in. I'm a bit twitchy, like there's something I need to check, but I resist the urge. I look them all in the eye when I speak to them. I have more to say and they do too, because I don't have a phone covering the middle of my face.

Once the kids are down that night, I point out to Matt that I haven't used my phone. He's pleased but sceptical. This has been tried before.

'And I found an amazing quote from Rob Delaney: "The currency of love is focused attention".'

He smiles a bit.

'I told you about that ages ago,' he says. 'But I don't think you were listening.'

Matt

The other night, Anna asked if I wanted to leave. I didn't use the safeword and accounts weren't due.

I was a little thrown, because that question is new.

But the pattern is not and this is what tends to happen.

A domestic issue will have been mishandled. Someone will have done a shitty job performing a minor logistical task, which will have inconvenienced the other person. A school uniform will go unwashed, or a piece of work will have been overlooked. And things will escalate, because it's never actually about that thing. There will be no shouting, just disappointment. We might be sat on the sofa, ignoring a box set, or walking home to relieve a babysitter, huffing in whispers whenever anyone walks by as we try to do a convincing impression of a couple not having an argument on the way back from dinner.

Much of it will focus on my inability to discuss feelings, as though there are deep mysteries in my head rather than just fleeting thoughts about what to eat next.

If I have problems, I prefer to let them stew in the back of my mind until I know how to fix them, not parp them into the ear of someone else. When times are tough, I'd rather just swear more at technology. The other day I shouted 'twatty little bastard' at an Asda self-service till and felt much better for it. To the outsider it looked like a minor breakdown; to me it felt like therapy.

Anna likes to talk things through, while I like to change them or ignore them. A few years ago, she spent some time in a job with a pretty poisonous atmosphere. Everyone there was deeply unhappy, and every night she would detail the psychological horrors of the place. I would tell her she should quit, I could support her for a bit, and did she fancy Thai or Indian?

I know that solutions are not always what's required, but I can't get beyond the simple equation that every issue has an action that can correct it. And so, when my solutions get ignored, I shut down a little. She calls me as closed as an unripe clam.

But the irony is that I'm married to someone whose face turned away about three years ago, with her eyes zoned in to a distant digital world.

Anna's smartphone is the most important tool in her working

life. In 2015, when she started Mother Pukka, Anna became prolific on Instagram, posting daily, often more than once, and took great care over her imagery. She wrote honestly about everything to do with our lives. And alongside the self-deprecating humour, she began campaigning for more employers to offer flexible working.

It wasn't unusual to come home and find her filming in the kitchen, shooting with our eldest (and then only) daughter, showing how to 'distress' a shop-bought cake to make it look homemade. I began to contribute as well. We began to write about our experiences with miscarriage.

And what kept us going was the response. Anna began to get hundreds of messages from women who said they felt less alone after their own miscarriages, or in the postnatal fug, or encouraged to put in a flexible-working request to their boss. The follower count kept ticking upwards. It reached 10,000 and kept going.

We'd both been journalists for more than a decade, writing for national newspapers and glossy magazines, but found that for the first time we could write honestly about things that mattered to us and some of those things seemed to connect with others.

It began to earn an income. Brands got in touch to ask about sponsored Instagram posts. Anna got asked to speak on panels. And when we pitched an idea for our first book, *Parenting the Shit Out of Life*, four different publishers said yes. We finished it a week before our second daughter was born.

Anna had created a job that meant she could continue to work and still be there for the kids. The follower count sailed past 100,000 and kept going.

But it was all-consuming. I'd return from work and we'd get the kids fed and bathed, her with one eye on the phone. Maybe one of us would cook, and then she'd spend hours tapping away. She got hundreds of DMs a day, and they're hard to ignore when it's someone confiding about a miscarriage or postnatal depression. The hours between 7p.m. and midnight became the most important part of her working day, but she'd often start the moment she woke up, rolled over and reached for her phone.

I saw the advantages, and the hard work, but it also began to grate. When I spoke to her she often wouldn't respond. If she paused for a moment, she'd be staring mutely ahead like she was in a waking coma. I got snappy when I saw her with her phone and wanted to snatch it off her. I wanted to throw it against a wall. She was there, but she was absent. I'd bring down our youngest for her feed, and hand her over silently, as Anna latched her and kept tapping away.

And there were critics to respond to. Some said, 'You're only doing this for money,' to which she typically said, 'Yes, I'm a writer, and this means I can be paid to write.' Some said, 'You're exploiting your children,' to which we typically said, 'Maybe, but we don't think so: we're careful what we show and ultimately this is to allow us to work and still see them.' Usually it was civil – curiosity more than criticism – and she'd happily have the discussion. A few anonymous accounts sent abuse.

And then she got asked to judge some awards. She will have told you more by now, but I can tell you what it was like to watch.

She spent weeks in an intense bubble, answering every comment, apologising a hundred times, as the anxiety built and our youngest daughter pawed at her chest. She asked me to keep away, and said a man can't be seen to defend her. I told her to ignore it. But of course, when it's you who's being attacked, that's a little hard to do. After a month or so the comments eased off and the chat boards quieted.

But it also made her a target. For a year afterwards, new accounts popped up – usually with blank avatars and following only her – to fire a few messages of abuse into her DMs or comments and then slip away. People invented stories about her.

And I became resentful at the anonymous blob of snark. That a – usually, but not always – faceless social media or chat board account can invent a lie and push it out unchallenged. That it will gather momentum on WhatsApp groups, and that these things can arrive at once in a flurry of abuse or criticism in the middle of a toddlers' play date or a rare dinner for two. That twenty or a hundred critical messages ('I'm so disappointed in you . . .', 'I can't believe that you . . .', 'You're such a cunt') can sit like a rat in the skull, scratching away, while 10,000 supportive ones wash off in an instant.

But there's also a resentment – an unhealthy, unfair resentment – that she can't just set it aside: that when I say 'It's not worth worrying about' (perhaps humanity's most unhelpful phrase), she continues to worry.

She's drifted away in this blue glow, but she won't let me help her. She wants me to be there, but she doesn't want to try my advice. And then I get angry with her because the problems persist.

So I call in some expert help – from three of the country's most revered therapists – to see how people in relationships are supposed to communicate. I am a therapy sceptic, so this goes against my natural instincts. My feeling is that if it's really that bad, tell a pal or partner. If it's not, stop grizzling. I realize this contradicts the (mostly good) trend towards openness about mental health. But I view therapists a bit like hypnotists or faith healers: spooky mind-manipulators whose spiel only works if you're willing to convince yourself that it has.

Their neatness also troubles me, as someone who tends to find himself always looking a bit shabbier than everyone else in the room. The men all seem to have perfectly shaved skulls or very angular cuts, and the women tend to look like they've just stepped out of a glamorous American legal drama where they right injustices and flirt outrageously for sixty minutes every Wednesday night.

I'm also uncomfortable with the fact they may know things about me that I don't know myself, and could be sitting there thinking, 'Entry-level narcissist with underlying guilt complex. Let's see if we can stretch this out to six months.'

None of these assumptions is fair, but it does mean I approach these therapists with a resolutely narrow mind.

The first is David Waters, a Brit recently relocated to New York. He was on the editorial launch team at *Men's Health* magazine in the nineties and stayed for a decade, while also writing for most of the UK's national newspapers. After a painful break-up with a boyfriend several years ago, he retrained and built up a psychotherapy business.

I confess to my therapy scepticism and he admits it's not uncommon, particularly for men.

'Of the heterosexual couples that I work with, it's usually her driving the therapy session rather than him,' he says.

I'm reminded of a friend of ours who told her husband they were going for a lunch date, only to take him to a marriage therapist as a surprise. They have since separated.

'The guy might be there slightly reluctantly. Although that can flip quite quickly and suddenly he starts to see the benefit,' he says, 'but ultimately, relationships over time are the closest to being in therapy without actually being in therapy. You have to face your own selfishness and your own demons because your partner, someone that you've been living with for a number of years, is holding up a mirror to you. What we see reflected back isn't always that pretty. We have to see our selfishness and at times our cruelty.'

There's certainly some truth to that for me. There are times when I'm impatient and not willing to listen because I feel I've listened enough. Most of the issues we've faced have been ones that have affected Anna more. I've written in the past about the impact of miscarriage on men, but Anna was the one who physically lived through them. The social media pillorying fell on her shoulders, with me as a gormless, arm-stroking bystander.

She has deep and complex relationships with friends, family and colleagues to discuss; I have a few drinking buddies and call my mum once a year to tell her what train we'll be on when we come down to visit.

For a long time I was very proud of my ability to be, as I saw it, a rock of stability and a source of empathy: to sit quietly and listen, saying in my kindest voice that everything will be OK. It is an ugly reflection in my own mirror, but perhaps my empathy pool has run a little dry now. Perhaps, when I feel I've done enough caring, I become snappy about minor logistics rather than explaining that

I may not be the rock I've always tried to portray and want some caring in return.

So I ask David for some practical tips.

'There's a very powerful tool, which I use with couples, called differentiation. It's about how you navigate conflict. It's not about winning, that's for sure. It's about saying, "When you do X, I feel like this." We find it very hard to articulate, but actually we tend to get a much more profound conversation that opens up.'

I ask him for a few more specifics.

'Well, "You never do the washing-up. I do everything around here." That would be the attack. A very understandable defence would be, "Well, I'm at work all day. If it wasn't for me, the bills wouldn't be paid." You're defending yourself with another attack. You're just battling it out by lobbing weapons at each other. To that initial, "You never do the washing-up" you might come back and say, "I feel really disappointed, because I see that you do so much. And I feel there are probably things I do that maybe don't get recognized."'

It sounds simple, but suspiciously like I'd be talking about my feelings. Almost as though, rather than silently swearing about the hair tongs, I should be saying, 'Darling, I'm disappointed that you often leave the hair tongs where I step on them, because it feels like you are invalidating my concerns about toe-scalding.'

Such emotional sense does not come easily. That is not the man I am, but maybe it is the man I should be.

I turn back to Charlotte Fox Weber, who told us to sit nose to nose.

While I accept that I could sometimes be more sensitive in my phrasing, I still feel that the biggest obstacle to us reconnecting is the collection of plastics, metals and minerals that sits in Anna's hand every evening.

'There's a terrible joke about a child who said to his mother, "Mommy when I grow up I want to be a phone so that you'll look at me," and I think that applies to relationships across the board,' Fox Weber says. 'It is increasingly recognized that phone addiction is a real addiction. It's not just a kind of pesky habit, it can be extremely compulsive.'

The newness of smartphones means that there are few studies on the subject, but those that exist each tell a similar story. One by Korea University[2] found that teenage boys diagnosed with smartphone addiction all had higher levels of GABA (which inhibits neurons) and lower levels of glutamate-glutamine (which sparks brain signals) than non-addicted peers. This makes people less attentive (are you still there?).

Smartphone use has been linked to the addictive drip of dopamine in the brain that keeps our reward centres ticking over (much like with those dive-bombing pigeons and Tinder) and can cause addiction. And that addiction can make you depressed, according to the *BMC Psychiatry* journal, which looked at twenty-two peer-reviewed papers on the subject and found that 'the positive correlation between smartphone addiction and depression is alarming.'[3]

---

2   'Neurotransmitters in Young People with Internet and Smartphone Addiction: A Comparision with Normal Controls and Changes after Cognitive Behavioral Therapy', Hyung Suk Seo et al., Korea University, November 2017

3   'The relationship between addiction to smartphone usage and depression among adults', *BMC Psychiatry*, 25 May 2018.

It's beginning to make me wonder if, like our porn sites, our smartphones need a health warning.

I do the Iowa State University test for 'nomophobia' or fear of separation from your smartphone, and score 90 out of 140, just a few short of the 100 level for 'severe nomophobia' and the need for 'an intervention'. I send it to Anna and she scores 132.

'I think that being aware of it as a problem is really important,' says Fox Weber. 'Not in a shaming way, but everyone knows that phones are a problem, so it's about interrupting that pattern in a very specific way. Coming up with a rule: we are not going to have phones at the dinner table or go to sleep with my phone in the same room.'

So we do those things. I buy a box to keep our phones in. They will be put away at certain hours. That may help. But I still feel that I'm dancing around the bigger issues of how we communicate and that I remain an emotionally lumpen dolt in need of an Ikea-manual-simple guide to my wife.

I put some specifics to Andrew G. Marshall, the sharp-eyed, shaven-headed therapist who told me to stop worshipping my children. He is also the author of twenty books, including his most successful: *I Love You But I'm Not in Love With You*. He gives pretty short shrift to my claims of emotional divviness.

'That's one of the common mistakes that we make: this idea that men are crap at relationships and therefore they're the ones who have to change,' he tells me. 'I don't actually believe you mean it, which is possibly one of the problems as well. Men will admit that they're crap at relationships and must do better, but actually they're very angry about the idea that they're not listened to. They're open to being patronized, but they're incredibly angry about it as well, so it doesn't make for a very good combination.'

I put three questions to him, to see how useless I may or may not be.

First, the huffing. How much harm do my muttered 'fuckssakes' – about laundry, hair tongs, bills and the like – actually do?

'My suspicion is it does have an impact on your relationship because you have a forever-being-fed resentment that's just underneath the surface,' says Marshall. 'You're irritated with her about something, but actually, either you don't want to go there because you think, "Why should I bother, because there's no point having the same argument?" or you've done that so often that you're actually not even aware that you're annoyed.'

Second then, is the emotional chats. Whenever Anna asks how I am, my response is typically 'fine' because I generally believe that I am.

'When she asks how you are feeling, that's a bloody good chance to bring it all up. "I'm feeling fed up", "I think we need to re-look at ABC again". Have that conversation. You need to explore and understand before you reach action, but you've got to action already. You're saying, "Pick up your hair tongs," but we don't actually know what the real issue is. It's probably going to be more complicated than just the tongs. There might be issues about money or sex or ten million other things, and it's only when we actually really understand it that we can actually move to the action phase.'

And third is the smartphone addiction and my response to it.

'The time to talk about it is not when you get to the point you're so exasperated you're saying, "For god's sake, can't you put that thing away?" Because immediately, the whole conversation is going to go badly.'

I explain a little more about Anna's work and the unpleasant rumblings in the underbelly of social media. While the scale of it for her may be unusual, the nature of the issue is pretty common.

'Often when there are long-running issues, one party just says, "I've done everything I can. It's over to you now." Or in that incredibly unhelpful way, they say to men, "man up" or to women, "get over it". I don't think that's really very helpful.'

Of course, I know that he's right. I probably am suffering a little from 'empathy exhaustion'. (I've just made that term up and am not a psychotherapist. They prefer the term 'compassion fatigue'.)

He then talks me through what he calls 'the drama triangle', which looks a little like this:

THE DRAMA TRIANGLE

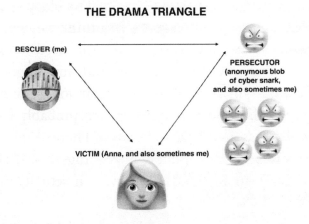

At the bottom is the victim (Anna), on the right is the persecutor (anonymous blob of cyber snark), and on the left is me (rescuer). According to the theory behind it, any one person can switch to any of the roles at any time (and even occupy more than one at once).

'You were in the rescuing mode, weren't you?' says Marshall. 'You were going to try and rescue her from all this. When you fail to rescue her, you get upset and then you become the persecutor and she's still in the victim place. Or you feel, "I've done all these things to try and help her, she's now having a go at me about it," and now you're the victim.'

There is a certain truth to that. I feel aggrieved that she hasn't followed any of my suggestions, and more aggrieved still when she starts digging at me for not being supportive enough. I also sometimes dig at her about not listening, which puts me firmly in the place of persecutor. So where to next?

THE WINNER'S TRIANGLE

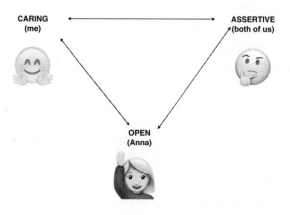

Why, the winner's triangle, of course.

'Here, all you have to do as the rescuer is care rather than rescue, and there's a big difference. And when you become the persecutor, you have to be assertive rather than domineering. Domineering is "We'll fix it like this", whereas assertive is "I have my opinions, you have your opinions, they're both equally valid, what are we going to do about it?" It's very much adult to adult rather than parent–child.'

This rings a loud bell for me, and I remember the time that in the middle of a minor row I – teeth-grindingly exasperated – called Anna by our eldest daughter's name. No one likes to feel their complaints are being equated to a child's demands for a Cadbury's Creme Egg.

But there's also work that Anna can do in this new triangle.

'Whoever is in the victim place has to go into the open mode. Being a victim is closed off. You're either in a ball saying, "Don't hit me," or you're saying, "Nothing is ever going to affect me again." But in the open mode, they can begin to say, "Why has this affected me so deeply?" So one person is listening, one person is assertive, one is open, and you can begin to see that actually all of those places on the triangle are equally good. How do you get from rescuing to caring? It's listening without trying to come up with a solution.'

If left alone, he suggests, 'she's going to feel angry that she had a crisis, and you were there for the first six months, but after that, you clocked out.'

I have a shivering aversion to anything that feels like a PowerPoint presentation of human emotion, which the triangle does (mostly because I made it in PowerPoint), but it's hard to argue with the sense of it, and the clarity that twenty minutes with Marshall has brought after two years of ignoring the problem.

'We've got all the myths about love: that love is all you need, love will build a bridge, love will conquer all, ain't no mountain high enough because I'm so full of love for you. And we think that we can neglect our relationship because we love each other, we can put each other low down on the list of priorities after the children, after the guinea pigs, and after work. It doesn't matter that you love each other: love needs to be fed. Love needs to be nurtured. You can't just take it for granted.'

And maybe that's the problem. It never was the tongs or the bills or the laundry. It's that I want her to be as she was: someone light and unburdened who makes me think 'Oh, wow, we could do anything' instead of 'Oh god, we've got to do so much.' That's not because she's lost her lightness, but because I have a little. I have allowed myself to become weary and burdened, instead of hopeful and blasé.

And I don't want to bring these things up in the nice moments, because it tends to ruin those.

I'm reminded of something David Waters said when I spoke to him: 'A happy ending is misleading, because I think a true loving relationship is an adventure that just keeps growing. There's nothing more tragic than the cliché of Valentine's evenings couples who have obviously been together a very long time, sitting, gazing at their food and not at each other.'

But, I wonder, how do you make sure that you don't end up like that?

10

Stick or Twist

Where's your happy ending?

Anna

There's talk of a 'lightbulb moment' when it's clear that you want to meander towards incontinence with someone. You just *know*. But I think a slowly-turning-up-the-dimmer-switch moment is more realistic. Anyone can get high on oxytocin and proclaim their undying love in those first heady months. It takes muscle to fan the embers twelve years on.

One dimmer-switch moment comes from a tetchy phone call after we've read each other's chapters. I'm in the seaside town of Whitstable, in a small Victorian terrace, trying to write these final words away from The Needs (perhaps that's the real answer: abscond).

Matt is tending to the homestead. I've just finished reading his chapter on the Portuguese free-love commune and this leaped off the page like a frog with violent flatulence: 'the electric promise of sex hangs in the air, and I found myself wondering about some women I spoke to: "If I lived here, might we have something?"'

It appears he wants to have sex with someone else.

I'm on the phone to him. He's found my lost debit card in the tumble dryer and the conversation is laced with implications of my financial and administrative ineptitude.

I snap at him about his lack of contact while I've been away.

'What's wrong? Why are you angry?'

'I don't like your tone.'

'There's no tone.'

'There's a tone.'

After the call, I send him this on WhatsApp: 'Sorry I was short with you but you sometimes come across as abrasive, which makes me defensive.'

I accompany this with a screen grab from psychologist Silvan Tomkins' theory of nine affects:

'Everyone has a personal script of how they understand and relate to their emotions. There are a lot of people who have absolutely no idea about other people's internal states. Instead, they'll react to those people by thinking they exaggerate everything. So some people will see exaggerated behaviour in what are actually completely normal emotional patterns.'

Seventeen minutes pass.

I can hear Matt's sigh from sixty miles away. There will also be an eye roll and an inner monologue about 'emotional guff'.

I offer some balance with an extract from the book *F*ck Feelings* by Michael and Sarah Bennett:

'Some people don't express feelings well through words but they express them through actions. They show up. They take up responsibility. Their way of expressing feelings and showing love is to ask you how your septic tank is working.'

I summarize with: 'I hope your septic tank is OK.'

Matt responds: 'My way of showing feelings is making tea and smutty gags. I'm currently looking at car insurance.'

'I'm researching places to stay for Howie's wedding.'

'Is this sexting?'

This is the dimmer switch going up a tiny notch. I'm starting to realize that I'm not hypersensitive and Matt's not as emotionally constrained as a shellfish.

I'm also starting to think that the national curriculum Key Stage ten should include:

1 How to file a tax return.
2 How to iron a shirt.
3 How to say sorry.

And the last of those should carry extra credit. I message again to ask if he wants to sleep with a Portuguese woman. He says, 'Most of them weren't Portuguese,' which he believes to be funny, then assures me he doesn't. I tell him it's OK to want to (The School of Life advises this), just not to 'seal the deal'.

Then I say sorry for thinking the worst of him when he's been doing his best. And sorry for scoring points when we should be on the same side. He's sorry too. It's what might be described as a sorry scene.

But we did at least manage to stop, consider each other's feelings and discuss them. That is enough to raise the dimmer a bit. I wonder how easy it is to raise it up and keep it there for all the years ahead.

I want to speak to a happy old person.

It's 6.25a.m. and the sun is slowly pooling over Whitstable Harbour. The air is briny and warm. I'm here to speak to a man who has handled plenty of fish and knows the sea well. His name is Derrick West, he's ninety, and the UK's oldest fisherman. He agreed to meet me, but only if I could get there before his shift starts at 7a.m.

He's worked here his entire life. He's been married to his wife, June, for more than seventy years and has faded tattoos of a ship on one arm and a seagull on the other. He's never lived outside of Whitstable and owns West Whelks, a fishery on the harbour that specializes in crustaceans and molluscs.

I apologise for being a few minutes late. I haven't slept properly in three nights because Matt's words and looming deadlines have been pinballing about my head. I flit between thinking I'm a rubbish catch and a need to heed eighty-four-year-old sex blogger Joyce's advice to 'cling on, my lovelies'.

Derrick is a man of few words but his face is set to smile at all times. His son Graham is hauling green nets weighed with whelks onto a nearby scale as he hollers, 'You won't find a happier man than Dad.'

So how did Derrick get to celebrate seven decades with one person? How's he still smiling?

He jokes about the size of my sunglasses and tells me to take them off. My eyes are red and I mumble about hayfever, which is not common by the sea.

'I think we need to stop putting pressure on one person to be The One,' he says, holding my hand in his: 'I get very cross with these young boys who go out there alone fishing. You have to think in case you go overboard, who is going to help you out?'

I'm a little taken aback by this firm grip from a stranger but it's kind and anchoring; I wonder when I last reached out to a stranger.

I ask if June isn't The One to save him when he goes overboard.

'She isn't,' he says quietly. 'I won't always be here. She might not be. But this place I have,' he gesticulates towards the harbour, 'these people I see every day on the seafront. My son Graham. My next-door neighbour. Happiness is all around us and to pin it to one person, well, that's never going to end well. I love June but she can't be the only one to save me.'

I wonder about the pressure I've put on Matt, and wonder if I've expected him to be this hunk of manly rock who can mend me when he's probably needed to break and be fixed too. I wonder if I've taken his 'swallow and defecate method' at face value, when I should have heeded his mum's whispers of 'He's a softie underneath.'

I think we've failed at something my parents have succeeded at: breaking together.

It reminds me of something Bethany said a few days earlier about unhappiness. She told me: 'I was supposed to be happy. I was the transgender poster girl of the University of Oregon journalism department. I wore rainbow dresses and smiled for the camera until one day when I couldn't be the happy transgender poster girl any more. I had found my happy ending publicly but privately I was very sad.'

Perhaps there hasn't been room for Matt to be sad. And I think I know the things he would have been sad about: being unable to say what he thinks for fear of tipping me over the edge; watching me become an anxious person illuminated by an iPhone.

It feels like the world puts happiness at the centre of aspiration.

It's the carrot we're meant to chase like donkeys along Brighton Beach. Get the grades! Bag the promotion! Marry the person! Have the kids! Buy the house! Enjoy the life! Or, in Bethany's case, 'Be the transgender poster girl!' Then what?

There is shame in unhappiness. We're fed images of gurning couples on films and TV and social media, but never shown the beauty of a wife holding her wife's hand through a failed IVF attempt. We're shown the Olympian bodies of Love Islanders, but we're never party to the lows once the cameras stop.

There's beauty in brokenness. Matt and I have been so focused on chasing sunshine moments that I think we haven't properly looked at the clouds. There have been birthdays, anniversaries and weddings in our iCal, but nothing that recognizes our biggest achievement, which has been sticking together even when we've been falling apart at the seams.

Is the key to happiness being able to comfortably sit in this unhappiness? To not see it as failure but to see it as the gritty mortar that holds things together?

Maybe it's about opening our doors in a world that increasingly distrusts its neighbours. Who is living next door or sitting opposite you? Why are you staring at your phone when you could be making someone feel less alone? Why are we looking down when we could look up?

Bethany put this in her bio on dating site Harmony: 'I am not your experiment, I am here to be loved.' She got one response in a year. It was from a woman down the road who she didn't fancy but now counts as a close friend; someone who would haul her out if she went overboard.

I head back on the train to London, to get a view from someone closer to home.

Seventy-five-year-old Cordelia 'Dee' Tocqueville is the UK's longest-serving lollipop lady and happens to patrol the zebra crossing on my way to work. I've passed her twice a day for two years and often wondered about the story behind this strict ('Please come on, children') yet kindly community figure.

We take seats on a graffitied park bench as she explains that she has a forty-six-year clean record of ensuring children cross the road safely, other than one time: 'It was back in 1974 when there weren't seatbelts and a car went round the corner and a toddler fell out of the door. Everyone was fine!' she chirps.

Dee plays Uno on Tuesdays with her friends and is also a powerful cribbage player. She met her husband Don ('Yes, we were Dee and Don, which sounds like a children's television programme!') in 1963 at a party near her local pub and he asked her to go on a date to a wrestling match.

'It wasn't your average first date,' she says. 'A few months later he handed me a big cardboard box with "6th May" written on it. He pointed to the date and said, "That's the day we're getting engaged." And that's what happened – he was a man of his word.'

In 1984, Don passed away.

'The word "widow" is like living in a shadow,' says Dee. 'It is a lonely word and I am not a lonely person. I loved his company but I love my own too. I enjoy a bowl of Bran Flakes in the morning and reading a serial killer book before work. I enjoy seeing the children crossing the road safely. I enjoy being part of something. I think before you can be happy with someone, you have to be happy alone.'

I think back to the family dinners where I've ridiculed Matt's need for solitude. I've taken it as a slight on me when it's just part of who *he* needs to be. Being alone doesn't equal loneliness, I think, and the dimmer switch goes up a bit.

There are parallels in Derrick the fisherman and Dee's life experiences. They seem open to the world around them instead of piling everything on the shoulders of the person next to them. There's a sense of community that I think we're desperately seeking online and failing at offline.

Dee continues: 'Because the chances are one of you will end up alone – and I don't mean that pessimistically, just realistically. The chances are stacked against being together forever. But I am very happy knowing what I love. Even if Bran Flakes might not be to everyone's taste.'

I've imagined Matt's knock knees and grey beard as he slopes around, clutching a mug of tea the colour of soil. I've imagined the small flat we'd live in with a delicatessen round the corner so he can always have a steady flow of his favourite cheeses. I've imagined us reading books together until our eyes go and having extended chats about the boiler. What if I've just not told him this enough?

I think the mould creeps in when you think your life might be better elsewhere. They say the grass is always greener but maybe you just need to water yours a little better. That's not to say stick with an arse of a human, just that other lives sometimes look a little more alluring because you don't have to live them.

As my mum says: 'Don't compare your garden to others, there's always going to be a fancier water feature over the hedge.'

It makes me think of those drawings that can be seen two ways. There's a famous one by Danish psychologist Edgar Rubin where some people see a vase, while others see two faces. It depends on what you're looking for and where you focus your attention. Maybe our brain can play similar tricks on us when looking at those we love: some see the flaws and no longer see the good, even though it's right there.

So what have I seen in the process of writing this book?

1 Matt and I want to be with each other after a few days apart. There's the initial relief of uninterrupted sleep away from the kids, then it's just a bit rubbish. Matt admits that when he was away for a few days working on the final edits of his pages, he made up an invisible friend called Dave who he spoke to in a Scottish accent about why he never did the tea run. Distance doesn't make the heart grow fonder but it makes you more aware of the small things (like flowers brought in from the garden) that make a big difference.

2 Matt has sought out tangible solutions to our problems. I've sought the human story not the scientific response. And this isn't as binary as man seeks numbers, woman seeks hugs. It's just that we look at the world differently and we can, perhaps, learn from each other instead of banging heads.

3 And this is not something I ever imagined writing: Matt isn't my world. He's someone who could go and live on a free-love commune if he so chooses, even though I would prefer it if he didn't. He still might go on to have a truly happy ending with someone else. I, in turn, might end up in a throuple or boiling whelks for a living. I love him, but I cannot take him for granted. We cannot take each

other for granted. We cannot live in this fantasy world of 'love conquers all' because it sometimes doesn't.

☆☆☆

I had a sticker on my bedroom wall when I was a teenager that read: 'It's better to regret the things you've done than the things you haven't'. The words were under a photo of a girl doing a 360-degree turn on a snowboard and, despite half-hearted attempts at Milton Keynes indoor snowdome, I'm yet to pull it off.

A few years ago, palliative nurse Bronnie Ware wrote an article called 'Top Five Regrets of the Dying', from her time spent with people on their death bed. These were the five:

I wish I'd had the courage to live a life true to myself, not the life others expected of me.
I wish I didn't work so hard.
I wish I'd had the courage to express my feelings.
I wish I had stayed in touch with my friends.
I wish that I had let myself be happier.

I think of the anger of miscarriage we've carried. I think of the times we haven't held hands, haven't kissed and haven't chosen to be kind to each other when the opportunity has always been there, because one day the opportunity might not be.

I've left the following interview until the end because I've not been sure how to ask the questions.

I first met Rachel Clements online. She commented on an Instagram story I posted where I tried on an Ann Summers corset, which broke as I removed it. We united over a gusset, which is not a usual springboard for friendship.

How you go from this frivolous exchange to asking how someone feels about their life ending is something I've been painfully aware I could get wrong. Rachel is thirty and has an incurable form of pulmonary fibrosis. She has 24 per cent use of her lungs. She is unlikely to live to see these words in print.

She lives in Ely, Cambridgeshire, with her three children and her forty-five-year-old husband, Richard, a Ford car salesman, who picks me up from the train station with their middle child, three-year-old son Louis, in the back seat.

Richard and Rachel met at a showroom where he was selling cars and she was working on reception. It was an office manager called Sonia who told them they needed to sort out their sexual frustration, which they did and which led to them getting married two years later, in 2013. Rich has always known about Rachel's illness.

We drive past a Tesco near the showroom and he tells me that is where they had their first lunch date.

I ask him the most blunt, bumbling question, and immediately wish I hadn't: 'How are you?'

He says, like most people suffering inconceivable sadness, that he is fine. I don't imagine it's easy to unpack all this to a near-stranger. We sit in silence and he winds the window down.

Their house has an 'I'll be there in a Prosecco' welcome mat on the porch. Their youngest son has just stopped breastfeeding and as the three grown-ups talk, Louis throws a Thomas the Tank

Engine book at Richard's feet in attention-seeking rebellion. Rachel's fourteen-year-old daughter makes up the family of five.

Richard untangles the two boys, who keep ducking under the wires of Rachel's oxygen tank, herds them into the kitchen and asks if we want tea.

Rachel has an ethereal air about her, with white-blonde hair and piercing blue eyes.

'The hardest thing is wishing time to speed up so my boys can remember me, and then wanting it to slow down too,' Rachel says. 'I'm aware that I don't have time. I'm aware of time. I feel the huge pressure of time. I need to make time count.'

She says that making time count doesn't just mean writing letters to her boys for the birthdays she's going to miss, or making memory boxes. But that it's in having normal feelings: being angry, being sad, reaching out and cuddling up. 'I call Rich a dickhead still. He calls me Bub.'

I think of my dad calling my mum Big Bird.

'I still do that thing where I won't add kisses to a text message when I'm cross. He isn't treading on eggshells and neither am I because we're already in pieces, to be honest. I can't sit here and sugar-coat it, like we're living each day like it's my last. We're not. I can't. We're arguing. We're crying. We're breaking.'

I think of what my parents said about breaking together and wonder how that translates to a darkness that weighs as heavily as this. Rachel and I speak for an hour, with pauses intermittently when she needs to gather her breath.

I feel invasive being there, like I'm stealing time that she could be spending with her family. But she wants to share her story as widely as possible, so her kids can remember it, and to try to raise money through crowd-funding to cover their mortgage so Richard can care for the family once she's gone.

Her focus is on the practical and how things will be when she's not there, but she also seems to want to share some of her anger at the hand she's been dealt.

Richard drives me back to the station, first proudly showing me the mobility scooter and oxygen tank he's neatly fitted into the boot. He lights up when speaking about the practical ways he's made their life better. He says: 'There is nothing on Google to help me with the future. You can't just type in "What do I do?"'

We say our goodbyes and I head to the train. I'm not sure what to say as we part. You can't say, 'good luck' or 'see you soon'. I feel lucky to have spoken to Rachel and Richard, and to have been party to their quirks and quibbles – the moment he brings her iced water without her asking and the look they exchange: a unique code that only these two know.

They're brave and strong, but they're also living a daily tragedy and it doesn't seem very fair. But things aren't always fair, and none of us can know when they will go bad. One thing we do know is that our time is finite and, if we let it, it can run away from us.

The dimmer switch has been going up for me, making me realize that for my happy ending, I need to make more time for the people I love. To stop grabbing for my phone the moment the kids are asleep and start grabbing for Matt instead. To see that time wasted on scrolling or sulking is time lost for good.

My happy ending will be with Matt, just as long as I can make time for him.

Matt

She's read my pages and it hasn't gone well.

Until today, I've felt pretty sure I do a good job of being a Loving Husband and a Nice Man. Turns out I'm a grotty perv who thinks he's a modern-day suffragette because he can operate a spin cycle.

We shared our chapters with each other a few days ago and both held our breath a bit. They were a strange couple of days, each of us saying, very quietly, 'So, um, where are you up to?'

I was a little worried that some bits might surprise her, but I'd also written that I knew immediately that I wanted to grow old with her, and that I miss her after a couple of days away. I'd written that I like her face and her slightly wonky nose. These things, I thought, should be reassuring. They reassure me.

These were her key 'learnings':

1 I fancied all the hippies.
2 I didn't think about her when I stayed with the monks.
3 I'm a dick about the laundry.

I've read hers too, of course, and this is what I've discovered:

1 She cries more than I thought.
2 Porn is very definitely an issue.
3 I'm not putting my cock in a shoe for anyone.

Writing a book with your partner is a tense process, especially when that book is about your lives. Over about nine months, we have been saying things like: 'I'm going to a free-love commune' (me) or 'I've met a really interesting throuple' (her) and keeping our conclusions secret.

We've also talked about her social media experience, and the impact it has had, and the places it led her to, both good and very bad.

And there are also niggles around working on a 'creative project' together. I have strong feelings about adjectives and their appropriate use. Anna has strong feelings about ignoring my opinions. Carole, our editor, may have to add 'part-time marriage therapist' to her CV.

So what have I really learned from her pages? Perhaps that she worries a bit too much about my minor grumps, but also that I'm a bit quick to dismiss her concerns. That if left, the niggles may really form a stalagmite at the heart of the marriage, and that they are more constant than they've ever been.

So is that something to just live with? Do you just bumble on in a haze of 'could-be-worse' until the days when you've got your teeth in a jar and a catheter in your belly?

It makes me wonder how people feel at the actual end, in those moments before they hop off this mortal coil to whatever comes next (or doesn't). I decide I need to speak to someone about dying.

Anna Lyons is one of the UK's only 'end-of-life' doulas. In the same way that a birth doula will prepare people for having a baby, an end-of-life doula will prepare people for death. Since 2001, she has helped lots of those who were close to the end, and I want to know what she's learned.

'People regret working really hard, not spending time with their family or their friends. They regret wasting their life in a job they don't love,' she tells me.

And what about relationships? I ask her.

'One lady I worked with desperately wished she hadn't stayed with her husband for sixty years,' she says.

The woman had been from a generation where divorce was taboo and, 'felt really pissed off that she was made to stay in a loveless marriage for her entire adult life,' Lyons tells me. 'She nursed him while he was dying, and after he died she spent quite a lot of time being very, very sad and lots of people assumed it was because she was so devastated at the loss of her husband. But she was devastated at the loss of *her* life. He had died when she was in her late seventies. She lived till her late nineties and never really felt able to meet anyone else.'

The other common regret she hears is that people couldn't make good relationships work.

'When you're dying alone, people think about what could have been – the person they wish they'd fought harder for or they had tried harder with. They're really common regrets of relationships, whether it be platonic or romantic or familial.'

But maybe it's easy, with hindsight, to know who you should have tried harder with and who you should have got away from sooner. How do people know in the moment?

I put in a call to an old mate called Noel, who recently separated from his wife. They have two daughters and have decided to share the family home while renting a small flat. One parent spends half the week at the house with the kids while the other is in the flat, and then they swap.

We started out as journalists at about the same time, and his girls are just a little older than mine. And being from Yorkshire, he also prides himself on speaking plainly.

'You want to ask me probing, emotionally wrenching questions about my divorce, so you can profit off it for your book?' he asks.

I explain that yes, I do, but 'profit' is quite a loose term in book publishing these days.

Mostly, I want to hear how he knew it was all over and that their issues were something more than the daily niggles that can happen when people have jobs and kids and feelings.

'It's definitely nothing to do with bickering. It's way deeper – the realization that there are massive fundamentals that you just don't agree on,' he says. 'Once we started unpicking some of the issues, then those fundamental differences came to the fore quite strongly. That's when your eyes are opened, and it's like, "Jesus Christ, we've been living what is essentially a lie for a number of years."'

I ask what the differences were.

'We had no shared purpose, we have no shared interests. We'd spend a lot of time in separate rooms, just following our own likes. We started doing stuff together less and less. When the kids come along, they can be a real distraction from your own issues. We started spending less time together outside of the children. Once we started looking, it just became obvious that we'd massively grown apart.'

The separation is still raw, he tells me, and the process is not easy, particularly with kids asking when everything will be back to normal. But neither of them has any doubts about the choice they made.

And Noel's tale is relatively typical. 'Drifting apart' is given as the second most common reason for divorce, according to Co-op Legal Services, behind adultery and just ahead of 'money issues'. ('Different parenting styles' comes in at six, with the slightly harsh 'changes in appearance' at seven. Maybe it's time to shed my holiday weight from 2012.)

But whatever the reason, once you've decided it's over, it seems that the best thing to do is quit. People talk about 'staying together for the kids', but what kind of warped idea of a happy relationship is that likely to leave them with?

Researchers at Montclair University in the US recently studied[1] data on American families from 1987 to 2003. They wanted to see how divorce affected children in those marriages. They found that kids from 'high-conflict' homes – those with constant arguments – where the parents stayed together were much more likely to end up divorced themselves than those whose parents split up or stayed together but were in 'low-conflict' marriages. (They didn't investigate 'no-conflict' marriages, because they weren't unicorn hunters.)

So staying together for the kids is a terrible idea. If you want a happy ending, stay together because of how you feel for each other or accept that things have ended and move on.

But that's not where we are. We're together because we want to be – I just wonder if we want to be as much as we did before, and in the same ways.

---

1   'Conflict or Divorce? Does Parental Conflict and/or Divorce Increase the Likelihood of Adult Children's Cohabiting and Marital Dissolution?', Constance T. Gager, Scott T. Yabiku and Miriam R. Linver, *Marriage & Family Review*, January 2016.

When I started researching this book, I saw a TED-style talk online called 'Why You Will Marry the Wrong Person' by Alain de Botton. He's probably Britain's best-known philosopher, which is a bit like being France's best-known morris dancer, given our suspicion in the UK for all things that involve quiet contemplation. But he's also probably written more insightfully and prolifically on love and happiness than anyone in the country, from his first book, 1993's *Essays in Love,* which sold two million copies, to *The Course of Love,* written twenty-three years later.

So I get in touch, and arrange an interview at his office in leafy Belsize Park. It's an area of mansion blocks and immaculately turned-out Georgian terraces and the air feels a little fresher.

De Botton's office is on the ground floor of one of these mansion blocks, and we sit in a plain reception room with a puddle-shaped, glass-topped coffee table between us as I faff about with recording equipment.

De Botton is married himself, with two children. And the main reason we all marry the wrong person, he tells me, is that our idea of happiness is an unattainable dud in the first place.

'The notion of being uncomplicatedly happy forever with one person is just not true to who we are. It's an unimaginative picture. It's beautiful that we want to live happily ever after, and it's touching and it's poignant. It's also profoundly wrong,' he says.

It's relatively new as well, having crept into popular culture as an idea some time around the middle of the eighteenth century, before which you married based on a trade-off of livestock or land or power and hoped not to hate each other for too long before the pox got you. But a few hundred years of fairy tales have set an unrealistic expectation for us.

'The assumption is that the one area where you won't make a mistake is in whom you marry. But the overwhelming conclusion of an overwhelming majority of people is that, to some extent, they are with somebody with whom there is friction, there is conflict,' he says. 'And our society makes that realization look like a tragedy, rather than what it in fact is, which is part of existence and therefore something that we should probably learn to live with, even learn to laugh at, but certainly embrace and get curious about, rather than be terrified about.'

It does seem to me a little unhelpful that love, whether it's with your childhood sweetheart or a steady flow of free-sexuality-practising ecologists, is the one area where the expectation is that you will 'just know'.

You don't 'just know' how to juggle or make risotto or ride a bike. You may have seen those things happen, but you wouldn't expect to stick out your hands and magically keep three balls moving through the air. You'd practise, maybe ask for advice or watch a YouTube tutorial. And yet choosing a partner from six billion other adult humans, and then having a loving relationship with that partner – when they have had a million tiny experiences feeding in to who they are, what they want, and what they're afraid of (and will often not understand those things themselves) – is expected to be something that comes to you as instinctively as an infant reaching for a boob.

De Botton's solution is to do a little work, and part of that work is being the tiniest bit fake.

'We don't generally believe in editing ourselves with our partners, but there are maybe ways in which holding back, or having some secrets, might be a good idea. I don't mean an absolutely awful secret, like "I've stolen all the money" or "I've got another family squirrelled away", but just maybe that you don't like your mother-in-law. Maybe keep that in. I think that couples who stick together probably have a certain amount of diplomacy.'

That may be a little late for us, given the book we are writing. But in truth, my diplomacy levels have been waning for the last couple of years. I used to want to shield Anna from all negativity, even those tiny daily grumps. If she'd moved my keys somewhere and I couldn't find them, I'd laugh about her manic tidying. If she brought home a friend who I thought was a bit of a plonker, I'd give my personable best and tell her afterwards, 'Yeah, she's great.'

But now I hide a little less. I huff about the keys, I pull a face when she mentions the friend. I thought this was a good new level of honesty – of 'being true to myself' – but it's actually just that my manners have slipped.

De Botton also touches on something that every professional I've spoken to along the way has said: your ideas of relationships and 'happily ever after' almost always come down to your parents. They are the building blocks for our later adult lives, either because we choose partners like them or go for someone who is the exact opposite.

'Many of us have learned about love in childhood in ways that are less than optimal. Maybe we loved somebody who was depressed, maybe we loved someone who left us feeling humiliated, maybe we loved somebody who found our freedom very difficult and needed to constrain us in order to build themselves up,' he says. 'The child of a parent who was distant and rather unemotional is going to make a beeline for adults who are quite distant and unemotional, and then respond to the adult in the same way that they might have responded to that parent.'

As he says this, I distinctly remember the time – and it's only happened once – when we were packing for a trip, discussing travel logistics, and Anna accidentally called me 'dad'. We brushed over it pretty quickly.

But also, as the first-born in my family, I have always felt confident in the love that came my way from my mum, and that I didn't have to do anything at all to work for it. Whenever we're all visiting her, my younger sister sifts through the family albums to do a picture stock-check and prove there were many more of me. 'See!' she will shout. 'GOLDEN CHILD!' While that's lovely (for me, less for her but she'll be fine), it might make me a bit blasé about any loving affection that comes my way.

Then there's the whole 'absent dad' thing, which no doubt adds an extra muddle of what psychotherapists dramatically call 'childhood scars'.

De Botton suggests trying an online 'attachment types' survey as a piece of work that people can do to better understand who they are. I have a quick look after our interview and there are three main attachment types: avoidant, secure and anxious. Even before taking the test, I kind of know where this might be heading.

I take the *Psychology Today* test on my phone as I head back to the Tube. It takes ten minutes and costs US$6 to get your results.

I am 'dismissive-avoidant', it says: 'They tend to require a lot of space . . . have a cynical view of others . . . prefer to rely on no one but themselves . . . detached from their emotions . . . perceived as cold and unloving . . . The only thing they dislike more than having to depend on others is being someone else's leaning post.'

It's like this brief internet survey can see into my soul.

Dismissive-avoidants also have 'very little fear of being abandoned' and feel that they 'deserve to be loved by others'. On a scale of 0–100, the survey rated my self-esteem at 89, but my 'need to please' as an 8. That is not a typo – I got 8/100 on the 'need to please' scale. Frankly, you're lucky I've written this book and should feel blessed to have it in your hands.

I send the link to Anna to see what she gets. Later that day she sends back her result. 'Secure' individuals, it says, 'Tend to have better-quality relationships . . . they are better at resolving conflicts . . . interact with their partner in a more positive manner.'

Secure sounds better. It is the healthiest of the attachment styles. Fortunately, the internet also tells me that 'secure' and 'dismissive-avoidant' can be a passable match, so long as the dismissive one gets his head out of his arse (I'm paraphrasing).

Specifically, according to author Jeb Kinnison, 'The dismissive will tend to drive the secure partner towards attachment anxiety by failing to respond well or at all to reasonable messages requesting assurance.'

There are some quite loud bells ringing there.

The secure can fix the dismissive, 'but at great cost in patience and effort . . . If this does not happen, a secure is more likely to give up on the relationship and move on.'

I'm reminded of the row we had a few nights before, when she asked, for the first time in twelve years, if I wanted to leave. I huffed 'of course not', arms folded and leaning back against the kitchen countertop, while she stood in the doorway, eyes red and lower lip wobbling, before announcing that she would 'fuck off, then'. I can't remember what sparked it, but I do remember thinking it was all a bit unnecessary.

'I told you I wanted to live with you in 2006,' I thought. 'Why do we have to keep going over it?'

Maybe I need to review my dismissive-avoidant ways before she starts to wonder if actually it's her that wants to leave.

Because I do want her to stay. And sometimes it takes a little nudge to remind you.

The night after that row, we were still on slightly tense terms when Anna called down from the bath. The kids were asleep and she was surrounded by lit candles and peculiar scents.

She had found a bruise on her left breast and asked me to switch on the light.

It was huge – dark black and purple with yellow edges, and spread halfway across her chest. She hadn't noticed it that morning and didn't know where it came from.

We both did some googling, but neither of us wanted to share the details with the other.

'It's probably fine,' we both agreed. 'But worth checking out.'

But the internet wasn't saying it was fine. The internet was saying this is almost certainly a sign of inflammatory breast cancer. IBC is a particularly aggressive form, and by the time large bruises show, you're usually at stage three with a cancer that has spread to other lymph nodes.

'I'll get you booked in tomorrow,' I said, and as we went to sleep I told myself that self-diagnosing online was always a bad idea.

The next morning we were quiet, did the school run together and then made some calls. It might take a couple of weeks for a scan through the NHS, we found, but eventually got an appointment with a clinic across town. They had a same-day service that we put on the family credit card.

We were nicer to each other that morning, and a little more considerate.

'It's probably nothing,' she said.

'Definitely,' I said. 'But good to be sure.'

And then we went about our working days. Her slot was 2p.m. to 4p.m., so I fetched the eldest from school. We did homework and had a snack, but I wasn't really in the room. I was picturing a clinic in west London, with nurses in pale blue and posters of smiling old men demanding that you get your prostate checked.

And I was wondering what the next couple of hours might mean for the rest of our lives and how we would tell the girls. Whether things would be operable, or if we'd just be looking for a nice place by the sea to spend a couple of months together. It was something I physically felt. My mouth was dry and my stomach knotted.

The eldest and I were on our way to get the little one from nursery when Anna called.

'It's fine,' she said, and I gave one of those stunted sigh-laughs that people do when they realize the train they've been running for has been delayed. 'The doctor looked worried and put me straight in for a scan, but it was fine. They think it's from some kind of impact.'

We'd been in the car with her mum a few days before when she'd had to do an emergency stop, and I guessed that it might have been that. I'd never spoken so excitedly about seat-belt positions.

'Well, anyway, good,' I said, 'because I wasn't sure if I'd be best going straight to Bumble or should have a little fun on Tinder first.'

She laughed, fortunately, because that was a joke that really could have gone either way.

We were much nicer to each other for a few days after that. But it shouldn't take the fear of a fatal disease to make you nicer to the person you've decided to spend the rest of your life with. That should really just be how you are.

I shouldn't be huffing about hair tongs, I should be calmly discussing why they annoy me.

I shouldn't be sitting in the drama triangle, shifting from rescuer to persecutor to victim. I should be in the winner's triangle, being caring and open and, when needed, gently assertive.

I should be stopping to ask, whenever a prickle of pique runs up my neck, not 'What do I want?' but 'What does love need now?' Because those free-loving hippies might have some wonky ideas about spirituality, but that's about the most important question I can think of for any person to ask at any time.

It might feel a bit like a sentiment that should be stitched in beads, but sometimes the clearest ideas are the simplest, and when I've stopped myself, and taken a moment to ask that question internally, I have been nicer and my life has been better.

So what does love need me to do? It needs me to stage a gentle intervention for Anna with her phone, and physically keep it from her at certain times, and tell her how much she is missed and that if that doesn't get fixed then she will be physically there but emotionally missed forever.

I need to remember what Panos said in a sun-dappled courtyard in a Greek monastery: that the river keeps moving and we must too. That our past relationship is gone – that every relationship ends every night and has to be built again every morning.

I need to look at her face every day – really stop and stare and breathe it in – just like Charlotte Fox Weber told me, to remind myself who she is and why we're here in the first place.

I need to remember something De Botton said, right at the end of our interview, about 'despairing cheerfulness' and the fact that many people 'get to a point of a particularly beautiful harmony, because it's been so hard-won'.

And, perhaps more importantly, that he said, 'a happy ending means realizing once and for all that there is no such thing, but making your peace with it and realizing that right next to "happily ever after" is a wonderful alternative, which is "good enough".'

And I need to realize that this isn't just settling: 'good enough' is a remarkable achievement for any combination of humans, given all the peculiar things that humans are and want and need.

And I need to remember all those old folk in MRIs at Stony Brook University, whose reward centres lit up like day-glo rave sticks when they saw pictures of their life partners.

These things are true if you are two, or three or a whole platoon. They are true if you're same-sex, mixed-sex or inter-sex. They are true if you've decided to love no one but yourself. It may sound like I'm using *Shrek* as a life philosophy, but 'good enough' is a beautiful place to get to and 'happily ever after' doesn't exist.

I also need to remember something Dan said when we were having beer and pizza in my local pub. Three pints in and he casually offered, in his drifting Essex accent: 'Well, it was John Stuart Mill who said "Ask yourself if you're happy and you cease to be so."'

That's Dan who ties complicit women to chairs, is known as 'Seventies Dan' among his younger colleagues, and calls chamomile 'lesbian tea' (the second of those things being a result of the third).

He hadn't even googled it, it was just something in his head. 'England's greatest philosopher,' he said, before slinging back the dregs of his San Miguel.

And his quote makes a lot of sense (the John Stuart Mill one, not the one about chamomile, which does have a certain floral refreshingness and no proven compatibility with one sexual preference over any other). If we're all constantly asking ourselves how happy we are, then how will we ever have a chance to be so?

The happiest people I know are my daughters, aged two and six, who can't see an open space of more than ten feet in front of them without running into it, arms flapping like epileptic octopuses. They can't see a bed without jumping on it or a snack without eating it.

They don't stop to ask how happy they are, they just are. They have an unquestioning acceptance of the hilarity of all things, and no one lives more in the moment than they do.

But I also need to realize that they need us less than we think, and they are going to be fine if Anna and I are.

I need to remember that their happiness is directly linked to ours, because the best way to ensure you create loving humans who respect themselves and the world around them is to love whoever you're raising them with.

All of these things require work.

They all require being a little less selfish and a little more kind. But, honestly, what the fuck else are you doing with your time? There is nothing more important for you to do than this.

So be kinder to the ones you love, and ask the same of them.

There is no happy ending, unless you allow it to happen.

In memory of Rachel Clements
05/09/1988 – 25/01/2020

Acknowledgements

Firstly, we'd like to thank everyone who we've quoted in these pages. Thank you to those friends and strangers who allowed us to peek into their lives in the most intimate way. Thank you to our families, who allowed us to share more of their lives than might reasonably be expected.

Thanks to Heart radio for opening up the door to so many interesting interviewees through the *Ellie & Anna Have Issues* show and podcast. It is the show's producers, Elena Guthrie and Lawrence Hall, who put us in touch with Saamirah and the throuple: Cathy, Thomas and Nicole.

A huge thanks needs to go to our literary agent, Abigail Bergstrom, who has that rare ability to encourage while critiquing. Everyone needs the trusted friend who tells you there's spinach in your teeth.

Thank you to all those academics and researchers whose work has been so helpful in separating whimsy from fact and helping to explain why we sometimes feel the ways that we do. And thanks to those who took the time to explain months of work and complex conclusions in easily quotable ways.

Thanks to these organisations for gathering all that work in navigable libraries, much of it available for free: academia.edu, the

American Psychological Association's PsychNet, JAMA Network, PMC and the U.S. National Institutes of Health's National Library of Medicine, Research Gate, Sage Journals, Semantic Scholar, Springer Link, Taylor & Francis Online. You have taken us down hundreds of curious wormholes.

Thanks to the stat gatherers at the UK Office of National Statistics and US Census Bureau and General Social Survey. People don't often thank stat gatherers, but without you, we'd know much less.

Thanks to the many journals that first bring interesting research to public attention, including, but not limited to: *BMC Psychiatry, Journal of Sexual Medicine, Psychologies, Psychology Today, Science.*

Thanks to Relate and Alain de Botton and The School of Life, which do so much to make the big questions feel easier to manage.

Thanks to Frederick at Tamera, who gave up several days of his life to guide Matt around and introduce him to remarkable people whose stories could have filled a book on their own.

It's also here that we need to thank Phillip Bodenham, whose Whitstable AirBnB cottage was where we wrote a significant chunk of the book to escape the infant hollering. We were paying to stay there, but without him we wouldn't have found Britain's oldest fisherman, and his love of the area and recommendations helped us feel less isolated when in the writing hole.

And we'd also like to thank everyone who we spoke to, in person or online, but whose words we couldn't use for one reason or another – those interviewees who generously gave up time to speak to us, including all those followers of @mother_pukka and @papa_pukka who shared their stories: each tale revealed something wonderfully human, and we're sorry we couldn't use more of them. Three hundred or so pages really aren't very much with all those tales to tell.

To our girls, who weren't really sure what we were doing but continue to use our first book as a doorstop.

And thanks to you for taking the time to read this book. None of us have much of it, and we hope you found this to be time well spent.